The Duel

Giles Hunt's previous publications include *Mehitabel Canning: A Redoubtable Woman*, based on the letters of the woman who was George Canning's guardian from the age of six, and *Launcelot Fleming: A Portrait*.

The Duel

Castlereagh, Canning and Deadly Cabinet Rivalry

Giles Hunt

I.B. TAURIS
LONDON · NEW YORK

Published in 2008 by I.B.Tauris & Co. Ltd
6 Salem Road, London W2 4BU
175 Fifth Avenue, New York, NY 10010
www.ibtauris.com

ISBN: 978 1 84511 593 7

A full CIP record for this book is available from the British Library
A full CIP record for this book is available from the Library of Congress

Library of Congress catalog card: available

Typeset in Perpetua by A. & D. Worthington, Newmarket, Suffolk
Printed and bound in Great Britain by TJ International Ltd, Padstow, Cornwall

Contents

List of Illustrations		vii
Acknowledgements		ix
Introduction		xi
1.	Origins	1
2.	Boyhood and Youth: Castlereagh	7
3.	Boyhood and Youth: Canning	15
4.	The Young Politician: Castlereagh	29
5.	The Young Politician: Canning	47
6.	Contrasting Fortunes	69
7.	Cabinet Colleagues	85
8.	The Year of the Duel	109
9.	The Duel	127
10.	The Aftermath	143
11.	Long-Term Consequences: The Two Foreign Secretaries	155
12.	Death Comes To Us All	175
	Appendix 1	187
	Appendix 2	193
	Appendix 3	195
	Notes	199
	Select Bibliography	205
	Index	209

Illustrations

Charles Pratt, 1st Earl Camden. As Chief Justice of the Common Pleas (1761–66) he had granted the radical Wilkes a writ of Habeas Corpus. He became Lord Chancellor in 1766. His daughter Frances became Castlereagh's stepmother and Camden took a paternal interest in the boy's education and early career. (National Portrait Gallery)   8

George Canning, aged five, drawn (possibly by Reynolds) shortly before he went to live with his uncle Stratford. (By kind permission of the late Miss Daphne Gale)   17

Canning's aunt, Mrs Stratford Canning, with her daughter Bess. Canning's uncle Stratford and his wife Mehitabel (Hitty) brought him up from the age of six. (Romney started this portrait in 1778 and did not finish it until 1784)   17

Emily, née Hobart, Viscountess Castlereagh, at the time of her marriage – 'as fine, comely, good-humoured, playful (not to say romping) a piece of flesh as any Illyrian'. Copy of painting by Lawrence (National Trust). The original is at Mount Stewart.   34

Paddy Turned Knife Grinder ('For Aid when Hibernia calls, Sure Paddy's the devil's own grinder'). Castlereagh sharpens his sword, helped by Beresford and Clare, while Grattan primes his pistols. (Published by Mr Meury, 21 Nassau St, Dublin)   37

Billy Pitt drives the Union Coach, packed with Scots members with Dundas on the roof throwing coins to Irish members packed in behind and shepherded by Castlereagh (far left). John Bull is loudly protesting. (Published by Mr Meury, 21 Nassau St, Dublin)   40

Pitt, driving the Union Coach, is shot by Lord Chancellor Loughborough, depicted as a highwayman, while John Bull with his cudgel tells Castlereagh, inside the coach with 'the scarlet woman of Rome', to 'give her up'. Castlereagh is firing his pistol at the highwaymen. (Published by Mr Meury, 21 Nassau St, Dublin)   41

William Pitt as Prime Minister, aged 44, by Hoppner. (National Portrait Gallery)   48

George Canning *c.*1798, by Hoppner. (By kind permission of Sir Andrew Buchanan, Bart.)   61

Henry Bentinck, 3rd Duke of Portland. When Portland was Home Secretary, Lord Minto said of him, 'The Duke of Portland will look at his nails and raise his spectacles from his nose for a fortnight before he answers me.' His procrastination as Prime Minister was part of the reason for the duel of 1809. (National Portrait Gallery)   86

Spencer Perceval succeeded the Duke of Portland as Prime Minister in 1809 and became the only British prime minister to be assassinated (in April 1812).   88

Canning, Castlereagh (and Mulgrave) pulling together harmoniously. The King told Canning that seizing the Danish fleet was 'a very immoral act. So immoral that I won't ask who originated it. I have determined not to ask that question'; but, Canning told his wife, 'all in the most perfect good humour, laughing even at his own difficulties'. ('British tars, towing the Danish fleet into harbour' by James Gillray, hand-coloured etching, published by Hannah Humphrey, 1 October 1807. National Portrait Gallery)   92

Canning in 1809, shortly before the duel. Lawrence, the artist, thought he seemed pensive and preoccupied.   124

Castlereagh in 1809, by Lawrence. Mrs Arbuthnot spoke of his 'remark-ably fine commanding figure ... smile sweeter than it is possible to describe ... benevolent and amiable countenance ... an air of dignity and nobleness', but to political enemies Castlereagh was a figure of hate. What Hazlitt saw in this portrait was 'the prim, smirking smile of a haberdasher'. (National Portrait Gallery)   129

Cartoon depicting the duel between Lord Castlereagh and George Canning on 21 September 1809 entitled 'Killing No Murder, or A New Ministerial Way of Settling the Affairs of the Nation'. (George Crui-kshank © The British Museum)   142

Lord Camden, 2nd Earl and 1st Marquess, was Castlereagh's uncle. Canning called him 'Chuckle', and after the duel Castlereagh was bitter about his failure to tell him what his colleagues had been saying.   147

Acknowledgements

First and foremost, I must acknowledge the generous help given by Professor Rory Muir. He encouraged me to attempt this book, and read most of it in draft, thus eliminating various errors (which does not make him responsible for any that remain). He also directed me to several sources that I would not otherwise have known about and which, thanks mainly to Cambridge University, I was able to find.

I am grateful to Lady Mairi Bury for putting me on the track of Castlereagh's private correspondence, now in the Public Record Office of Northern Ireland. Most of the material about Canning I had already researched for *Mehitabel Canning*, and is now in Leeds Public Records Office; I am grateful to the Earl of Harewood for having given permission to quote from the Canning archives freely. Nottingham University have very helpfully put the Portland papers online.

More people than I can name have helped and encouraged me in various ways; in particular my cousin John Gleave took a great interest and took a lot of trouble to investigate Castlereagh's psychological state at the time of the duel; he had been the senior consultant neurosurgeon at Addenbrooke's Hospital, Cambridge, so his expert opinion was invaluable. Sadly, he died before this book could be published.

My thanks, too, to Guy Garfit for the illustrations that were in *Mehitabel Canning*, and to Andrew Buchanan for the considerable trouble he took to send the publishers a copy of his Hoppner picture of Canning. My daughter Elizabeth also mastered the arcane science of taking and transmitting digital photograph of the prints in this house.

Last, but by no means least, I have learned again how very lucky I am to be married to a wife who, instead of complaining at my immersing myself in the early nineteenth century rather than being useful in house or garden, has constantly encouraged me to write this book, and has read each chapter in draft making comments that managed to be useful without being discouraging; not for nothing was she once secretary-cum-nanny to a renowned author and playwright. It is not a platitude but the sober truth to say that without my wife this book could never have been written.

Introduction

Shortly after five o'clock on the morning of Thursday 21 September 1809 two men set off in a curricle from St James's Square. They were bound for Putney Heath, where they arrived soon after it became light. They were joined by another pair who had set out from Brompton. At seven o'clock a duel was to be fought; the weapons were not to be swords (as might have been the case 50 years earlier) but pistols. Duels were starting to be frowned on by 1809, so when one did occur care had to be taken to choose a time and place where it was not likely to be observed. What made this particular duel so extraordinary was that it was being fought between His Majesty's Secretary of State for Foreign Affairs, and His Majesty's Secretary of State for War and the Colonies, and at the height of the Napoleonic Wars.

Rivalry, even personal enmity, between cabinet colleagues is not unusual, but when newspaper columnists today talk of politicians 'coming to blows', they do not as a rule mean anything physical. Admittedly there is still a line in the House of Commons that members must not cross because the two sides once had to be kept at arm's length, when the 'arm' included a sword in the hand. But even when duels were still quite common, for cabinet colleagues to shoot at one another was a shocking event, and for the Foreign Secretary and the Secretary of State for War to do so at a time when England was at war and the country's very survival under threat was bizarre in the extreme. What had got into Canning and Castlereagh to make them behave as they did? Was this duel simply a personal quarrel, or were there deep political undercurrents at work – a simmering hostility between the old eighteenth-century world dominated by landed interests, and the new nineteenth-century world where wealth and power were starting to get into the hands of manufacturers and bankers? History depicts Castlereagh as a Tory reactionary, while Canning was considered dangerously liberal both in his foreign policy and in his views over domestic policy, where he realized that the 'struggle between property and population' (as he put it) was bound to lead to the end of aristocratic dominance.

Certainly the different social and political views of the two participants provide a fascinating background to the duel on Putney Heath that September morning of 1809; and, those differences apart, their contrasting personalities might seem to suggest that they were instinctively antagonistic to one another. Canning was brilliant, but had the reputation of being ruthlessly ambitious, unreliable and too clever by half. He had earned that reputation after Pitt resigned in 1801 over the King's refusal to agree to Catholic emancipation for Ireland; he insisted on resigning too, against Pitt's express wishes, and proceeded to carry on a bitter factious opposition against Pitt's chosen successor, jibing that 'Pitt is to Addington as London is to Paddington'. As Foreign Secretary Canning had been brilliant, but controversial (as when in 1807 he persuaded the cabinet to agree to the bombardment of neutral Copenhagen to prevent Napoleon getting his hands on the Danish fleet). The grounds for Castlereagh's challenge to a duel seem to show Canning in a very bad light; he had told the Prime Minister that unless changes were made in the government (which everyone assumed would include moving Castlereagh from his office as Secretary of State for War), he would resign. Surely Castlereagh had good grounds for complaint against a colleague who had been intriguing against him behind his back; little wonder that when he eventually found out what had been going on, he challenged Canning to a duel.

As a result of the duel, a weak government lost two of its more able members. Castlereagh remained out of office for two and half years until he was appointed Foreign Secretary early in 1812, and Canning for four more years after that – having, to his subsequent bitter regret, refused a generous offer from Castlereagh to step aside and let him become Foreign Secretary again in the summer of 1812. Castlereagh then remained Foreign Secretary for ten years while Canning either languished on the back benches or held the less important post of President of the Board of Control. After Castlereagh died in 1822 Canning became Foreign Secretary again, and a very good one too (though some would say that he merely had to build on the solid foundations laid by his predecessor).

Castlereagh lacked Canning's brilliance, but he was calm, resolute, hard-working and conscientious. He seems to have been the *beau ideal* of an English aristocrat – tall, handsome, cultivated. As Irish Secretary in the closing years of the eighteenth century he had played a crucial part in persuading the Dublin parliament to pass the Act of Union, and as Secretary of State for War he devised an effective recruitment policy – a vital achievement that had eluded his predecessors. When, later, he was Foreign Secretary he became one of the principal architects of a peace settlement that kept Europe free from any major war for a hundred years. True, he was scurrilously attacked by the poet Shelley as a merciless reactionary ('I met murder by the way, he wore a mask like Castlereagh') but that simply shows that, like the Duke of Wellington, he was above courting cheap popularity.

Such were my impressions from the history books I read at school. I concluded that Castlereagh was a far more admirable character, and a better statesman, than Canning. But more recently, I read some family letters centred round Canning's aunt and realized that my earlier impressions of the man just could not be correct. His private letters – which he could not possibly have thought posterity would ever see – show him an honourable and principled man who cared deeply for his country and was fiercely loyal to his friends. True, he was ambitious, but no more so than most of his colleagues; and I began to think that the reason why some of them accused him of being devious was that he could think more quickly and clearly than they could, so that he saw dangers and opportunities that others had not thought of (such as the fatal consequences if Napoleon acquired the Danish fleet). Unlike most men he perceived that social trends were making 'population rather than property' the deciding political force. I also came to realize the surprising fact that in 1809 Canning was the only member of the cabinet who was neither a peer nor the son of a peer, so that it was easy to label him as a social upstart who by implication could not be trusted. All this, coupled with Canning's inability to suffer fools gladly and a devastating wit, explains why many people resented him; but unprincipled he most certainly was not. His private letters explain why his friends were so devoted to him, and why *The Times* reported after his funeral that 'regret was exhibited in the conduct of the assembled multitude yesterday more strongly and intensely than, we believe, was exhibited at the death of any subject within the memory of the oldest person now living', whereas at Castlereagh's funeral some of the crowd booed and hissed at the coffin.

So should we see Canning as the hero and Castlereagh the villain – the accomplished pistol shot who challenged a political opponent who had never before handled a pistol in his life? Unfortunately, that thesis will not stand up either. The mask of villainy simply will not fit Castlereagh. He was just as much a man of principle as Canning, and in his personal life was kind, generous and loyal.

The intriguing question therefore remains: what really did lie behind that ominous meeting on Putney Heath early in the morning of 21 September 1809?

CHAPTER 1

Origins

Castlereagh and Canning stemmed from very similar roots. Each man's father belonged to the Irish Ascendancy, a status defined by Catholics as 'a Protestant on a horse'. Canning's mother was Irish by descent although she had been brought up in England, while Castlereagh's mother was an aristocratic Englishwoman, which may be why in some ways Castlereagh seemed more English than Canning, whose mother was Irish by birth and who certainly considered himself an Irishman (writing to a cousin he calls Ireland 'our country') and had a temperament to match. But in public perception it was Castlereagh rather than Canning who was thought of as an Irishman, because he had been born and brought up in Ireland and had started his political career in the Irish House of Commons, where he had imbibed the ethos of the Protestant Ascendancy. Canning, on the other hand, was born and brought up in England and, except for a summer holiday visit to his grandmother when he was 16, never went to Ireland.

Both men's fathers were heirs to estates in Northern Ireland originally granted to their forebears by James I at the time of the Ulster Plantation, and both families had managed to increase their inheritance by judicious marriages. Castlereagh's grandfather, Alexander Stewart, had not expected to inherit the family's thousand-acre Ballylawn estate in County Donegal as he was a younger son, and was apprenticed to a Dublin merchant. He seems to have had a shrewd business sense; before long he had established his own firm, and when at the age of 32 he inherited Ballylawn on his elder brother's death, he did not simply settle down as a country squire on its £400-a-year income, but went to seek his fortune in London. He found it in the person of a cousin, Mary Cowan, who was the daughter of a Londonderry alderman and half-sister and heiress of an Indian nabob, Sir Robert Cowan. Alexander Stewart married Mary Cowan, and her fortune enabled him to buy the Newtownards estate in County Londonderry. He had hoped that his purchase would give him

1

the nomination to the local parliamentary borough, but found to his chagrin that it did not. Determined nonetheless to get into politics, which could be the road to riches (a more high-risk route than marriage, but potentially even more lucrative), Alexander accordingly got himself elected for Londonderry. Alas, he was almost immediately unseated for alleged bribery and corruption; but for his descendants, this failure proved a blessing in disguise, as it made him decide to eschew politics and spend his money instead on improving his estate. He built a country house, Mount Stewart, on the Newtownards estate, a pleasing Georgian country house in the style of Adam which remains in the family to this day. Alexander also bought property in Dublin which rapidly increased in value – the mid-eighteenth century saw a housing boom all over Ireland, before the troubles began once more – and collected pictures, including a Nativity by Rubens, all of which stood his son Robert, Castlereagh's father, in good stead.

The Stewarts had originally come from Scotland (the area around Castle Douglas is still called 'the Stewartry') and as Presbyterians were precluded until quite late in the eighteenth century by the Test Acts from standing for parliament. This had put them at some social disadvantage, although it had not stopped Castlereagh's great-grandfather from raising a regiment to fight on the winning side against James II in 1690. His son Alexander (Castlereagh's grandfather) remained stoutly Presbyterian and sent his son Robert to finish his education not in England but at the soundly Calvinistic University of Geneva. When after his time at university he returned to Ireland, Robert 'had the good sense' (as Montgomery Hyde puts it) 'to fall in love with the daughter of a powerful if somewhat greedy landowner and parliamentary borough proprietor in the north of Ireland'. No doubt Alexander was delighted at seeing his son following in his footsteps and showing such good sense in his choice of a wife, but Lord Hertford's reaction was very different; he did not consider young Robert at all a suitable match for his daughter. However, in 1765 Hertford became Lord Lieutenant, and that gave Robert a chance to press his suit; as the son of a respectable Dublin family he had the entrée to receptions and balls at the Castle, and made full use of his opportunity. Before long Lord Hertford had to give way, and Robert Stewart married Lady Sarah Seymour-Conway on 3 June 1766. On her part, it can only have been a marriage for love, and although her money and position probably played a large part in Robert's thinking, there is no reason to believe that he was not genuinely in love as well.

The Cannings' Garvagh estate in County Down was larger than the Stewarts' Ballylawn estate, and they too had made 'good' marriages in successive generations. Canning's great-grandfather, like Castlereagh's, had raised a regiment to fight on the side of the Protestant William III against the Catholic James II in 1690, and when peace was restored he married the daughter and heiress of Robert Stratford of Baltinglass, in whose honour they named their son Stratford Canning. (To anyone trying to unravel the Canning family history, their limited repertoire of Christian names is exasperating; not only was Canning's grandfather called Stratford, but so was one of his uncles and *his* youngest son, who after being launched on a diplomatic career by his illustrious cousin ended his days as Lord Stratford de Redcliffe. Equally confusingly, Canning's father and one of his first cousins were also called George, as he was.)

Canning's grandfather Stratford inherited the Baltinglass estate as well as Garvagh, which made him a considerable landowner; and following his father's example, he too increased his inheritance through 'a good marriage'. His wife (Canning's grandmother) Laetitia was daughter and sole heiress of Obadiah Newburgh who owned a sizeable estate in County Cavan and a property in Kilkenny. In order to demonstrate his position in society, Canning's grandfather, just like Castlereagh's, set about building a larger country house on his estate (both men also had houses in Dublin). Garvagh was originally built in the Palladian style, was much altered in a pleasing, unpretentious manner in 1813, but unlike Mount Stewart has not survived. The third Lord Garvagh's affairs had to be managed by the Commissioner in Lunacy, the estate was sold in 1923 and in the 1960s the house was demolished to make way for a new school.

Castlereagh's and Canning's grandfathers were thus very similar in both wealth and social class, but with that generation the resemblance ends. Stratford Canning, who had a keen sense of his own position in society, must have been green with envy when the son of his contemporary, Alexander Stewart, married the Lord Lieutenant's daughter while his own eldest son had been packed off to England for 'forming an unsuitable attachment' against his father's wishes. While Castlereagh's father was living with his bride in some style in the fashionable quarter of Dublin in a house belonging to his father-in-law, Canning's father was struggling unsuccessfully to earn his living at the Bar in London.

Fortune seemed to be smiling on Robert Stewart and his bride, but their life was not all bliss; their first child died in infancy – an all-too-common tragedy in those days, that also befell Canning's parents. But their second child, the future Lord Castlereagh, was born on 18 June 1769, with presumably the best nursing care and attention that money could buy – a much more propitious start in life than Canning was to have. But there was one experience that they both suffered: when each was a year old, he lost a parent through death. In Canning's case it was his father; in Castlereagh's his mother, who died in childbirth (the baby was stillborn) on 17 July 1770. The best medical care that money could buy did not amount to very much in the eighteenth century.

Losing his mother when only a year old did not deprive Castlereagh of any outward sense of security; he was in no sense a loveless orphan but went to live with his Stewart grandparents at Mount Stewart, where life in 'the big house' in that beautiful Irish countryside, with fishing in the streams and lough, and wild country to scramble in, must have been idyllic. A boyhood spent in those surroundings gave Castlereagh a love of the countryside, and a start in life that Canning never had, but losing a mother in infancy was bound to affect him emotionally; no grandmother, however loving, can fully take the place of a mother, and lack of mother-love when he was young may help explain why Castlereagh, though basically kind, could sometimes be extremely ruthless. It may be, however, that a hard streak was inevitable in anyone brought up as a member of the ruling class in what was in fact an occupied country. Castlereagh was born only a few weeks after the Duke of Wellington (coincidentally on 18 June which would later become Waterloo Day), and in her biography of Wellington Lady Longford, who had herself married into the Ascendancy, wrote:

> It is tempting to trace some of the resemblances between the two political allies [Wellington and Castlereagh], especially their cool detachment, to a common source – their membership not only of the aristocracy but of the Irish Ascendency. Taught from childhood to feel all the aloofness of an Ascendency class, utterly apart from the native Irish who were their neighbours, it was only when their eyes were raised to distant horizons [i.e. the continent of Europe] that the glance was friendlier.[1]

Meanwhile, on 17 March 1757 Canning's father at the age of 26 had sailed from Dublin 'with a Bill in my pocket on a Merchant in London for £37:10s and 8 guineas given me by my Father to pay my travelling expenses. From that time to 1st October 1760 I received from him precisely the sum of £580 and no more.'[2] George was called to the Bar and became a member of Lincoln's Inn, but failed to make a success of the law. He got involved in radical politics, which probably did not help (he was a friend of Wilkes), and wasted time and money writing poetry which he published at his own expense. He confided to his younger brother that one volume alone, 'I do assure you cost me very near £400 in hard cash', and admitted that 'time is precious and perhaps I have already hazarded too much of it'. One poem contains the lines:

But hence, Despondance! Hell-born Hag, away.
Oft lowers the morn, whence radiance gilds the day;
Hard if all hope were dead, all spirit gone,
And every prospect closed at thirty-one.

So, Welcome, Law! Poor Poesy, farewell!
Tho' in thy care the loves and graces dwell.
One Chancery cause in solid worth outweighs
Dryden's strong sense, and Pope's harmonious lays.

But alas, lucrative Chancery cases failed to materialize, and if George hoped that his father might relent, he was disappointed: 'From 1st October to this day [13 May 1766] I have not received from him, directly or indirectly, a single shilling,' he wrote. It must be confessed that old Stratford Canning seems to have been a most disagreeable old man. His youngest son – Canning's uncle Stratford – was disinherited just as the eldest son had been, and for the same reason – marrying against his father's wishes. Stratford, like his eldest brother, left Ireland for London, but unlike his eldest brother he succeeded, after a difficult start, in establishing himself, and within a few years was a prosperous banker. If Canning's father had realized how implacable his father was, he too might have buckled down to work and prospered, but whereas Stratford as the youngest son had always known he must make his own way in the world, George seems to have thought that as the eldest son he was bound to inherit eventually despite his father's anger.

The final nail in George's financial coffin was his marriage in 1768 to Mary Ann Costello. She was of good family – her uncle was a Gentleman Usher to Queen Charlotte – but her widowed mother was virtually penniless, and in old Stratford Canning's eyes that was inexcusable. He grudgingly agreed to make his eldest son an allowance of £200 a year, but only on condition that he sign away his birthright, Esau-like, to his brother Paul whose aim in life, as Stratford's wife Mehitabel rather tartly put it, was 'at all costs to stand well with his father'. Paul made a thoroughly 'suitable' marriage – to Jane, the sister of Colonel Spencer (who later became engaged to Canning's aunt Frances (Fan)). Spencer jilted her, later had a fling with Princess Augusta, and, as General Sir Brent Spencer, became second in command in the Peninsula, where Wellington found him 'a very puzzle-headed fellow' – he habitually called the river Tagus 'the Thames' – and in 1811 managed to have him sent home. Paul's son – another George Canning – married Castlereagh's half-sister; she died in childbirth, and perhaps if she had lived personal relationships between Canning and Castlereagh might have been less cool.

Since Canning's father found that neither the law nor his father would support him, he tried his hand at the wine trade. But that failed too, and by the time his son, the future Prime Minister, was born on 11 April 1770 in Queen Anne Street, Marylebone, George was on the verge of bankruptcy. On his son's first birthday, 11 April 1771, he died. His brother Stratford reported that the cause of death was 'an inflammation of the bowels'; the *Memoirs of Canning* (1828) say that he died 'of a broken heart'. Probably both diagnoses are correct.

George's death was a traumatic experience for his widow. He died deeply in debt – the bailiffs came and removed the actual bed on which her husband had died – and the beautiful but penniless Mary Ann was left with a baby son of one year old and expecting another child; a boy was born on 23 December 1771 but died a few years later.

The effect on Canning of losing a father in infancy was quite different from the effect on Castlereagh of losing a mother. Far from being deprived of a mother's love, Canning until the age of six was almost constantly with his mother, with no nurses or servants to come between them. Mary Ann undoubtedly spoiled him, but also implanted in him an unusually affectionate nature; he remained devoted to her throughout his life, and showed great affection to all his relations including the half-brothers and sisters born subsequently to his mother, and had more close and lifelong friends than many politicians. But by no stretch of the imagination could Canning's earliest years be called secure. While Castlereagh's solidly based childhood at Mount Stewart gave him a natural self-assurance, the first six years of Canning's life with a mother who was struggling to earn a living, frequently on the move and never quite sure whether she could make ends meet, meant that his early years were spent against a background of constant uncertainty and insecurity.

These contrasting childhood experiences help to explain why in later life Canning often seemed to be over-anxious to explain and justify himself, whereas in the same circumstances it would not have occurred to Castlereagh that there was any need to do so. They also make one wonder how it was possible that in that age of aristocracy a child brought up in such conditions could ever have become Prime Minister.

CHAPTER 2

Boyhood and Youth: Castlereagh

The first eight years of young Robert's life at Mount Stewart were enviably free from restraint. His father had been elected to the Irish parliament and spent most of his time in Dublin, so Robert was brought up by his grandparents. Grandparents notoriously tend to be more indulgent than parents, and the countryside around Mount Stewart gave plenty of scope for a boy who enjoyed outdoor life. When he was six his father re-married. Frances Pratt was the daughter of Lord Camden, so for the second time Robert Stewart's bride was a daughter of an English peer. The marriage made little immediate difference to young Robert, as his father remained in Dublin and his new wife soon had her hands full with bearing and rearing children.

Frances's father, however, was to have a crucial influence on her stepson's future career. The son of Sir John Pratt, he had been born in 1714, educated at Eton and King's College Cambridge, and called to the Bar in 1738. He had had a distinguished legal career, becoming Attorney-General in 1757, and Lord Chancellor in 1766, having been raised to the peerage as Lord Camden the previous year. By the time his daughter married Robert Stewart, however, Camden had been in opposition for several years, and apart from a spell as Lord President of the Council in Lord Rockingham's government in 1782 would remain so – he was opposed to Lord North, and was a liberal-minded Whig. As Chief Justice of the Common Pleas he had provoked the government's fury by declaring general warrants illegal, and thus securing the release of the radical Wilkes.[1] Such was the liberal-minded man who treated young Robert as his own grandson.

Camden's letters show a touching affection for the boy; he told his son-in-law (31 January 1777) that he had received 'a very pretty letter from my friend

7

Charles Pratt, 1st Earl Camden. As Chief Justice of the Common Pleas (1761–66) he had granted the radical Wilkes a writ of Habeas Corpus. He became Lord Chancellor in 1766. His daughter Frances became Castlereagh's stepmother and Camden took a paternal interest in the boy's education and early career.

little Robert' then aged six, 'and I shall answer his letters as soon as I can get some information about the Magic Lantern'. More significantly, on 11 August he wrote:

> you have thoughts, I hear, of putting Robert to school. I am very happy … to have an opportunity of approving your plan. … Whether a private or public education is best, has long been an undecided controversy; but I am sure that an education at home is the very worst. Robert is a charming boy and has excellent natural parts, but if he grows up under your roof he will be utterly spoiled. Forgive me this freedom.

The boarding school chosen for Robert, when 'shades of the prison house began to close around the growing boy' at the age of eight, was Armagh Royal School. This was a Church of Ireland foundation, and presumably Camden suggested it on the grounds that, although Robert had been baptized in the Presbyterian Church, he ought to grow up in the Established Church to avoid discrimination under the Test Act. Armagh provided as good an education as any school in Ireland, but the régime was harsh and tough; according to a (perhaps not totally reliable) book of reminiscences, *Realities of Irish Life* by W.S. Trench, the older boys even fought duels with pistols (could that have given the future Lord Castlereagh ideas?). It must have been hard for an eight-year-old boy who had never left home, but Robert had learned to hold his own in rough-and-tumble with the local Newtownards boys. A letter he wrote at the start of his first term shows a determination to keep a stiff upper lip whatever he might have been feeling inwardly: 'At present I am highest in my class – no boy shall get above me. I am resolved to study very close when at my Book, and to play very briskly when disengaged.' [2]

Perhaps fortunately for him, young Robert only had to endure four years at Armagh Royal School. When he was ten, he was reported as being 'delicate, and wasted in his left arm by an issue previously applied'; this could suggest a mild form of polio, or some injury during games. Whatever the cause, the trouble cleared up and there is no subsequent mention of any weakness in his left arm, but it may have been one reason why, after his grandfather Alexander Stewart's death, his father moved him at the age of 12 to a private school at Portaferry, much nearer Mount Stewart. At about the same time Frances Stewart had a slight breakdown, hardly surprising considering the number of children she had borne (she eventually had 11), and decided to live for most of the year in the quieter surroundings of Mount Stewart. She proved a very good stepmother, and from the age of 12 to 17 Robert's upbringing during the holidays was almost entirely in her hands. Frances treated young Robert exactly like her own children, and he was in every way part of her family – eight girls (one of whom as we have seen married Canning's first cousin but died in childbirth) and three boys, two of whom died young. The surviving son, Charles, became an alarmingly gallant cavalry general, a head wound in a skirmish having further excited a naturally impetuous temperament, and eventually became the third Marquess of Londonderry.

Young Robert seems to have blossomed under the kindlier regime at his new school but the teaching was not as good as at Armagh, so he also had a tutor. Unfortunately the man entrusted with that task was the local rector, James Cleland, whose subsequent behaviour as a magistrate shows him to have been a vindictive bigot. Cleland's influence may help explain why his pupil later behaved so ruthlessly during the rebellion of 1798, and so far as religion goes, the rector would be unlikely to have instilled virtues like tolerance and forbearance – or, indeed, very much in the way of Christianity. Castlereagh seems to have accepted religious belief as a matter of course; it would not have occurred to him to doubt the existence of God, but nor would he have given the matter a great deal of thought. He would have accepted the Bible as a matter of course as the basis for morality, but would have seen no need to be over scrupulous in observing its precepts. He always conformed to conventional religious observances – at the Congress of Vienna he would not entertain or attend balls on Sundays – but on the other hand saw nothing wrong in billeting his militia in Bandon Church, telling his wife (4 January 1797):

> the scene [was] truly ridiculous ... all the pews filled with redcoats, eating bread and cheese, and a large quantity heaped on the Communion table. ... Your friend ... suddenly appeared in the pulpit with his bugle horn and made the church ring with his music. The ridicule of it made the soldiers forget their wet clothes.

This attitude was very different from the evangelical Protestantism of political colleagues such as Liverpool or Spencer Perceval.

By the time Robert was 12, the American War of Independence had developed into a European conflict. Robert's father, like Canning's, had been a strong partisan of 'Wilkes and Liberty' and had supported the revolting American colonies, but when France, unable to resist fishing in troubled waters, declared war on Britain and Ireland, that was a very different matter. Robert Stewart had no time for the French and like many Irish gentry raised a Volunteer regiment on the Newtownards estate. In that heady atmosphere of patriotism young Robert was thrilled, as any boy would be, by the military bands and smart uniforms; at a Volunteer review in 1782 his father let him lead a small contingent in a mock attack on Belfast, and 40 years later Castlereagh's obituary in the *Belfast Newsletter* (20 August 1822) recalled how 'young Stewart rushed forward in the ardour of his soul, grasped [a captured gun] in his arms, then mounted its carriage and with tears of triumph huzzaed to the main body, and called them to come on'. These early memories may explain Castlereagh's exceptional zeal as colonel of his battalion of the Derry militia 12 years later, though whether his military experience made him a better Secretary of State for War is doubtful. (Some years after the Second World War, Sir Francis Festing, when Chief of the Defence Staff, found that ministers with little or no military experience (usually Labour) were much better than those (usually Conservative) who were under the delusion that previous service as captains or majors had given them a sound strategic grasp.) Not until one day in 1813, in the wake of an advancing army in France when he saw hundreds of corpses and almost no living people, did Castlereagh see what real war, as opposed to soldiering with the militia, actually meant.

Undoubtedly, young Robert could have made a good soldier; he possessed plenty of courage and resourcefulness, and could normally keep a cool head in a crisis. When little more than a boy he confronted and saw off a poacher much bigger than himself, and during his first summer vacation from university showed outstanding coolness in the face of danger. He was sailing on Lough Strangford with a 12-year-old boy when they capsized. The boat sank; the boy could not swim. Castlereagh was a very poor swimmer, but managed to grab hold of the boat's tiller and a plank that had floated to the surface and, remembering from a science lesson that the human body could float, made them both keep quite still, face upwards and with body rigid. And thus they stayed for nearly half an hour until they were spotted from the shore and rescued.

When Robert was 15 Lord Camden told him:

> I am very much pleased and flattered with your letter, it invites a correspondence which I hope will never be discontinued, for besides the family connection, which looks like affinity, between us, the affection and esteem I have for your father, and your own personal merit, would of themselves entitle you to my friendship. ... I am, my dear Robert, yours most affectionately, Camden.

It was thanks to Camden that Robert went to Cambridge rather than Trinity College, Dublin, and he constantly gave shrewd advice – some of which, coming as it did from a seasoned man of the world, may not have been good for his character, but which was certainly beneficial to his career.

In September 1786 when he was 17, young Robert left Ireland for the first time and set off for England. His father went with him, and they took their time on what was in those days a long journey. They sailed from Kingstown (now Dun Laoghaire) to Holyhead, and thence by laborious stages through Wales, calling (as had become almost *de rigueur* for fashionable travellers) on 'the ladies of Llangollen', Lady Eleanor Butler and Miss Ponsonby, and so across England to stay with his mother's family at Sudbourne Hall near Ipswich, where Lord Hertford was pleased with what he saw of the grandson whom he had probably not met since his infancy.

Cambridge towards the end of the eighteenth century was at its lowest ebb. Dons were often sunk in port-sodden torpor or else absent altogether – Wilberforce wrote particularly scathingly about the Fellows of Trinity Hall who neither resided nor possessed any academic qualification (though admittedly some were practising law in London), instancing one Fellow who lived permanently at his home near Rye and alarmed the natives by his habit of emerging from bathing in the sea stark naked but with a beard that came down to his waist. Canning told his aunt after a visit to some Etonian friends at Cambridge: 'I have great reason to congratulate myself on having made choice of Oxford. Not but what Cambridge is very pleasant, but it does not seem the kind of place at which I could do much – indeed nothing but mathematics is required to be done.'[3] The dons, he considered, were snobs and toadies, and he was shocked to find that 'the Master of Trinity had the insolence to order that ... the Commoners ... should pull their caps off to the little prince [William of Gloucester] whenever they met him; to which some, and I should hope all of them, instantly refused to comply'.

Robert went up to St John's as a Fellow Commoner, which meant sharing with noblemen certain privileges such as wearing gowns with gold or silver trimmings and using the combination room. The privilege was granted not because of birth, but for a fee; Oxford had a similar system (Canning said that one reason why he was glad he hadn't gone to Cambridge was 'that there is infinitely more difference between commoner and Gent. Commoner than there is at Oxford, where I scarcely perceive it'). However, Robert did not spend all his time drinking, hunting and gambling like many Fellow Commoners, and St John's was a better college academically than most, and was beginning to produce good mathematicians. He made several friends, and went to stay during one vacation with Frederick Hervey at Ickworth. Lord Bristol, the earl-bishop, was away (presumably either building his splendid Palladian mansion in his Irish diocese or collecting art treasures on the Continent) so only Lady Bristol was at home. For most of the Christmas and Easter vacations, though, Robert stayed either with his mother's family at Sudbourne, or with Lord Camden in London or Bath; for the long summer vacations he went home to Ireland.

At the start of the Michaelmas term of 1787 Robert was not at all well and kept to his rooms for most of the term. Despite that – or perhaps because of it, since he could not socialize so worked instead – he was placed 'in the first class' at the December half-yearly examination. He stayed at Cambridge during the Christmas vacation and missed a visit to Bath, where, Lord Camden told him:

> you would have liked the Party ... [and all the] Plays, Balls, Concerts, Puppet Shows and Conjurers. ... But I do not write to tell you what you have lost by your unhappy illness, but for the more serious purpose of begging you to quit the College and quit the scene. ... So order a Post Chaise and come directly, and do not let the term business [i.e. keeping term] detain you for a moment. ... College life is too sedentary, and your Mind as well as your Body want some relief. ... Though the College learning is very valuable the society there is Pedantick, you may study Books at Cambridge, but you must come into the great world to study Men.

Camden was no admirer of academe; when Robert was slightly incapacitated by some accident, he wrote (28 November 1788), 'Divines will tell you that these untoward accidents are providential visitations for your good. ... Why, it may bring you to consort more with books than with wranglers', though he was afraid that this reflection was 'but little comfort, especially to a young man who loves hunting and shooting more than preaching'.

Despite Camden's urgings, Robert did not 'order a Post Chaise' and join the party at Bath, and on getting a report on his illness from Lord Bayham, his eldest son, Camden realized that it was better that Robert should remain quietly at Cambridge until he was well enough to travel. He missed most of the Lent term and the whole of the Summer term, for much of the time staying with Lord Camden, who considered that he would learn more of the ways of the world and of politicians in London than Cambridge could ever have taught him. He did not return to Cambridge until the Michaelmas term of 1788, and when he did he found undergraduate life dull and constricting. Perhaps Camden may have regretted recommending the advantages of London life, for he now reverted to more Polonius-like advice, warning against 'plunging ... into all the profligacy and dissipation' of London life and advising that 'you are more likely to acquire a taste for books [in Cambridge] than in London where the young men have forgot to read or write'. But in spite of this sage advice Robert decided to leave Cambridge for good at the end of the Michaelmas term, and not stay to get a degree.

Nowadays that would be a strange decision for a conscientious young man to make, but in those days a degree mattered little for the eldest son of a wealthy and influential father. So in January 1789 Castlereagh, as henceforth we will call him, ceased to be an undergraduate, and returned to Ireland where very soon he would embark on the political career that would last the whole of his life without interruption.

CHAPTER 3

Boyhood and Youth: Canning

The contrast between Castlereagh's early upbringing and that of Canning could hardly have been starker. After Canning's father died, his mother found cheap lodgings on a farm in Holborn. As well as her one-year-old son, she was expecting a second child – the boy was born on 23 December 1771, eight months after his father's death. Mary Ann and her two children were saved from actual destitution by her own family and by her brother-in-law Stratford, but she was very badly off. Swallowing her pride, she implored her father-in-law to continue his £200-a-year allowance, but he replied that he had 'no more connexion with you than I had ten years ago'. He was only prepared to make a small allowance to her children, 'during the infancy of one child or two I think forty pounds a year a sufficient allowance; as they grow up and of course require a further allowance I mean to increase it proportionately, but with regard to an allowance as a maintenance for yourself, I must beg to be excused'.

In January 1773 Stratford Canning (junior) became engaged to Mehitabel Patrick, whose father had been a Dublin merchant and near neighbour of the Cannings but had died without leaving his daughter enough money for old Stratford to consider her a suitable match for his son. She immediately offered to look after Mary Ann's two sons so that she could 'find a situation in a good family' as a companion or governess. But Mary Ann was determined to keep her sons with her, and 'under the protection of' the Duchess of Ancaster and with the backing of Garrick' went on the stage to earn a living. She was very beautiful, but alas no actress; Garrick gave her the lead in *Jane Shore* at Drury Lane, but it was a flop. (Lord Glenbervie's journal for 20 January 1819 says 'Went to see "Jane Shore"... had not seen this play since Canning's mother

15

made her debut in it. ... She acted in it most wretchedly, and never attempted it, I believe, a second time. I had gone there on purpose to support her'.) Before long, Mary Ann was reduced to touring the provinces, living with her two sons in a series of theatrical lodgings. To make matters worse she took up with an actor-manager called Reddish, who drank and had a reputation for dishonesty and a violent temper (he eventually died in York Asylum); nowadays her two little boys would probably have been on the 'at risk' register. Mary Ann never married Reddish but they had children – two sets of twins who died young, two sons Charles and Samuel, and Charles's twin sister.

By 1776 Mary Ann's second son had died, and she at last agreed that Stratford and Mehitabel (Hitty, as her family called her) might have six-year-old George to live with them. This was not the traumatic uprooting that some biographers have suggested, as the boy already knew his uncle and aunt well; as Mary Ann testified, Stratford had been 'ever willing to extend the helping hand' long before her son went to live with him. For all that, going to live with his uncle and aunt certainly changed his life dramatically. His aunt Hitty never took his mother's place in his affections, nor did she try to, since she had a strong fellow-feeling for Mary Ann and both had been 'unfortunate in being an object of that severity which never softens' (i.e. old Stratford Canning's temper). You could disapprove of Mary Ann, be exasperated by her, but she was vivacious, lovable and loving. Canning loved his mother very much, wrote to her every week of his life and visited her, often at great inconvenience, whenever he could. Mary Ann's trouble throughout her life was that she was rather too inclined to trust to 'the luck of the Irish' and hope that 'something would turn up'. Alas, all that turned up after Reddish was a Bristol linen draper called Hunn, who saw her on the stage and married her. Although the marriage produced five more children (making 14 in all for Mary Ann) it was never happy. In 1792 Canning told Hitty:

> my Mother is thank God in good health and considering all that she has undergone, in wonderful spirits. Her husband and she, I am afraid, do not live together on comfortable terms – live together indeed they do not. ... What will become of them, God knows. At present he is employed in the very lowest station that a mercantile house affords, that of rider to a tradesman at Bristol.

And three years later, Canning wrote in his journal, 'He is a scoundrel. Good God, that she could ever link herself to such a fellow.' It must have been an enormous handicap for a rising politician in the eighteenth century to have an actress mother married to Mr Hunn, but Canning never tried to distance

George Canning, aged five, drawn (possibly by Reynolds) shortly before he went to live with his uncle Stratford.

Canning's aunt, Mrs Stratford Canning, with her daughter Bess. Canning's uncle Stratford and his wife Mehitabel (Hitty) brought him up from the age of six.

himself from her, and did all he could to help both her and her brood of Reddishes and Hunns. When he came into £400 a year on his grandmother's death he insisted that his trustees give £50 of it to his mother, and when Pitt later obtained a pension for him he arranged for it to go to her instead.

Canning's uncle, like his father, had been disinherited for making an 'unsuitable' marriage. There is a folder containing letters between Stratford Canning *père* and *fils* on which Hitty has written 'to be examined and destroyed'; later she crossed that out and instead wrote 'need not be destroyed', adding in the shaky handwriting of old age 'Letters to S.C. Sent from his son S.C. previous to the year 1773 when all intercourse ceased between them' (there are also some letters from father to son). The letters belie any assumption that his sons must have been reprobates to have incurred their father's wrath; their crime was simply that they failed to use marriage as a means to increase the family's wealth and importance. But despite failing to marry for money, by 1776 Stratford was prospering as a partner in a merchant bank, Borrowes and Canning. Besides his house in Clement's Lane in the City he also had one in Putney, which was then rural. He already had two children, two-year-old Harry and a baby girl, Bess. (Subsequently there were three more boys: William, who was ordained and became a canon of Windsor; Charles, killed at Waterloo as a colonel on Wellington's staff; and Stratford, who ended up as Viscount Stratford de Redcliffe, KG.) Old Stratford Canning had died in 1775 and his widow gladly agreed to pay for her grandson's education, so Stratford sent young George to Hyde Abbey, a preparatory school at Winchester with an excellent academic reputation. It was doubtless tough by present-day standards, but Canning cannot have found it too bad since in later life he always spoke well of it. When he was 12 he went to Eton, telling his mother in a pathetic, blotchy letter, 'Alas I am not half as happy as I was at Winchester.' [1] Before long, however, Canning came to love Eton, making many lifelong friends and showing academic brilliance. He could have become a Colleger (i.e. in the Scholars' house) but stood out against it. Four years later he told his old Hyde Abbey master, Dr Richman:

> I am now, my dear Sir, at the top of Eton School. I am the first of the Oppidants [sic]. ... I was to have been on the Foundation, but I did so dislike the idea, and saw so evidently the great difference of behaviour and respect paid to the one situation in preference to the other, that I prevailed upon my uncle (being aided by the advice of Mr Fox and Mr Sheridan, who gave their opinions in my favour) to give up the idea. ... A Colleger rises much slower in the school, and is consequently much later at the top. He stays till 19, an Oppidant [sic] till 17; two years ... to a man whose line is the Bar, [that] is surely an object.

Canning had decided to follow in his father's footsteps – but, unlike him, to succeed.

During the summer holidays of 1785 Stratford and Hitty took their nephew and their eldest son Harry to visit their grandmother in Ireland. Laetitia Canning evidently took to her eldest grandson George, and on her death 18 months later left him the small Kilkenny estate of Kilbracken, worth about £220 a year, which was part of her own dowry. Although Canning never went to Ireland again, the fact of being an Irish landlord, albeit on a small scale, gave him an insight into the Irish character and habits through his dealings with Mr Dogharty, his agent.

Back at Eton, Canning blossomed. He was the leading light in producing a schoolboy magazine *The Microcosm*, which was so successful that the printer Gally Knight bought the copyright for £50. It poked fun at pomposity and literary pretension, and although the in-jokes make no sense to us we can still appreciate, for example, the parody of some prosy eighteenth-century eulogies, in the imaginary 'biography of Mr Gregory Griffin':

> The voluntary sallies of Mr Griffin's wit were only to be equalled by the readiness of his repartee; of this the following anecdotes will give evidence.
> Mr G____ walking one day in the Street, was suddenly accosted by a friend of his who, pulling off his hat, addressed him with 'How do you do, Mr Griffin?'
> Mr G____ without the least hesitation or embarrassment instantly retorted 'Pretty well, I thank you sir. I hope you are well?'
> Another time, Mr Griffin was attacked in a large company by a lady, who thinking to catch him unprepared asked him very sharply 'How much two and two were?' 'Two and two, madam' said he with great quickness, and without betraying the least confusion, 'make *four*'.

The last *Microcosm* (July 1787) contained a 'Self-Obituary of Gregory Griffin' which is of some historic interest. Bell's *Life of Canning* imagined that 'Mr Griffin' who 'was at the age of six years employed in learning the rudiments of my mother tongue, spinning cock-chafers on corking pins, and longing for bread and butter ... the utmost stretch of my intellect was the acquisition of the same bread and butter' was really a pseudonym for Canning himself. But rough though his first six years were, Canning had never sunk to quite the level that many biographers, following Bell, believed. Once an assertion gets into print, it is hard to dislodge.

On 22 May 1787 Stratford Canning died, aged 43. This was a big blow to his nephew, as well as to his own children. Canning called him 'indisputably one of the best of men in every respect, as a parent, a friend and a Christian', and his uncle had very largely filled the gap left by his father's early death.

His aunt Hitty could not take over as Canning's guardian because she was a woman; but luckily Canning had twice been to stay with William Leigh, a Norfolk rector who had married one of his Canning aunts (Bess, widow of Westby Perceval of King's County), and he now wrote to ask Leigh to be his guardian:

> To you, my dear Mr Leigh, as my nearest male relation (older than myself) I have in some measure a natural right to apply. ... But I am well aware of the trouble which must attend the employment. ... You will be so good as to direct your answer to this letter to me at Eton, whither I shall return tomorrow [25 May] after calling on Lord Macartney, who has been kind enough to interest himself very much about me. Oxford was I know, and I believe Christ Church the College, which my Uncle had designed for me, though he intended writing about particulars to a Mr Jackson who has two Sons at Christ Church himself.

His uncle's death had put Canning in a difficult situation. He was barely 17, and clearly did not know how far the plans for his university education had got – he had not even realized that 'Mr Jackson' was in fact the Dean of Christ Church. It was a stroke of luck that his father's old friend Lord Macartney was in England (having just declined the post of Governor-General of Bengal), as his intervention seems to have pricked Leigh into overcoming his reluctance to take on the responsibility of becoming Canning's guardian and trustee. It was lucky, too, that Macartney was a friend of Dr Jackson, who agreed to give Canning a place at Christ Church; left to himself Leigh would have sent him to Cambridge. Even so, all was not entirely plain sailing; Canning wanted to go to Christ Church as a Gentleman Commoner, partly because he thought that ordinary commoners at Oxford were as much looked down on as they were at Cambridge, and partly because the Dean pointed out that a Gentleman Commoner could take his degree after two years instead of three, a great advantage to anyone destined for the Bar, assuring him that the extra expense 'was not so considerable by any means'. Macartney came down in favour of the idea, but Leigh, rightly, put his foot down, realizing that Canning's income was not enough to allow of any unnecessary expense, however 'inconsiderable'. Canning, as one might expect, disagreed; he told Richman, 'I have been involved in a great deal of unpleasant perplexity with regard to entering as a Gentleman Commoner. ... Mr Leigh wrote a letter to Lord M in which he stated his objection [so] Lord M returned an answer agreeing to accede to Mr L's sentiments.'[2]

That episode brings home how insecure Canning must now have felt. His father was dead, his mother had married the appalling Hunn, and the unexpected death of his uncle and guardian had left him with no obvious person to turn to for advice. He knew that Stratford had wanted him to go to Oxford, as did his father's old friend Lord Macartney, but Leigh, his 'nearest male relation', wanted him to go to Cambridge. Macartney thought he ought to go to Oxford as a Gentleman Commoner (as did Sheridan, a close family friend), and had Stratford been alive he would almost certainly have thought so too – he could easily have upped his nephew's allowance to cover the expense. Canning seems to have enlisted Macartney's support for the Gentleman Commoner idea *without* telling him that Leigh had already vetoed it. In the circumstances, that is perhaps forgivable, but it makes one wonder if the deviousness that Canning sometimes displayed to get his own way may have had its origin in his being left without any firm support at an age when he most needed it.

Dr Jackson managed, but only just, to fit Canning in at Christ Church in time to count as 'keeping term'. A letter to Mrs Leigh (dated 'Dover Street, Novr. 5th 1787') was written 'amid the pangs of hairdressing':

> Yesterday was the fatal day that queued me, and robbed me of half the acquaintance I have in the world, for I do not suppose 1 in 5 would be able to recognise me in my present situation [Canning's hair had been cut short and was now being pulled back into a fashionable though uncomfortable queue]. I have not perhaps benefited myself much by the removal, for though it has relieved my mind I find the weight is only transferred, and my tail by its repeated pulling makes me perceive that, like King William, 'I have it behind'.

There is a portrait at Harewood House said to be of Canning, painted by Reynolds in 1788 and typical of portraits of boys leaving Eton at that period with their long, flowing locks. If that portrait is of Canning, then the date must be wrong, but the picture illustrates how the transition from schoolboy to undergraduate was marked by a change in hair style; Canning's visit to the barber was, as it were, a rite of passage. He was not, as Castlereagh was, strikingly good looking, but his portraits show a lively, intelligent face. The Lawrence portrait of 1809 shows very little difference from the Hoppner one some 15 years earlier, except that by the age of 39 he had gone bald on top. It is a curiously modern face; Canning looks remarkably like Ian Macleod who died in 1970 when Chancellor of the Exchequer, and who, like Canning, was considered by more right-wing colleagues to be 'too clever by half'.

Once at Oxford, Canning told his aunt:

> I do not expect to do very much in the studying line this term, as the
> mathematical lectures do not begin till next term. However, not to be totally
> idle I am reading a Greek play with Ld H. Spencer to Mr Pett [his tutor] who
> is so bashful a man that it is with the utmost difficulty that I can get anything
> out of him. ... He is however exceedingly clever, and one of the best men
> in the world. ... Luckily for me Ld H. Spencer had come to Oxford about a
> week before me, and though very *fresh* was able to inform me of a variety of
> circumstances in which I should have been at a loss how to conduct myself. I
> was on Wednesday last elected a member of the Eton Club [whose] uniform is
> pretty enough, a dark chocolate coat, large white buttons with E on them, buff
> silk waistcoat and black silk inexpressibles [trousers]. It is wonderful what a
> number of Clubs there are here. ... The uniform of the Resurrection Club is
> a black coat with death's head buttons. The cause of this institution is that the
> anatomical lectures have been at a stand for some time past for want of a body,
> and this Club is formed for the purpose of endeavouring to procure one. I am
> not yet so far gone in the study of anatomy as to wish to become a member.

Canning formed many lifelong friendships at Christ Church, including 'Jenkinson, Lord Hawkesbury's son. He is very clever, and very remarkably good-
natured. We talk together on every subject but one, *Politics*; and that, having
sounded one another in two or three slight skirmishes, we now by a sort of
tacit compact mutually avoid.'

Jenkinson's father, who became Lord Liverpool, was in Pitt's cabinet, while
Canning followed family tradition and was an ardent supporter of Fox.

Canning was to have spent the summer vacation with Hitty's friend Mrs
Crewe, the 'toast of the Buff and the Blue', a leading Opposition hostess. But,
as he explained to the Leighs (26 September 1788):

> I found that [my mother] was to be in Chester and would be playing there
> exactly at the same time. ... I should indeed have been very glad of an
> opportunity to see her under any circumstances, but to be under the necessity
> of seeing her in such a situation, while it was not yet in my power to rescue
> her from it [would] be a useless and a painful gratification. ... I hope in God
> the time will come when it will be in my power to effect something more
> permanent for her ease and comfort.

Meanwhile he asked Mrs Crewe 'that *her name* should be prefixed to the bills'
for his mother's benefit night, and she gladly agreed. Canning must have felt
his mother's plight very acutely; a few months earlier Mrs Sheridan had been
to a play with the Crewes and told Hitty:

Who should I see acting there, but Mrs Hunn, G. Canning's mother. I should not have known her, had not Mrs Hesketh told me she had been *one* of Mr Reddish's wives – I cannot tell you my dear Woman how shocked I was when I saw how wretched, and miserable her vices have made her. She was very big with child, and thinner, older, and more ugly than you can imagine when you recollect her, as I did. I fancy she knew me, for she never took her eyes from my face, which quite distressed me – but her Husband! What a creature! I never in my life saw anything so vulgar, and illiterate; with *her* understanding and talents (for she certainly *had* both) [how could she] make such a choice!

The following year, in September 1789, Canning did visit Crewe Hall, and a letter to his cousins gives a good description of a country house party in those days:

At ten – or rather from ten to twelve – at any time – breakfast in a large gallery of God knows how many feet long, in which there are billiard tables, Trou-Madame and a variety of other games for wet weather, together with a very fine collection of books. After breakfast, riding, and driving, which I do with great success on a coach-box which is prefix'd to a phaeton. On Saturday I drove the Bp [of Peterborough] and Mrs Crewe to Etruria (Mr Wedgewood's work-place) about fourteen miles, and coming back drove so fast that the poor Bishop roared aloud for mercy. ... At four or five or six or seven, according to the day, dinner; in the evening cards, books and conversation, and at eleven supper, after which Mr Crewe, Mr Greville and I generally sit till about one. ... The perfect freedom with which one does what one likes, nobody asking why or wherefore, is charming.

He also had the chance to go shooting, and claimed that 'I trust in a few days I shall be able to hit [his cousin] Willy's bottom at ten yards distance'. When Mrs Crewe took him on a visit to the dowager duchess of Leinster at Buxton, they found the guests reading a play. Among them

was the Provost of Dublin College, Hely Hutchinson, an old man of about 70 or 80. This old fool proposed they should get up this play and read it before all the company. In the morning Lady Lucy Fitzgerald who is a very good natured laughing sensible girl proposed having a play bill printed. Now it was very evident that if play bills were printed, the whole affair would get into the newspapers. This never occurred to the Duchess, but it did occur to me and made me all the more eager, and the playbill was accordingly wound up with 'And Pierre, by the *Right Honourable Hely Hutchinson, Provost of Dublin, Secretary or State for Ireland* etc. etc.' Just as we were setting off to have this printed arrived a message to say that the old Provost was in such a rage as never was seen.

Canning sounds from his letters to have been thoroughly bumptious. He could seldom resist a temptation to puncture pomposity by a cutting remark, or occasionally by a practical joke, but Mrs Sheridan reassured Hitty, saying:

> I must say a few words to quiet the apprehensions you seem to entertain of G. Canning. I assure you that it is not only my opinion but the opinion of all I know Man or Woman that he is not only the cleverest, but the most pleasing young man possible. His manner is perfectly modest and unassuming, he never puts himself forward, nor adopts any one foible of the Boys of the present age. S. desires me to tell you that so far from thinking he is likely to be hurt by living in the World, it is *his* opinion that it is the greatest service to him. ... If George has any fault, it is that he is too grave, or rather too old in his manner for his age, and the commerce of the world will rub off a *little* of the Latin and Greek, and give him an additional brilliance without decreasing his sterling value.

Certainly Canning was not neglecting his studies. During his third year at Oxford he was awarded a Studentship (i.e. fellowship) at Christ Church – 'a creditable thing and a profitable thing enough, seeing that it brings God knows how much meat and drink and lodging in the year, and what is best of all, it was given ... without being in any degree solicited for me' (i.e. it was on merit). He stayed at Crewe Hall again in 1790 and 1791, and, thanks to Mrs Crewe, met people such as Pepper Arden the Attorney-General and the courtier Sir Ralph Payne, whom it was useful for an aspiring politician to know. In 1790 the house party all went on a trip to the Lakes which Canning ungraciously described as 'great pieces of water ... and boats, which you may sail or row in if you please, which you will find pretty much like sailing or rowing anywhere else – except indeed that here you will have the advantage of being wet through for it always rains – at least I guess so, as we were drenched every day regularly',[3] though later on he came to love the Lakes and often went there for holidays.

The Sheridans too played their part in making sure Canning lived 'in the world'. On his way back to Oxford for his last term, he had stayed with them in London and was

> introduced to the Prince of Wales ... at a grand supper and catch-singing. I was charmed beyond measure, and far beyond my expectation, with the elegance of his address, and the gentlemanliness of his manner. He did me the honour of a good deal of conversation, and asked me, as his father had done before him [when Canning was at Eton] whether I intended to be Lord Chancellor? to which (as you may easily guess) cocking my hat fiercely over one eye, putting my arms akimbo, and hollowing with a loud voice, I replied

'Yes – damme' [a take-off of Lord Thurlow].

And just before going down from Oxford for good that June, Canning was twice invited 'to meet Mr Fox and his lady (Mrs A) [Mrs Armistead whom in 1796 Fox eventually married] ... and have paddled about with them and Lord Holland and other folks on the water, and dined by the side of clear streams at Clifden, on cold viands of the most exquisite flavour'.

Although Canning was set on a political career, reading for the Bar had to come first – unlike many of his friends he had to earn his living. He spent most of the law vacations at Christ Church, where as a Student his expenses were 'merely 8d a day for rolls and butter' since he got dinner and supper free, whereas in his London lodgings dinner was 'about 7 shillings, and an oyster and a tiff of something good at night' cost one and sixpence, leaving '8s 6d balance in favour of Ch. Ch.'. He wrote rather wistfully on Christmas Day 1791 to his cousin Bess:

> you I suppose are preparing to eat roasted Turkey with a zeal which would do honour to a Bishop. ... I am quite alone, about to sit down to a solitary mutton chop and mince pye – and to drink a merry Xmas to you all, after dinner, in a small tumbler of wine and water ... my only relaxation from the fatigues of legal investigation is the reading of the first lesson of the morning and evening Service – aloud – which I do every day in the College Chapel in my quality of a *Student Bachelor of Arts*.

But although his days were being spent in 'law – law – law', politics was never far from Canning's thoughts. Like Castlereagh, he had been brought up as a fervent supporter of Fox and the Opposition Whigs, and welcomed the French Revolution with open arms – as Wordsworth put it, 'in that dawn 'twas bliss to be alive, and to be young was very heaven'. But before long, events in Paris began to make some Whigs have second thoughts – Burke with his *Reflections on the Revolution in France* was the first to express what would previously have been thought heresy, that 'Liberty, Equality, Fraternity' might be fine in theory but could have unacceptable side-effects when put into practice. Just as Castlereagh was starting to be what his County Down constituents called 'Pittized', so too with Canning. He had always hero-worshipped Fox, who was not only a family friend (and godfather to Hitty's third son, Charles Fox Canning, killed at Waterloo) but the most brilliant politician of his generation, but in his letter describing his Clifden picnic with Fox he mentions 'the poor King and Queen of France' – a phrase that a few months earlier he would not have dreamed of applying to a Bourbon monarch (it would be fascinating to know what, if anything, Fox had to say on that picnic about recent events in France).

The trigger for Canning's decision to change his allegiance from Fox to Pitt may have been the young Opposition MP Charles Grey's founding of the 'Association of the Friends of the People' in April 1792. Even Windham thought this call for democracy ill-timed – 'you don't set about to repair your house during the hurricane season' – and Canning not only felt the same, but also disliked its author personally. Grey had not endeared himself to Sheridan's friends by trying to push himself forward during the Regency crisis of 1788, and more recently, and far worse, he had seduced the glamorous Georgiana, Duchess of Devonshire (like Princess Diana two centuries later a daughter of Lord Spencer; she had supported Fox in the Westminster election wearing a fox's brush on her head and kissing everyone from babies to butchers). In the spring of 1792 Georgiana, in order to avoid scandal, had to go to France for Grey's baby to be born. France in 1792 was no place for a duchess, and Grey was responsible for her being there. Personal dislike of the man coupled with disapproval of his ill-timed Association of the People may well have given Canning the final push that decided him to turn his back on the party and policy of Fox.

It so happened that two people who might have persuaded Canning not to turn to Pitt were otherwise occupied. At about the same time as the Duchess was giving birth in Paris, Eliza Sheridan gave birth to a baby girl fathered by Lord Edward Fitzgerald (who six years later died in Dublin from wounds received while resisting arrest as a ringleader of the Irish rebellion). Hitty, whom the Sheridans always called 'Sister Christian', had been so shocked at Eliza's adultery that she refused to see her, but when Sheridan told her that Eliza was very ill, Hitty went to her at once. After the baby was born, Eliza's condition deteriorated sharply, and in April she went to Hot Wells near Bristol in the vain hope of a cure. Sheridan persuaded Hitty to go with her – 'her friend, whom she loves best in the world, Mrs Canning, I have prevailed on to accompany her. ... There never was in the World a more friendly act than her doing so. She has left her daughter and all her children whom she dotes on for this office.' For two agonizing months Hitty was constantly at her bedside, and after Eliza died on 18 June she stayed on for the funeral at Bath Abbey a fortnight later. When she did eventually return to London Hitty was busy helping Sheridan sort out Eliza's possessions and catching up with her own domestic affairs; also, Eliza on her deathbed had made Hitty promise to take charge of her baby, Mary, which of course she did. As a result, neither Hitty nor Sheridan, who might have had some influence on Canning, saw very much of him that summer, and when they did they had more pressing things to think about than his political views. When eventually Hitty heard that her nephew had deserted her friend Fox and thrown in his lot with 'that monster' Pitt she was horrified. Unlike Castlereagh, who was persuaded to throw in his lot with Pitt by his grandfather, Lord Camden, Canning was most certainly not encouraged to do so by any family pressure – on the contrary. Hitty felt that her nephew was betraying all that his uncle Stratford had stood for; coming at a time when she was emotionally drained and exhausted, Canning's decision seemed to her to be self-seeking apostasy, and she upbraided her 22-year-old nephew as if he were still a schoolboy. In a long and patient reply (15 October) Canning affirmed that,

> the sort of argument which never did, or will, or in my opinion ought to make an impression on my mind, is that which is derived from example only – as when one hears 'Such a one thought so', brought as sufficient ground for one's self being so to think. ... I flatter myself that you will not think that I have set up for myself a surly, selfish, impudent confidence of opinion – nor will you accuse me of having been 'got at', 'talked over', 'come round', 'taken in', and other such elegant phrases.

The letter was sent from Crewe Hall, but if Canning thought that such an impeccably Whig address would mollify his aunt, he was mistaken; she was never reconciled to Canning's political views and stayed a staunch Foxite all her life.

Canning, however, had made up his mind. On 15 August (not having dared, or at any rate cared, to tell his aunt) he had called on Pitt at Downing Street at his own request, and Pitt, who knew a good thing when he saw it, promised to find him a Commons seat as soon as possible. Thanks to his uncle and aunt having rescued him from the tender mercies of Reddish he could start on a political career with many advantages: the best possible education, a capacity to amuse and a first-class brain. He did also have one disadvantage that can easily be overlooked by anyone living in the twenty-first century: he was not a lord, nor the son or even cousin of a lord. That counted for more than we today could think possible, in the eyes both of the King and of the ruling political class. The avidity with which peerages were sought, even Irish ones that did not convey a seat in the House of Lords, may seem extraordinary to us, but it was not motivated simply by snobbery or social climbing and a wish to boast of aristocratic lineage – after all, both Castlereagh's and Jenkinson's fathers were born commoners – but being a lord or an heir to a peerage gave weight politically. Eton and Christ Church had given Canning several aristocratic friends such as Lord Henry Spencer, Granville Leveson-Gower, or Morpeth, who accepted him as a social equal, and the fact that he had to earn his living made no difference since many a younger son of a peer had to do the same. But during the course of Canning's career he was frequently criticized as being an upstart, and what would be considered normal ambition in other politicians was seen to mark out Canning as an adventurer on the make — especially as political opponents could point out that he was the son of an actress and therefore socially outside the pale.

CHAPTER 4

The Young Politician: Castlereagh

In the same year that his son came down from Cambridge, Robert Stewart was created Baron Londonderry in the peerage of Ireland. (He subsequently became a viscount in 1795 and Earl of Londonderry in 1796, which was when his eldest son became known as Viscount Castlereagh, and Marquess of Londonderry in 1816.) Although an Irish peerage did not give its holder a seat in the Westminster House of Lords (so that even when Castlereagh eventually became Marquess of Londonderry he remained in the House of Commons as an MP), there was in 1790 an Irish parliament at Dublin. When Robert Stewart, on becoming a member of the Irish House of Lords, had to give up his seat as an MP for County Down, he was determined that his son should take his place, so in 1790 young Robert found himself a parliamentary candidate. The fact that he was still under 21 and thus ineligible for election did not seem to worry anyone, and he set to work with a will. He stood on a radical platform of parliamentary reform and the curbing of corrupt government patronage, all very unlike his later political views. He also stood for the repeal of the Test Acts that disenfranchised Catholics, so as a product of Armagh Royal School and Cambridge University he also needed to reassure the dissenters of County Down of his *bona fides*. With this no doubt in mind, he often spoke (according to his obituary in the *Observer*) from chapel pulpits during the campaign.

Electioneering was robust. Robert's opponent was Lord Hillsborough, eldest son of the Marquess of Downshire, who looked on County Down as his family fiefdom. Robert's supporters called Hillsborough 'an absentee, a whoremaster, a pimp, and an adulterer', and his supporters retorted with the text 'Go, boy, tarry in Jericho till thy beard be grown.' The French Revolution was stirring political passions to an even hotter pitch than usual, and the 'Northern Whig Club' formed in Belfast drew up Robert's election manifesto. The fact that he started his political career drinking toasts to 'President Washington and the United States of America', 'A Happy Establishment to the Gallic Constitution', and 'Our Sovereign Lord the People' (the same toast that later led to Charles Fox having his name struck off the Privy Council when he proposed it) helps explain why in his later career as a rather right-wing government minister Castlereagh was accused of being unprincipled.

The poll was opened seven weeks before Robert's 21st birthday so that his nomination was illegal, but objections were brushed aside by a friendly sheriff, and at the end of three months' furious campaigning Hillsborough topped the poll with 3,534 votes. However, as it was a two-member constituency Robert, in second place with 3,114, was also elected. Success had not come cheap: the family property in Dublin had to be sold together with the collection of books and pictures, and plans for enlarging Mount Stewart were not put into effect (which for later generations probably proved a blessing). It has been calculated that Robert's election cost his father £60,000 – at least £3 million today.

The new parliament was adjourned after only two weeks, so Castlereagh (as we will henceforth call young Robert even though he did not assume the title for another six years) could rest and recuperate at Mount Stewart until the new session began in January. For the gentlemen of the Protestant Ascendancy the journey to Dublin was worth the discomfort of winter travel along the atrocious Irish roads, for there was, as Arthur Young wrote, 'a very good society in Dublin in a parliament winter, with dinners and parties, and balls and suppers, every night of the week'. Lord Cloncurry reckoned that Dublin society in the 1790s was 'as polished and brilliant as that of Paris in its best days ... with a conviviality which could not be equalled in France'. The Ascendancy was a close-knit society where everyone knew everyone else, but that did not stop quarrels and duelling – Lord Camden had warned that 'the Irish are captious and quarrelsome, especially when they are in liquor' (which was quite often) – although it certainly made for conviviality.

Ireland was governed like a colony; the Dublin parliament could huff and puff, but the real decisions were taken in London. Many of the bigger landlords lived in England and never saw the abject poverty of their tenants. When Lord Bessborough, for instance, came into his inheritance on his father's death in 1793 he went over to Ireland and set eyes on his 27,000-acre estate for the first time in his life; and not until 1808 did Lady Bessborough go with him to Ireland for her first visit. What she saw evidently distressed her; her mother Lady Spencer wrote (29 October 1808): 'Would to God, my dear child, it were in your power to do as much good there as your heart would dictate.

... I sincerely wish you might make an annual or biennial visit there – and if it was not for that vile herring pond – how I should like to go with you.' The Irish Sea was indeed a barrier; a man might be an admirable landlord of his English estates but leave his Irish property to be managed by an agent who might or might not be honest or capable. Those of the Ascendancy who were landlords and came to Dublin for 'a Parliament winter' were usually too taken up with the social whirl to notice the dreadful poverty in the slums surrounding Dublin's fashionable Georgian squares. The ruling class only became aware of the poor on their doorstep when an enraged mob from time to time descended on College Green and tried to seize and beat up any MPs they could catch. Castlereagh, therefore, served his political apprenticeship in a milieu that taught him to despise the mob and hold firmly to the principle that one must never give in to its demands, even if they are reasonable, as that might only encourage further demands. He might drink to 'The Sovereign Lord, the People', but when the 'people' came brandishing cudgels and demanding justice, his whole upbringing taught him to brook no nonsense and call out the troops if needs be. Growing up in that world must also have inclined him to think that the corruption and jobbery that he had previously attacked were in fact natural and inevitable and must be accepted as the norm.

Lord Camden realized that real political power lay in Westminster, not Dublin. He also realized that his grandson was exhausted and jaded after his election campaign and was finding County Down society distinctly unappealing. Seizing his moment, he suggested (23 January 1791): 'Would there be any harm in professing yourself a friend of the Pitt administration in England, though you are in opposition to the Castle [i.e. the Dublin government]?' Camden's concern for his step-grandson is very touching; he had become a true guide, philosopher and friend. Castlereagh took his advice. When on 21 February the Irish patriot Grattan moved for an inquiry to look into the East India Company monopoly, Castlereagh supported the motion, 'since it was only a motion for inquiry', thus giving the impression of hearty support without actually having to declare himself against the monopoly. Even so, his speech ruffled some feathers at the Castle, the Lord Lieutenant complaining that the young man might have shown more gratitude for his father's peerage, while the Chief Secretary commented that his conduct in combining an anti-government speech with 'a long panegyric on Mr Pitt ... needs no comment'.

When the 1791 session ended in June, Castlereagh set off on a short tour of the Continent. On his way through London he bought a copy of Burke's *Reflections on the Revolution in France*, and on the Continent he met several French émigrés whose views strongly reinforced Burke's arguments. He concluded that, bad as the Bourbon monarchy had been, the revolutionary principles were 'unsafe'. His County Down supporters, however, had no such reservations: the *Belfast News-Letter* reported that at the Bastille Day celebrations on 14 July the Volunteers had marched triumphantly through the streets followed by members of the Whig Club wearing uniforms and green cockades – 'the wearing of the green' – while a float represented a figure of Hibernia in chains receiving the image of Liberty from a Volunteer. Castlereagh was finding it increasingly difficult to please his County Down constituents and yet at the same time support Pitt. When the East India monopoly came up again, he voted with the government, and his constituents called him 'a half-blooded fellow ... the meanest of the human race' (and doubtless more besides).

Parliament apart, however, Castlereagh was enjoying himself. Young, good-looking, the wealthy son of a peer, he was elected as a matter of course to Daly's Club in Dublin, and in County Down took his natural place as a JP, supporter of the Down Hunt and local landowner. In the autumn of 1792 his second visit to the Continent was curtailed by the fighting in the Low Countries, and he was one of the few to predict correctly that the ill-trained French revolutionaries would defeat the professional armies of Austria and Prussia. When Britain declared war in January 1793, however, Castlereagh surprisingly sided with the small radical minority who thought that the declaration did not commit Ireland, even though the Opposition leader Grattan supported the war. Castlereagh's political principles still seem to have been in a state of flux, but a year later he came to see (as he told Camden's son Lord Bayham) that the existing Irish system of parliamentary government was so corrupt that it simply would not work. The choice had to be made between governing Ireland 'by reason', with the consent of the governed, or 'by force', imposing British rule. Since under the first option Catholics would inevitably form the majority in the Irish parliament and thus set it at odds with Westminster, Castlereagh preferred the second option, government 'by force', even if that meant abolishing the Irish parliament and reverting to direct rule. His whole upbringing made him dislike the idea of direct rule, but he was clear-sighted enough to realize that it was the lesser of two evils, because sooner or later Catholics would have to be given the vote, and in any Irish parliamentary election they would form a majority. Castlereagh was essentially a pragmatist; a few years later as Chief Secretary he would use corruption in order, as he put it, 'to buy out and secure for ever the fee simple of Irish corruption which has so long enfeebled the powers of government' – in other words, compensate borough-mongers for the loss of a right that they should never have had in the first place.[1]

Despite his youthful radical fervour, Castlereagh was never at heart a liber-
tarian like Charles James Fox. When war was declared in January 1793, any
doubts that he may have had about its legality were soon swept aside by patriotic fervour. He became lieutenant-colonel of a Derry militia battalion and
took his duties very seriously – duties that mainly involved the curbing of civil
unrest. In February of the following year, Lord Camden became seriously ill,
and Castlereagh hurried over to England in time to see him before he died.
It proved a momentous visit. When Camden died in April, his grandson felt
the loss keenly; not only had he been very fond of his step-grandfather, but he
was now also bereft of his counsel and advice. However, while still in London
he met and fell in love with Lady Emily Hobart. Her father, the second Earl
of Buckinghamshire, had died the previous year; a Norfolk man, he had been
an MP for Norwich from 1747 to 1752, but the pinnacle of his career had
come after he had succeeded his father and been a (not very successful) Lord
Lieutenant of Ireland (from 1777 to 1780), so Castlereagh was following in
the tradition of his father. The couple were married at St George's, Hanover
Square, on 9 June 1794; they were blissfully happy, and remained so throughout their marriage. Emily was extremely attractive – Dr Haliday, the secretary
of the Northern Whig Club, said she was 'as fine, comely, good-humoured,
playful (not to say romping) a piece of flesh as any Illyrian'. Her husband, too,
was tall, handsome and good-looking, and like Emily had his full share of sex-
appeal – indeed, gossip had credited him with many 'gallantries' – and they
hated being parted even for a single night. Emily had little taste for politics
or diplomacy and had a penchant for saying or doing the wrong thing at the
wrong time, but she loved and admired her husband and loyally supported him
throughout his life.

Marriage was not the only result of Castlereagh's visit to England that
summer. On 25 May he was returned for Tregony, a Cornish treasury borough,
becoming an MP in Westminster as well as in Dublin. This was due to Pitt,
who had better judgement than his Lord Lieutenant (who had grumbled 'I have
no hopes of Mr Stewart; he uniformly votes against us'), and saw in young
Castlereagh a recruit worth having. Back in County Down, his constituents became uneasy; Dr Haliday had already feared that his MP had become
'Camdenized'; now he complained that he was 'Pittized'. For the time being,
Castlereagh's (and Emily's) youthful charm kept his constituents' criticisms
at bay, but he could not go on indefinitely riding two horses at once, being
Opposition member for County Down, yet loyally voting for the suspension of
Habeas Corpus at Westminster.

Emily, née Hobart, Viscountess Castlereagh, at the time of her marriage – 'as fine, comely, good-humoured, playful (not to say romping) a piece of flesh as any Illyrian' (see p 33).

The views about Ireland's future that Castlereagh had expressed to his cousin may well have been to some extent an early result of being 'Pittized'. Pitt had realized that reforms of some kind were necessary. The Irish parliament had been set up in response to grievances about trade alarmingly similar to those of the American colonists; you could say that the Dublin parliament was conceived during the Boston Tea Party. But the Regency crisis of 1788 alerted Pitt to its dangers; for while Pitt was doing his best to limit the scope of the Regency Bill, the Irish parliament had pledged loyalty to the Prince of Wales as Regent. If that situation were to repeat itself, the result could be devastating, with Ireland recognizing the authority of a prince who supported Fox's peace party while Britain was at war with France (indeed, as we saw, there was a move in the Irish parliament to deny that the declaration of war in 1793 covered Ireland as well as Britain). Simply abolishing the Irish parliament would be impracticable: it would mean Ireland having to be coerced by force, and the American war had been an awful warning of what might happen when that solution was tried. In Ireland there was the further complication that over three-quarters of the population were Catholics, who were treated as second-class citizens. Pitt and Dundas had succeeded in pushing measures of Catholic relief through a reluctant parliament in 1792 and 1793, so that Catholics then had the vote, were allowed sit on juries and could hold minor offices. But if they were allowed actually to sit in the Irish parliament, they would very soon control it, so Pitt was coming to the conclusion that the only solution was to unite the Irish parliament with the Westminster parliament, where there would be not the remotest danger of Catholics forming a majority.

In the same year, 1794, that Castlereagh married Emily and also became an English MP, the Duke of Portland together with several other Opposition Whigs joined Pitt's government. One of them was Lord Fitzwilliam, whom Pitt invited to go to Dublin as viceroy. Firzwilliam should in theory have been just the man to guide Ireland along that path; he was aware of its needs and sympathetic to reform. Unfortunately, although his heart was in the right place he was, to quote Lord Rosebery, 'absolutely devoid of judgment, reticence, and tact'.[2] Before his appointment had even been confirmed Fitzwilliam invited Grattan to London and tried to have Chancellor Fitzgibbon (later Lord Clare) dismissed. Pitt summoned Fitzwilliam to meet him, together with Portland and his colleagues in the government (Spencer, Windham and Grenville) and impress on him that he must not make speeches that would arouse unrealistic hopes among Catholics or undue alarm among the Protestant Ascendancy, and must not dismiss Chancellor Fitzgibbon. Unfortunately, this had little effect: as soon as Fitzwilliam arrived in Dublin he gave leave to introduce a Catholic

Emancipation Bill, inviting Grattan to propose the address of thanks for the Speech from the Throne, and Castlereagh to second it.

Possibly if the Duke of Portland, who as Home Secretary was Fitzwilliam's departmental head, had quickly and firmly restrained the wayward Lord Lieutenant, the damage could have been repaired; but the flaccid and vacillating Duke was not a man for decisive action. Fitzwilliam did not try to dismiss Fitzgibbon, but started to dismiss other Castle officials (Dublin's 'Castle' being equivalent to London's 'Whitehall'), including Beresford, who was not only a powerful political figure but was not officially under the Lord Lieutenant at all but in the Treasury department. The tragic result was that when Portland at last woke up and Fitzwilliam was recalled, everyone assumed that it was because he was a reformer, whereas the real reason was that he had flouted his instructions. Instead of bringing hope to Ireland, Fitzwilliam left little except suspicion and hostility behind him.

Fitzwilliam's successor was Castlereagh's uncle (who had been Lord Bayham until his father's death made him the second Lord Camden). He had inherited his father's political antennae for sensing the winning side, but not his father's intelligence; the Opposition peer Lord Charlemont called him 'a plain, unaffected, good-humoured man of pleasing conversation and conciliatory address'; Canning would nickname him 'Chuckle'. Only ten years older than Castlereagh, he was said (by Lord Grenville) to be 'in his nephew's pocket'.

His uncle's appointment as Lord Lieutenant was the defining moment in Castlereagh's career. It finally cut him off from his Whig Opposition supporters in County Down and made him generally unpopular with the Irish people. The new Lord Lieutenant's procession when he arrived in Dublin was attacked, the Primate's coach stoned and the Chancellor hit on the head by a stone through his carriage window; and when Grattan introduced his Catholic Relief Bill Castlereagh spoke against it. The die was cast; he had changed sides. After entertaining Camden at Mount Stewart, he spent the rest of the summer in camp with the Derry Militia, with Emily enjoying the role of colonel's wife. Meanwhile, Fitzwilliam's recall had been the match that set light to the fuse of Irish nationalism. The Orange Order, founded in 1795, led to a new sectarian bitterness: Orangemen were said to have driven 5,000 Catholics out of Ulster 'to hell or to Connaught'. The United Irishmen movement, which originally included Protestants as well as Catholics, was even more dangerous as it set up directories and committees on the Jacobin model, and armed and drilled by moonlight. Camden bleated anxiously for more troops to be sent from England; he was not the man to cope with a crisis, and to make matters worse

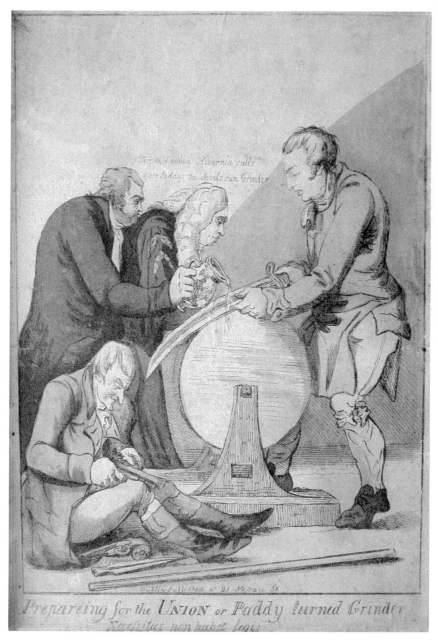

Paddy Turned Knife Grinder ('For Aid when Hibernia calls, Sure Paddy's the devil's own grinder'). Castlereagh sharpens his sword, helped by Beresford and Clare, while Grattan primes his pistols.

his able Chief Secretary, Pelham, was in England on sick leave. Camden introduced two panic measures: an Indemnity Act allowing what would normally be unlawful force to be used against rebels, and an Insurrection Act that made the taking of oaths a capital offence. He then caved in to the demands of the equally panic-stricken country gentlemen and allowed them to raise yeomanry regiments to enforce these laws (hence the Catholic definition of a member of the Ascendancy as 'a Protestant on a horse'), thus giving them carte blanche to harry, pillage and even kill anyone they disliked the look of.

Castlereagh not only acquiesced in these draconian measures but was actually a member of Camden's small unofficial cabinet that advised them. From now on, the radical young Opposition member who drank a toast to 'The Sovereign Lord, the People' was transformed into an agent of the state. In September 1795 he left Dublin armed with arrest warrants to round up United Irishmen in the Belfast area, many of whom had been his most loyal supporters. His first arrest was the 18-year-old Charles Teeling, who later described what happened:

> Lord Castlereagh was the personal friend of my father. ... He was triumphantly returned to Parliament ... pledging himself in language most unequivocal to the unceasing pursuit of parliamentary reform.
>
> Accompanying my father on a short excursion on horseback, we were met by Lord Castlereagh, who accosted us with his usual courtesy and politeness. We proceeded up the street together, when having reached [Lord Camden's house] where he was staying, we were about to take leave of his lordship. – 'I regret', said he, addressing my father, 'that your son cannot accompany you'; conducting me at the same moment through the outer gate, which to my inexpressible astonishment was instantly closed, and I found myself surrounded by a military guard. I expostulated ... and demanded that the gate should be reopened and my father should be admitted. My father entered; he looked sternly at Castlereagh and inquired the cause of my arrest. 'High Treason', replied his lordship.[3]

Castlereagh then entered Teeling's father's house with a military escort, and after pointing a pistol at his 14-year-old son ransacked the house and took away any papers that he hoped might provide evidence of treason, together with his pistols.

Teeling spent the next three years imprisoned in Dublin Castle in hideous conditions, his life only being saved by the kindness of Cooke, the Under-Secretary, who gave him parole when his health broke down. Teeling also lost two brothers, one executed and another dying as a result of imprisonment, while his father was kept in custody without trial for over four years and lost most of his property. Teeling's account of the rebellion may therefore be biased, but there is no reason to doubt that his arrest took place exactly as he described, and it illustrates why many Irishmen felt such a cold hatred for Castlereagh. Those who had given their time and money to get him elected to parliament, only to find him arresting men for holding the very views to which he had pledged himself, were especially bitter. When Castlereagh refused to let Teeling's mother see her son before he was taken off to Dublin, she told him, 'I was wrong to appeal to a heart that never felt the tie of parental affection – your Lordship is *not a father.*' (Castlereagh's inability to sire children may be a significant clue to some of his behaviour, but his occasional 'heartlessness' was probably the consequence of never having known a mother's love – perhaps the 'icy calm' for which he was noted when Foreign Secretary may have had the same cause.) There almost seems to have been a Jekyll and Hyde streak in Castlereagh's behaviour: he thought it quite natural to invite Teeling to supper after his arrest, apologize for the armed guards and converse in a most friendly way over several glasses of wine, and then send him back to prison. Teeling never saw his home again: by the time he was released it had been burned by the forces of law and order.

For the next few months, enforcing law and order claimed all Castlereagh's attention. He rode tirelessly round his father's estate, cajoling tenants to swear the oath of allegiance with a mixture of argument, threats and hospitality, helped by a squadron of dragoons (rather ill-disciplined – one troop had all its arms stolen while asleep in a barn), and by December over 300 tenants had taken the oath. Castlereagh told Emily, 'we had a very jolly dinner. Cleland [the Rector] quite drunk, Sinclair [a Presbyterian minister who had previously refused to take the oath] considerably so, my father not a little … the whole very happy, and God Save the King and Rule Britannia declared permanent.'

In December a French fleet was sighted in Bantry Bay, and the Derry Militia, full of martial ardour, marched south to oppose an invasion. Fortunately a gale thwarted the French plans, but the alarm gave Castlereagh a taste of being on the receiving end of military planning; his battalion was sent to Limerick one day, to Mallow the next, then to Cork and then to Bandon; two generals, Dalrymple and Smith, each thought he was in command. In March 1797 Camden gave General Lake carte blanche to search for and seize arms without a warrant and to impose curfews, the breaking of which incurred a fine of five shillings – those who could not pay to receive 100 lashes. Carhampton the commander-in-chief weakly protested that this was illegal, but Lake (whose motto was 'Damn your writing, look to your fighting') took no notice. Searches and arrests were used to pay off old scores (in 1970 a similar policy

Billy Pitt drives the Union Coach, packed with Scots members with Dundas on the roof throwing coins to Irish members packed in behind and shepherded by Castlereagh (far left). John Bull is loudly protesting.

in Northern Ireland led to people reporting any neighbour they disliked for possessing a gun, and if they had omitted to buy a gun licence, a common failing, they were sent to Long Kesh prison). It was a sure way of stoking up more hatred.

Throughout the summer of 1797 the grisly work of the assizes went on, making martyrs for Irish folklore. Camden appointed Castlereagh Keeper of the Signet, an 'office of profit under the crown' that meant that the holder had to stand for re-election if he wanted to continue as an MP. The post was a sinecure, but unlike the Chiltern Hundreds was worth something – £1,500 a year. In October 1797 Castlereagh was sworn in as an Irish Privy Councillor and became part and parcel of a government that committed many atrocities – 'the soldiers make no scruple of stripping men, tying them to a tree, and flogging them with bits and bridles', Lord Charlemont was told, while at Newtownards Dr Haliday witnessed 'burglaries, robberies, arson, murders … passed over without censure or any satisfaction to the sufferers'. In December Carhampton was replaced as commander-in-chief by General Abercromby, who was horri-

Pitt, driving the Union Coach, is shot by Lord Chancellor Loughborough, depicted as a highwayman, while John Bull with his cudgel tells Castlereagh, inside the coach with 'the scarlet woman of Rome', to 'give her up'. Castlereagh is firing his pistol at the highwaymen.

fied at finding yeomanry and even militia units often behaving as virtual lynch-mobs, with the regular army little better. Abercromby issued a general order saying he had found the army 'in a state of licentiousness which must render it formidable to everyone but the enemy', and directed that troops must not act against the civil population without the authority of a magistrate who was actually present.

It was at this juncture that Pelham's health broke down completely, and Camden asked if Castlereagh could take over his work as Under-Secretary until a successor could be appointed. It was a custom that the Chief Secretary must not be an Irishman, but since Camden 'had perfect confidence that his being a native of Ireland will neither sway his judgment nor his conduct' and the matter was urgent, Pitt agreed. Castlereagh's first official despatch as Chief Secretary required Abercromby to 'act without waiting for directions from the civil magistrates ... [and] crush the rebellion in whatever shape it shall shew itself by the most summary military measures', an order that flatly contra-dicted that of the commander-in-chief. Montgomery Hyde's *Early Life of Lord Castlereagh* comments that 'unlike Abercromby, [Castlereagh] possessed nearly ten years' intimate experience of the country, [and] informed the Commander that in his opinion little good could now result' from confining martial law to districts that 'were in virtually open rebellion'. Whether Castlereagh's judge-ment was really superior to that of one of Britain's few really good generals is doubtful; his order gave carte blanche to anyone in uniform to ransack houses, fire on crowds or flog 'suspects' until they died or confessed, whichever came first.

Not surprisingly, a full-scale rebellion broke out in the spring of 1798. Throughout the blood-soaked weeks that followed, Castlereagh showed himself calm, efficient and hard-working. He acted promptly on the secret intelligence that led to the arrest of most of the leading conspirators before their plans could take effect, so that the risings were crushed piecemeal. But the crisis was altogether too much for Camden, who sent his wife and children home and followed them shortly afterwards. He was a kind but ineffective man, whose weakness probably did as much harm as Castlereagh's ruthlessness. However, he did Ireland one great service by telling Pitt that his successor must be both commander-in-chief and lord lieutenant. Accordingly, Lord Cornwallis was appointed, and almost his first act was to curb Lake and forbid 'the infliction of punishment under any pretence whatever, not authorised by the orders of a General Officer in pursuance of a sentence of a general Court Martial'.

Cornwallis was disgusted by what he found in Ireland. Conversation among the 'principal persons of this country always turns on hanging, shooting, burning etc., and if a [Catholic] priest has been put to death the greatest joy is expressed'.[4] He soon decided to bypass the Privy Council junta, and to the fury of the ultra-Protestants announced an amnesty on 17 July. He also reprieved any ringleaders who were sentenced to death whenever the law allowed. What is interesting is that once a new lord lieutenant announced a more moderate policy, Castlereagh unhesitatingly backed it, and stood firm despite vigorous protests from the Protestant gentry. His conduct as Chief Secretary tells us two things: first, that he saw obedience to his superiors as an absolute duty, and secondly that he stuck resolutely to his guns once he had made a decision. Both under Camden and Cornwallis, Castlereagh believed he was doing what was right, even when it involved a complete *volte face*. It was not that he was an unprincipled Vicar of Bray, holding on to office at all costs, but simply, it seems, that he was not good at working out principles for himself. He was a first-class chief executive – hard-working, always reading the papers put on his desk, carrying out policy loyally and effectively; but he was no policy-maker. He could be humane and compassionate at a personal level, but at the same time implacable at an official level; for instance, he did his best to enable Lord Edward Fitzgerald to escape after his arrest for treason, but when he failed to escape said that his death 'will be of more service than if he had lived'. To some extent this strange mixture of compassion and ruthlessness seems intrinsic to Ireland, as those who lived through the 'troubles' of the 1920s testified; but Castlereagh's personality does seem to have had something erratic, almost irrational, about it.

Cornwallis was at first very doubtful about having a Chief Secretary who had been appointed by Camden, but before long he was writing to his friend General Ross, 'I have every reason to be highly satisfied with Lord C__ who is really a very uncommon young man, and possesses talents, temper and judgment suited to the very highest station.'[5] When Pelham finally handed in his resignation in November 1798, Cornwallis unhesitatingly asked for Castlereagh to be confirmed in office as Chief Secretary despite being Irish; and once again Pitt agreed. As Chief Secretary Castlereagh was leader of the Irish House of Commons, an experience that stood him in good stead later. Initially he did not find managing parliamentary business easy; when the Address from the Throne was passed by only one vote, Castlereagh realized he had been naive to suppose that 22 members who 'had been expected to vote *for* (most of them having distinctly promised support)' would actually do so. Two days later he was ambushed by a snap division, and the proposal for an Act of Union was negatived by five votes. But Cornwallis was determined to push the Bill through, and his contempt for the 'patriotic Irish gentlemen who are so enraged at the insolent interference of England … [but] if ever they dare go to their country-house beg for a garrison of English Militia or Scotch Fencibles', reconciled him to the need to resort to any means, including bribery if necessary, to win the necessary votes. By February 1799, the gloves were off.

Bribery took three forms: hard cash, 'jobs' (profitable offices or sinecures) and honours. Cornwallis dealt with honours, helped by the extraordinary Irish appetite for titles: barons clamoured to become viscounts, viscounts to be made earls, earls marquesses. Nineteen promotions in the Irish peerage and 20 new peerages were granted to help ease the Act of Union through.[6] Castlereagh was in charge of awarding compensation for borough-owners, at £15,000 for a seat, and he worked out a very efficient formula to reduce the number of Irish members by two-thirds so as to have 100 MPs in a Union parliament. He was at his best in this kind of detailed planning.

Castlereagh worked just as hard, but not so openly, in buying the votes of

MPs and peers. We find him writing to John King, a Home Office official, in February 1800, 'We require your assistance' (underlined), and on 1 March, 'When can you make the remittance promised? It is absolutely essential, for our demands increase.' Five weeks later Cooke reports, 'The Duke [Portland, the Home Secretary] is anxious to send you the needful. ... Mr Pitt will continue to let you have £8,000 to £10,000 for five years [and] I do not come [back from London] quite empty-handed.' If bribery failed, Castlereagh fell back on naked threats: when Carew, the MP for Waterford, said he would report the offer of a bribe to the House of Commons, Castlereagh replied, 'Do, and I'll deny every word point-blank.' Carew then said, 'In that case there will be nothing for it but for us to take a walk to the fifteen acres' (fight a duel), but prudently withdrew his challenge on being warned that Castlereagh had been practising his marksmanship for just such an eventuality.

Castlereagh's dealings with the Catholics, however, were honourable and above board. He was remarkably free of anti-Catholic prejudice – he had paid for a Catholic church to be built on his Newtownards estate – and his talks with the Catholic Bishop Troy and Lord Fingall, the leading Catholic layman, went well. He made it clear that he could make no promises about emancipation, but both he and they believed that the government would honour its commitments once the Union was in place. When this failed to happen, neither Lord Fingall nor Dr Troy held it against him: they realized that he was as dismayed as they were.

When the Union Bill eventually passed, Cornwallis's and Castlereagh's feelings of relief were short lived. First, the Duke of Portland tried to renege on promises by the government to grant peerages, pretending that the King objected to the list of peers, whereas it was really he himself who objected. Cornwallis called his bluff by threatening to appeal to the King, and Portland climbed down, in what for him was a short letter (a mere thousand words) assuring Cornwallis that 'nothing, certainly, could be further from my intention than to propose any measure for your Excellency's adoption that could place you in a situation of any distress whatever'. A few years later when Castlereagh was a cabinet minister in Portland's government, he would thus have known that the Duke was not only verbose, indecisive and woolly-minded, but also shifty; over the Irish peerages he simply did not tell the truth. If Canning had been more aware of that side of Portland, the duel might well have been avoided.

Much worse was to follow. During the autumn of 1800 there had been ominous rumours that Pitt was having difficulty in persuading some members of his cabinet, and the King, to grant Catholic emancipation once the Act of

Union was on the statute book. Cornwallis sent Castlereagh to London to urge the need for emancipation, and was still sanguine that a measure would go through 'whatever Lord Loughborough's opinion may be', but he was wrong. In January 1801 the King refused point-blank to agree to any 'concession' to Catholics, and Pitt resigned, though urging his ministers to continue in office under the new Prime Minister, Addington. Most of them did so (Canning being one of the few who did not), but Cornwallis and Castlereagh felt honour bound to resign since they had, in all good faith, encouraged the Catholics to believe Catholic emancipation would follow the Act of Union.

Castlereagh's time as Chief Secretary in Ireland had given him ministerial experience at a higher level than he could have had at his age in England. Cornwallis still had some reservations about him, but by 1801 told his friend Ross that Castlereagh had 'improved so much as a speaker as to become nearly master of the [Irish] House of Commons'. Cornwallis had got to know Castlereagh extremely well, both officially and at a personal level, at a time of his life when he was evidently far more awkward and angular than the polished statesman that he later became, and believed that 'the gratification which the Irish feel at the prospect of [Castlereagh] making a figure in the [British] political world, has much diminished the unpopularity which his cold and distant manners in private society had produced'. Cornwallis also considered that Colonel Little-hales his Military Secretary 'in the private management of mankind much surpasses Lord Castlereagh' – a surprisingly lukewarm verdict in view of what was usually said about Castlereagh's charm and ease of manner.

Perhaps there always was something rather cold and distant in Castlereagh's outward manner. Although he loved his wife Emily very much, his letters to her seem more like those of Lord Chesterfield to his son than those from a young husband to his wife – certainly they are much more formal than Canning's letters to his wife. For instance, a letter to Emily of 25 August 1796 is somewhat ponderous:

> I cannot tell you what pleasure your letter gave me. No lover could receive a declaration with more satisfaction, and as it is really the principal enjoyment I shall experience till I return to you, I expect that the indulgence will be commensurate with your affection and not sparingly administered. ... I am rather uneasy, dearest wife, about your riding Prince when I am not with you. ... Horses of that nature are never to be depended on. ... Ask your uncle for the mare, but don't torture me with the idea of your being exposed to danger.

Again, on his way to London (28 September 1796) what is clearly meant as playful affection sounds more like a schoolmaster writing to an (admittedly favourite) pupil:

> O <u>you of little faith</u>! So you suspected me of failing in giving you regular assurances of my affection, and you never recollected that when a traveller is on the road every day's journey makes two days difference to the letter which is to return.

Probably, though, Emily would have found her husband's letters neither irritating nor pompous. Lady Bagot, admittedly a gossip (she once caused a diplomatic incident when her husband was Minister at Washington and the Americans opened one of her letters and discovered exactly what she thought of them), was nonetheless percipient, and described Emily when Castlereagh was ill in September 1807:

> No one was ever so invariably good humoured, yet she sometimes provokes me; there is a look of contented disregard of the cares of life in her round, grey Eye that makes one wonder if she ever felt any crosses or knew the meaning of the word anxiety. She talks with indifference of Bombardments and Assemblies, the Baby and the Furniture, the emptiness of London and the massacres of Buenos Ayres, Lord Castlereagh's increasing debility and the doubtfull success of Mr Greville's new Opera, with so exactly the same expression of voice and countenance, that they probably hold a pretty equal value in her estimation.

It is difficult to think that their marriage was a union of minds; Castlereagh was more intelligent than Emily, although he read little or nothing apart from political writings. But he was musical – he played the harpsichord – and they both loved dancing. His other recreations were outdoor ones – riding, driving, country walks – that they could do together. The mutual physical attraction was, and remained, strong, and they loved one another very much. And at home in the country in Kent, Castlereagh was far from being 'cold and distant in private society', and unbent completely, not least with children.

CHAPTER 5

The Young Politician:
Canning

It has been asked, why did Canning change from Whig to Tory? The short answer is, he didn't. Pitt was always a Whig – his bust is in Brooks's Club to this day – and his was always a reformist government until the war made him put domestic reforms on one side; he only became labelled as a Tory because when he formed his last government in 1804 the King would not let him include Fox, so he had to fall back on some conservative reactionaries. Canning was always considered 'liberale'. He argued consistently, and to the detriment of his career, for Catholic emancipation, and strongly opposed the slave trade, always voting for any motion for abolition – in 1799 he put down a motion of his own, though he agreed not to pursue it himself but 'transfer it into Pitt's or Dundas's hands. ... I shall not give it up, unless one of them will engage to bring it forward; in which case it will be more sure of being carried and I shall for that end resign it with pleasure.' [1] Pitt did give notice that he would introduce a bill as a government measure, but it got crowded out by more pressing war concerns, and not until 1807 was the slave trade eventually abolished, thanks to Fox.

But leaving aside political labels (which were irrelevant at the end of the eighteenth century, as the only Tories left were a few country gentlemen who still drank to 'the king over the water') the fact remains that Canning did make a deliberate decision to forsake Fox for Pitt, and was sometimes accused, as Castlereagh was, of sacrificing principle to self-interest. It is true that if he was to enter politics without first making a small fortune at the Bar, then Canning had to obtain office quickly, because he could not live for long on his inheritance; and since Pitt looked set to remain at the head of government for the foreseeable future, he was clearly a much better bet. But there seems

William Pitt as Prime Minister, aged 44, by Hoppner.

little doubt that the deciding factor that made Canning (and Castlereagh) switch allegiance was seeing the French Revolution degenerating into a reign of terror. Fox still felt that the guillotine, however distasteful, was a price worth paying for liberty, but many of his followers were beginning to doubt it. If such people as the Crewes and Sheridan had thought that Canning had acted simply out of self-interest, their attitude towards him would have changed; and it didn't. Sheridan, despite being Fox's chief lieutenant in the House of Commons, remained a lifelong friend (indeed Wilberforce thought that he had brought Canning up – 'poor fellow, I wonder that he could have been so pure') and Canning in turn always refrained from attacking him in debate. With Fox, who had looked on him as one of his protégés, Canning's desertion did rankle, but until Canning started to be a thorn in his side, he remained friendly.

Canning did feel some embarrassment, however, towards the Duke of Portland. During his stay at Crewe Hall in 1791 Mrs Crewe had taken him over to Welbeck to introduce him to her kinsman the Duke. Portland was a leading Whig magnate who had been Prime Minister (with Fox at his side) before Pitt, and had several parliamentary seats at his disposal. The Duke was impressed with Canning and offered to nominate him for a seat in parliament, but Canning declined the offer, partly (he said) because it would have cost him money he could not afford but also because it would make him beholden to the Duke. He told his friend Frere, 'I will go over in no man's train; if I join Pitt, I will go by myself.'[2] In a letter to his young cousin Bess dated 4 July 1793, Canning pleaded that he had been too busy to write sooner because he 'had verses to make upon the Duke of Portland's Installation (which, as from all other plagues and troubles of this mortal life, good Lord deliver you)'. Canning meant the Latin Ode that he had been asked to deliver at the Duke's installation as Chancellor of Oxford University, and in reality he was particularly pleased to have been asked because, as he told his aunt, it gave him an opportunity 'of showing the D. of Portland – and of knowing that he feels it – that no difference in politics can impair my respect for his personal virtues'.[3] The Duke's feelings apart, the Ode was helpful to an aspiring politician. Lord Bessborough told his wife, 'Today we had speeches in the Theatre by young men of rank, and it all went off very well. ... One was remarkable good, written by a Mr Canning, and I will send it you next post.'[4] When debating why Canning switched sides from Fox to Pitt, it is worth noting that a year later Portland would do the same thing, and in company with some other leading Opposition Whigs join the government – Pitt was glad to have them but cynical about their motives: 'they see that their titles and possessions are in danger, & they think their best chance for preserving them is by supporting Government and joining me'.[5]

Canning's letter to his aunt contained more important news than his Ode; he proudly told her:

> My dear Aunt, I write rather to show you the outside of this letter than the inside [he had franked his own letter]. I have the honour to represent in Parliament the respectable Borough of Newton in the Isle of Wight – and without one farthing of expence or one farthing's worth of obligation to any person but one, Mr Pitt.

Newton, or Newtown, was a 'Treasury Borough' whose members were nominated by the Prime Minister of the day, and was often used to bring some up-and-coming government supporter into parliament (Palmerston sat for Newton a few years later, never quite managing to learn the borough's name).

As a newly elected MP Canning thoroughly enjoyed what his aunt called 'the fine world'. He had very little money behind him, but the Dean of Christ Church had sensibly advised him to use the £3,000 capital his grandmother had left him as income, since it would have been well-nigh impossible for an aspiring politician to live on the small income from his Kilkenny estate, and, as Dr Jackson pointed out, 'either you will succeed or you will not' – nothing venture, nothing have.

Canning attended the House of Commons assiduously and led a very full social life. His set of friends included Jenkinson, Sturges Bourne, Granville Leveson-Gower, Morpeth, Boringdon, Frere, Augustus and Edward Legge, Bobus and Easley Smith (brothers of the better-known Sydney Smith who had co-edited the *Microcosm* at Eton – 'Easely' had got his nickname from the way he pronounced 'aisle'), Frederick North, and Charles and George Ellis. Most of them were present or future MPs, and Jenkinson ('Jenky' of Christ Church days, later Lord Hawkesbury and then Lord Liverpool) would have a critical influence on Canning's later career. Besides constantly supping or dining with these and other friends, Canning was soon seeing much more than a new member might expect of the Prime Minister. A week after he arrived in London in November 1793 Pitt invited him to dinner.[6] There were about 12 other guests, of whom Charles Yorke and Jenkinson were up-and-coming MPs like himself, and the rest were all ministers. The dinner was 'pleasant, beyond any idea that I had formed of it. The company consisted of about a dozen people, three or four of whom I knew more or less intimately, but the rest I had never even seen before, [yet] I had not been a quarter of an hour before I was as completely at my ease as I could have been at Wanstead or Ashbourne.' Pitt's cousin Lord Grenville, the Foreign Secretary, had 'much less coldness and reserve in his manner than I had been taught to expect, and

what little there was appeared to proceed rather from shyness than haughti-
ness'. Dundas, Secretary for War and the Colonies, was 'unaffected, frank and
jovial'. Lord Mornington, the future Lord Wellesley, Canning already knew,
and 'liked him better now than I ever did – both because he appears generally very sensible and pleasant, and was very attentive to me. ... He is one of
Pitt's most intimate friends.' Lord Bayham, Castlereagh's uncle (later Lord
Camden), 'seems very pleasing and gentlemanly in his manners, and is very
much liked and well spoken of' (although Canning soon revised that opinion,
nicknaming him 'Chuckle'). Pitt himself completely captivated Canning: 'Mr
Pitt is, at the head of his own table, exactly what hits my taste – attentive without being troublesome – mixing in the conversation without attempting to lead
it – laughing often and easily – and boyish enough if it should fall in his way
to discuss the history of Cock Robin' (Canning and 'Jenky' had recently been
arguing at the Christ Church high table as to 'who dug his grave?'). A week
later Canning dined with Dundas. Many of the guests were the same, including Pitt, and this time they included Lord Mulgrave who later, like Camden,
would serve in the 1807–09 cabinet. He had just returned from Toulon where
he had been Lieutenant Governor during the brief British occupation of the
port, and seemed 'very good-humoured, and talks sensibly and abundantly'.

During these first months as a young MP and barrister, Canning burned
the candle at both ends. When not dining out, he would have dinner or supper
at the Crown and Anchor dining club in the Strand, or the newly formed Carey
Street Club which 'is not confined to dining or supping ... and is the same to
us lawyers that White's and Brooks's are to the people at the other end of the
town'. Early in 1794 he was elected to White's – 'Hetty glowed crimson on
hearing it', he recorded. Poor Hitty; she had been so proud of him three years
earlier, telling Bess that 'Brooks's fête is to beat White's all to nothing. There
is to be a fine Ode composed for the occasion. George is employed to write it
and I hope it will do honour to his muse.' As often as not Frere would breakfast
with Canning at his Lincoln's Inn lodgings. Besides having many formal invitations, Canning was welcome to call at any time on Mrs Crewe when she was
in London, on her friends the Markhams (he was Archbishop of York), on Lady
Malmesbury whose husband was abroad on a diplomatic mission, and on Lord
Stafford in his vast Whitehall mansion. He had met the Staffords when Mrs
Crewe arranged for him to stay a night at Trentham en route for Oxford and
he 'came away delighted with all the people I had seen, and half in love with
two or three of the Lady Levesons'; Granville Leveson-Gower became a lifelong friend, and Canning also stayed frequently at Wimbledon with the eldest
son, Lord Gower, whose wife was Countess of Sutherland in her own right,

and when they took a house in Albemarle Street he had an open invitation to dine or sup with them there. The life of an amusing but impecunious up-and-coming young politician could be a strange mixture of grandeur and economy: dinner with the Prime Minister or supper at a ducal mansion one evening, and a chop at the Crown and Anchor the next – and on days when the House adjourned much earlier or later than expected, so that he had either refused an invitation or had to miss one, he would sometimes go to bed hungry.

Canning spent most of the Christmas recess of 1793 at Christ Church, where he could live virtually free and use the library. When he wrote to Bess on Christmas Day he complained that 'a villainous Cold and Cough, of which the seeds were sown when I last saw you at Wanstead, grew up into a most thriving and vigorous distemper, and the cowardly disease took advantage of my journey on a coldish day from London to Oxford to make another attack on me'. From Oxford, he went to stay with Charles Ellis in Bedfordshire, revelling in 'a most comfortable house, full of books, and billiards, and battledore and shuttlecock, and good wine. The Ellises went fox-hunting now and again, and would have tempted me to accompany them by offers of the finest and safest horses. … But as I think fox-hunting one of the many pleasures without which one can very well contrive to pass through the world, I resisted their temptations' (how different from Castlereagh!). But the warmth and comfort of Wootton were followed by a 50-mile cold January journey to Wanstead, where a Twelfth Night family party was enlivened by Sheridan and his son Tom.

On the last day of January 1794 Canning made his maiden speech, on the subject of the Sardinian Treaty. He spent the morning pacing up and down his room rehearsing his arguments, and before leaving for Westminster 'sent for a bit of cold meat and a glass of white wine, for Jenkinson and all wise people had told me it was necessary to have some support to prevent a sensation of *sinking* and emptiness'. When he took his place in the chamber just behind Pitt and Dundas, he saw Frere and Sturges Bourne in the gallery, having arrived early enough to get places 'just opposite the situation from which I spoke'; he also spotted 'the two Legges, Adderley, and two or three Christ Church faces … who looked shrewdly as if they had smelt out the probability of my speaking'. Canning whispered to Pitt, 'If there comes on a debate I have thoughts of speaking', and his journal records the colloquy that ensued:

> P. 'You cannot chuse a better time.'
> C. 'If Fox opens, I think I will not speak immediately after him, but wait for Grey or some other young one.'
> P. 'I think you judge very rightly – and I think I can augur from Grey's looks

that he will probably give you an opportunity.'

C. 'Pray have you the dates and minutes of all the old Sardinian treaties about you? I want to look at them again.'

P. 'No, really I have not – but here comes Ryder [lately Under-Secretary at the Foreign Office] – he has them I know, and he shall let you see them.'

C. 'I have another treaty, which strikes me as being much more completely analogous ... the Prussian Subsidy of 1758 – What do you think of it?'

P. 'Good God – aye – it is exactly in point – it will do admirable. £670,000 if I recollect right. I am glad of it – it is the very thing.'

That colloquy shows how much Pitt thought of Canning, and why. But it did not save him from first-night nerves as he had to sit through four speeches, starting with Fox and ending with Grey, before seeing the Speaker 'pull off his hat towards me, and heard him cry and the House echo "Mr Canning". It was not fear [I felt], it was tumult.' Winston Churchill might have called this debut 'not a maiden speech, but a brazen hussy of a speech' (his description of A.P. Herbert's maiden speech in 1935), far more detailed and combative than convention expected. However, Canning had the grace and good sense 'to make some little apology for what I *modestly* called my presumption' in contradicting Fox, 'and to assure him that ... it was not for any want of admiration for his talents, or of respect and esteem for his person'. He sat down after three-quarters of an hour to a general buzz of acclaim, and as soon as he decently could went upstairs and dined with 'Jenkinson and Wallace and Ch. Ellis from the House, and Edward Legge and Aug[ustus] from the Gallery ... and the bumpers of port wine that I swallowed, and the mutton chops that I devoured, and the sensations that I felt, are not to be described'.

The pace was too good to last. Earlier that month he was honest enough to record in his journal an evening when, having dined too well, he 'was perfectly unfit to go to the Dss of Gordon's, but unluckily was incapacitated also from perceiving my own unfitness. ... What I said, or did then, the Lord knows, for I have only a very faint and dizzy recollection. ... I only know that I talked eternally, partly with Lord Carlisle (who is a person that I never venture to talk to when I am sober), and on waking [the next morning] wondered what I had been doing.' A fortnight after his maiden speech Canning felt 'not at all well'. For a whole week he dosed himself with quinine and camomile, 'determined to bully my complaint rather than yield to it', dining one day with Lord Stafford (after 'a pretty long walk, thinking it might do me good'), the next day with the Master of the Rolls. Then followed two large dinner parties, with Ryder the Paymaster-General, and with Charles Ellis's brother, and supper with some Irish cousins, the Bruces. Little wonder that by Friday he felt 'very shivery and unwell', despite which he went to the House, dined tête-à-tête with Jenkinson and 'stayed up chatting till about one'. The next day, a Saturday, he 'sent an excuse to the Archbp of York and dined at home'. But by then the fever had taken hold. By Monday his 'headache increased so did my languor and general uneasiness', and the doctor he was persuaded to send for 'did not seem to know what to make of me. It would turn, he thought, either to an intermittent or a low fever.' Luckily Hitty realized he was not well and came and 'sat with me the whole morning, which circumstance alarmed me very much and I therefore tried to persuade her that I was much better than I really felt myself'. For five anxious days he was in a semi-conscious delirium, probably with pneumonia, and at one point his condition gave real cause for anxiety. In the eighteenth century even members of the privileged classes had to have a fairly strong constitution to survive childhood, with even the grandest houses ice-cold in winter, journeys either on horseback or in unheated carriages, and medical science primitive. Canning must therefore have been reasonably healthy, but throughout his life he was constantly complaining of having colds, and he was not so robust as Castlereagh or, indeed, most of his political contemporaries.

Canning convalesced at Wanstead, where Hitty told him 'with glowing indignation' that her second son William 'was a most determined *bad politician*. I found that she had told me true. He had *quite proper* notions', and Canning promised to take his young cousin to the House of Commons for a debate. He did not return to London until 1 April, to find an invitation to dine that evening at Lady Malmesbury's, but his first visit was to his grandmother and aunt (his mother's sister) in Somers Town. Before long the social round was again in full swing, though from then on he took more care about his health: 'I have, in obedience to Dr Turton, left off a bad custom which I had of going down to the House *fasting*. … I either feed myself before I go out at about 3 o'clock, or call at Jenkinson's and get fed on my way – taking care however not to drink enough to puzzle one's self, nor to eat so much that one may be prepared for a dinner or supper after the debate.' His next speech was on 10 April, on the conduct of the war. By the time he was called, there was little left to say except that the situation would be worse if '*gentlemen on the other side* had held the government'. When he had sat down, Pitt and Jenkinson both warned him that he 'must expect a violent attack but I must not mind it'. Come it did: 'you cannot think what an odd feeling it is to sit and hear one's self abused before 3 or 400 people. I found however I could bear it without any unpleasant feeling.' Canning's 14-year-old cousin Willy 'had been highly edified and delighted, and had a mouth expanded to a size hardly human, gaping with attention'.

Soon after this Canning nearly ruined his friendship with Jenkinson. When he was staying at Addiscombe with Jenkinson's parents, Jenky told him that he was 'to be Colonel of a Regiment of Fencible Cavalry – and he would have me take *a troop* in it as *Captain*. It would be good fun enough. But I do not find the military disposition sufficiently strong within me.' Unfortunately, Canning could not resist a tease: a month later, egged on by Lady Malmesbury and the two Ellises, he composed a spoof recruiting handbill and had a copy printed:

> To all Brave, aspiring, invincible Heroes
> No republican Roundheads, but true Cavalleroes ...
> 'Tis the bold Colonel Jenkinson calls you to arm,
> And solemnly swears you shall come to no harm.
> We're no common Dragoons, made of Tailors and Barbers,
> But pure Cinque Port Horsemen, the pick of five harbours ...
> Those Infantry fellows, they send them to Flanders,
> If you go, they must find you some other Commanders;
> They stand to be shot at, our plan is more sensible,
> For the scampering away is what makes a true Fencible.
> If to land at a Seaport these Frenchmen should try,
> We'll presently trounce them – I'm Member for Rye.
> I shall tell them at first with the utmost civility,
> That I trust they won't stay to disturb our tranquillity ...
> But if they refuse on this warning to quit,
> I'll go straight up to Town and acquaint Mr Pitt.

George Ellis, 'who draws remarkably well', added a picture of a fencible sergeant, and at a dinner at Lady Malmesbury's at which Edward Legge and the Ellis brothers were present, Jenkinson was brought a sealed envelope with a bogus note from a printer saying that he 'has struck off 500 of the enclosed handbill and returns the original as desired. NB Unless further orders, bill-stickers will be about with the bills at six this evening.' Canning was looking forward to hearing how the joke had gone down, and was astonished to hear from Charles Ellis that 'Jenky is exceedingly hurt – we did all we could to soothe him ... but without much effect'. Lady Malmesbury 'sat down on a sofa' with him '*he* with *her* hand in *his* and *she muching* him and coaxing him for about two hours ... but she could get no answer from him but tears'. Jenky felt that Canning had betrayed their friendship by mocking him and laughing at him behind his back. Not until the last day before the Whitsun recess did Canning finally manage to convince his friend that no offence had been intended, upon which 'we shook hands ... and talked the whole business over again as laughingly as if it had been the affair of two other people'. This particular misunderstanding was partly because Canning could not take the Volunteers seriously, whereas Jenkinson most definitely did. (Incidentally, Pitt did not think much of them either; when the government proposed they should become liable for overseas service and a member protested that they should *never* go abroad, Pitt sardonically interjected, 'Except, I presume, in case of invasion'.)

This episode was not the first or the last time that Canning totally failed to see how hurting his wit could be, and part of the trouble was that among his own circle of friends this kind of humour was expected and appreciated. For example, Canning wrote Lady Sutherland a letter, ostensibly written by his manservant Fleming on his behalf, misspelling words so as to make not-very-subtle and rather coarse jokes such as 'ordures' instead of 'orders'. It said that William Leigh (who as a clergyman could not serve in the Yeomanry so was expected to produce a *substitute*) 'has not yet been able to get a *prostitute* and would be glad to know if Ld G[ower] had more than he wanted for his own *personal* service (*which her Ladyship could probably tell*)'. Lady Sutherland saw at once that the letter was a practical joke, and told Canning that all Trentham had been laughing 'to an unspeakable degree'; Jenkinson might have realized the letter was bogus, but would certainly not have been amused.

Before long, Canning was able to made amends for his 'recruiting poster' practical joke. Jenkinson fell hopelessly in love with Lady Louisa Hervey, whose father Lord Bristol, the earl-bishop after whom so many hotels were named, was of an uncertain temper and was, as usual, abroad. They felt they must wait to obtain his consent to the marriage before approaching Lord Hawkes-bury, who they expected would give his consent gladly, but Hawkesbury took umbrage at not having been told earlier and refused to do so. Canning knew Lady Louisa and her family, whose Wimbledon house was near the Gowers', and it was largely thanks to his sound advice and diplomacy that Jenky's father relented, and the couple were married on 25 March. It proved a very happy marriage, though Canning complained that 'marriage does give men odd turns to be sure' – no longer could he drop in on Jenky whenever he felt like it.

To Canning's credit, 'the fine world' (as Hitty called it) did not turn his head. He did not allow his constant invitations to most of the best houses in London prevent regular visits to his grandmother and aunt in their house in Somers Town, and if his mother came up to London he always made sure to see her. He also went to great pains to help his half-brothers, doing his best to obtain a commission for Samuel Reddish who was serving as a sergeant at Botany Bay, and fitting out 'poor Charles Reddish' with clothes to make him presentable for the job he found for him through Hitty's brother Paul Patrick. In May 1794 Canning received a letter from a Yorkshire schoolmaster, Mr

Milner, 'informing me that my mother's children had been with him Lord knows how long ... and that my mother was indebted to him £28.3.2d and he in great distress. God help him! and her! and me! and all of us! One circumstance amidst all the sadness of his letter which almost makes me laugh is that she has been sending him cart-loads of Collyssium (her eye-ointment) for payment, which the poor man complains nobody will buy.' In November, sadly, he 'heard from my poor mother of William's illness. I poked out a little bit of *paper* to send to the schoolmaster in hopes that it might make him more attentive to the poor boy's care.' In December, however, the boy died – 'another dreadful stroke to my poor mother' – and Canning sent Charles Reddish to his tailor to be 'measured for mourning' clothes. In July 1795 Canning felt that his 'poor old grandmother' was 'dropping gradually into the grave. No disease of complaint but universal decay of body and mind.' For some time she had been 'wishing most devoutly herself for her dissolution. Poor old soul she reads the psalms all day long, and they seem to afford her infinite consolation.'

That same month of July, Canning took his nine-year-old cousin Stratford to Eton for the last two weeks of the summer term so that he would not feel too strange when he went there in the autumn. The Provost, Dr Davies, could not resist showing off one of his star pupils to the King:

> He ordered his chariot and insisted on taking me up to the Terrace [of Windsor Castle]. The K. and Q. were walking in full Terrace. 'Stand this way' says Dr D. 'Here they'll see and speak to you immediately'. 'Probably not' said I, 'for I do not go to Court and it is likely they may not know me'. But he took pretty good care that they should [and] without any further provocation than a look from the King – 'Mr C., Sir, Mr. C. – Come to Eton to bring a little cousin, Sir – always happy to see a scholar that does us so much credit in the world, Sir' – and on he was going while I looked as foolish as might be. The K. and Q. good-naturedly did not laugh, but went through their string of questions and compliments, routed up the old story of the Microcosm, and hoped my little cousin would follow up my steps both at Eton and at Christchurch and elsewhere. If Hitty heard this, I thought.

To Hitty and her family George III was always 'Knobbs', and to her nephew, despite his change of political allegiance, Knobbs he remained. Canning was never a great royalist: when at the start of the 1795 session Pitt had asked him to second the King's Speech he tried, but failed, to be let off wearing court dress, and a nasty cold did nothing to diminish his impatience with the tedious ceremonial. He felt a very strong disposition to stay at home and nurse my cold, instead of encreasing it by going full dressed to the House of Commons. ... But ... much against my will I got up and dressed myself and went down to the House ... [whence] we set out in procession at about half past three for St James's, the Speaker in his gingerbread coach leading the way. This being New Year's Day the Court was much crowded, and we waited hours in a cold ante-chamber. ... At last our gracious Sovereign was ready to receive us. We marched up through the apartments – bowing – bowing – bowing till we approach the footstool of the great chair in which the King is seated, surrounded by his courtiers, and sticks white and gold. The Speaker with an audible voice reads the Address ... and the K. returns his answer. Then bowing – bowing – bowing – as before, we retire backwards out of the apartments.

At the end of the session, in July, Canning breakfasted with Pitt and had a long talk about his future. Pitt commiserated with him that there had been so few opportunities for him to speak, but pointed out that he had done better in that respect than most of his contemporaries, and that by giving way gracefully, although he had wanted to speak, he had done more to gain the approval of the House than if he had tried to push himself forward. Pitt also asked what kind of office Canning would like, to which the answer was that it must involve real work. He was due to be called to the Bar 'this term or the next', and although a sinecure office would enable him to practise as a barrister as well, to do that would damage his reputation 'in the eyes of the world'. Canning also said, when asked, that the Irish Secretaryship was the office he would like to aim at after experience in a more junior post. Pitt undertook to ask the Duke of Portland about an under-secretaryship at the Home Office that was about to fall vacant, but said that it was not in his gift but the Duke's. Canning came away from that talk with Pitt satisfied that before long something would be found for him.

Before going north to the Leighs at Ashbourne, Canning went to stay at Belmont with the Malmesburys. On the morning of his departure Lord Malmesbury, now back in England, asked Canning to put off his departure, and they 'passed the whole day tête-a-tête', talking over 'the Under-Secretaryships, the Irish Secretaryship &c'. To have the advice and support of someone who had 'lived for 31 years in the political world' was obviously a great help. Letters to Bess Canning suggest that by 12 October Pitt had asked Grenville to make Canning an Under-Secretary at the Foreign Office, that by 28 October the appointment was almost but not quite certain, and that by 13 November the 'official arrangements are in proper train – but not yet declared'. (He also told Bess that he had just voted for 'the Bill for saving all your lives – or as you profligate Republicans say, for extinguishing all your liberties' – in other words, the suspension of Habeas Corpus; *plus ça change*.) The appointment was eventually announced in December.

Canning would have been glad to serve in the Home Office because that was the department under which Irish affairs came and as an Irishman he wanted above all things to do something for his country. It is tempting to speculate what difference it might have made had he and not Castlereagh been Irish Secretary during and after the Irish Rebellion. But Canning was also interested in foreign policy: his maiden speech had been on the Sardinian subsidy, and he had planned to spend much of the summer recess of 1794 'constantly and wholly preoccupied ... in learning the French tongue'.[7] The Foreign Office had two Under-Secretaries: Hammond, a career diplomat, was responsible for the Northern Department, Canning for the Southern Department, which included France and Austria as well as the Mediterranean, and when Hammond was away on missions to Berlin or Vienna, Canning had to deal with literally all Foreign Office despatches. It was an invaluable apprenticeship, but very hard work: the war was not going well and keeping the Continental powers on side was increasingly difficult.

Grenville, the Foreign Secretary, was Pitt's first cousin on his mother's side. An intelligent and high-minded Whig aristocrat, had he lived a century later he would have won a First at Balliol, been on the committee of the Athenaeum and been acclaimed as statesman, patron of the arts, and an example of all that an enlightened peer should be. Canning liked him, but found him heavy – which indeed he was in more ways than one. In the words of a Brooks's Club satire:

> Nature, in all her dispensations wise
> Who form'd his headpiece of so vast a size
> Hath not, 'tis true, neglected to bestow
> Its due proportion to the part below;
> And hence we reason, that to serve the state,
> His top and bottom may have equal weight.

Grenville was kind to Canning, and frequently invited him to Dropmore for a weekend, but at least once, as he told his cousin, he would have preferred a weekend of 'peace and quietness' at Wanstead when Grenville had 'insisted upon my coming to relax and recruit at Dropmore – and I have of late refused him so often that I cannot avoid going – as though it is dull enough, the invitation is meant kindly'. It was always difficult for him to get away for a weekend, as 'sleeping in the country is quite out of the question, unless I would run the risk of having a quiet family knocked up at midnight by a messenger with Red boxes under his arm. ... Sunday was not always a *Sabbath* to me.'[8]

Canning's work as Under-Secretary was soon complicated by the fact that by 1797 Pitt wanted to try to make peace with France, while Grenville did not. The war was going badly: Austria had proved a broken reed and the Continental alliance was in ruins. Pitt realized that every effort must be made to see if France would enter into serious peace negotiations – as he wrote to Grenville, 'I feel it my duty as an English minister and a Christian, to use every effort to stop so bloody and wasting a war.' Canning felt, as Pitt did, that 'if peace is to be had, we must have it'; the country was close to economic collapse, with bad harvests and severe food shortages, naval mutinies at Chatham and Spithead, pressure on the pound, trouble brewing in Ireland and fever wreaking havoc among the troops in the West Indies. The cabinet was divided, but after hot debate agreed (with Grenville's dissent formally noted) to send Lord Malmesbury, accompanied by George Ellis as his first secretary, on a peace mission to Lille, which the French had, rather unpromisingly, designated instead of Paris as the place for negotiations to take place. Malmesbury was convinced that peace must be had if at all possible, and when leaks to British newspapers about possible concessions threatened to jeopardize the negotiations, Pitt told him to send his official reports to the cabinet, but to send fuller reports to Pitt and Grenville. This was a sensible precaution, since the King saw all cabinet papers and was not above 'leaking' details of any proposals that might disadvantage his Electorate of Hanover. But what was highly irregular was that Pitt also told Canning to read all despatches before the Foreign Secretary saw them, and remove anything that might make Grenville feel that Malmesbury was making too many concessions and so recall him. In the event, the peace talks were condemned to failure by a regime change in Paris, so Canning's 'censoring' did neither good nor harm – no harm, that is, except possibly to Canning himself. As he told Malmesbury, 'the instructions and opinions I get from the Minister [Grenville] *under whose orders I am bound to act* accord so little with the sentiments and intentions I heard expressed by the Minister [Pitt] *with whom I want to act* that I am placed in a very disagreeable dilemma'. Malmesbury later came to think that having been given so much privileged responsibility so young had been bad for him.

Certainly Pitt did treat Canning very much as a favoured son. He encouraged him to edit the *Anti-Jacobin*, a satirical magazine aimed at countering anti-government pamphlets and satirical tracts that were circulating. This gave Canning a chance to put his talent for satire to positive use (for once!). Verses such as those in *The New Morality* were a good antidote to pro-French anti-war

George Canning *c.*1798, by Hoppner.

propaganda aimed at well-meaning but woolly-minded liberals:

> France at our doors, *he* sees no danger nigh,
> But heaves for Turkey's woes th' impartial sigh;
> A steady patriot of the world alone,
> The friend of every country – but his own.

while the same poem debunks the new radicals who repudiated conventional ideas of right and wrong, dismissing those who suggest that everything is grey as being:

Too nice to praise by wholesay, or to blame,
Convinced that *all men's motives are the same;*
And finds, with keen discriminating sight,
BLACK's not *so* black, nor WHITE's so *very* white.

Not great poetry, but at the time and for its purpose quite effective – and the *New Morality* does contain one phrase that has entered the English language:

Save, save, Oh! Save me from the *Candid Friend* !

Canning felt the failure of the peace talks very much, and was aghast when Grenville wanted the negotiations published, as that would have broken faith with the peace party in France. Pitt realized that Canning was disenchanted with Grenville's policy, and in February 1799 moved him from the Foreign Office and made him a Commissioner of the Board of Control for India, a post (as Canning put it) 'of less emolument but more ease and dignity'. To make up for the drop in salary Pitt arranged for him to have a pension of £700 a year, which, however, Canning made over to his mother. Appointment to his new office meant he had to stand for re-election. In 1796 he had ceased to be member for Newton but had been found a new seat which, as he had told Bess, was 'one with new, live constituents, I would have you know; they live at a pretty little town called Wendover ... and I have no doubt they will be charmed with the honour of returning me as their Representative'. Re-election to so obliging a seat three years later was no problem: 'My first excursion in the course of the Easter Holidays must be to Wendover to have myself re-chosen after vacating my seat – and my second shall be to Wanstead – and then I shall go frisking and flourishing about, so happy in my new liberty, after three years of such slavery, as never was slaved!'

He certainly had 'slaved' at the Foreign Office. When he later became Foreign Secretary some ambassadors accused him, in turn, of being a slave-driver, but the underlings in the Foreign Office always found him kind and considerate. When a Foreign Office messenger was drowned, Malmesbury's grandson recounted how his grandfather and Canning 'gave themselves much trouble in arranging his affairs for his family. It is but one of many kind acts of this nature.' When Malmesbury's son Fitzharris was Under-Secretary he became devoted to Canning, and complaints of 'slave-driving' from ambassadors like Lord Strangford should be taken with a pinch of salt, as the diplomatic service was often used as a form of outdoor relief for impecunious members of the aristocracy. Canning certainly showed no favouritism. Bagot was a close friend, but that did not save him from more than one 'snub' while he was an ambassador: Canning's rhyming despatch, 'In matters of commerce the fault of the Dutch/ Is in yielding too little and asking too much …', had a serious purpose, to make Bagot acquaint himself with the latest Foreign Office cipher. And it worked. Bagot told Canning, 'I could have slain you! But I got some fun myself, for I afterwards put the fair decipher into Douglas's hands, who read it twice without moving a muscle or to this hour discovering that it was not prose.' Similarly, although Lord Granville (Leveson-Gower) was one of his closest friends, that did not save him from deserved rebukes when he was British Minister in Paris: 'the perpetual recurrence of dinner is exceedingly distressing', Canning wrote (31 December 1824), 'but did it not enter your mind that you might evade the force of that not unexpected impediment by beginning to write at a time of day when it does not usually present itself? Try that device.'

During August 1799 Canning went to stay at Walmer Castle with Pitt, who was Warden of the Cinque Ports. Among the guests was Dundas. His wife Lady Jane was with him, and had brought the daughter of Major-General John Scott of Balconie and his wife Lady Mary, friends of hers who had both died. Canning knew that Lady Jane was 'apt to have Misses with her', and that Joan Scott was an heiress, and that her sister was married to Lord Titchfield, eldest son of the Duke of Portland. He was determined not to let gossip add his name to the long list of suitors Joan had rebuffed, and 'carefully avoided sitting beside her at dinner'.[9] He told Bess on 9 August that 'before the end of next week' he would leave Walmer and 'pay you a visit at Wanstead', but two days later he had decided to prolong his visit, and by the end of the month was well and truly smitten. Joan, though shy and reserved, was attractive. Canning poured out his heart in a long letter to the Leighs, and by 2 September was able to report to Bess that,

> the Person upon whose stay mine depends in some measure, does not go till the 10th, and I think the circumstances encouraging enough to induce me to proceed. I dare not say to you how much I hope; and I dare hardly acknowledge to myself how much my happiness depends upon my not being disappointed – I know I have your prayers and good wishes, dearest Bess.

Lady Jane had clearly been matchmaking. She knew that Pitt saw in Canning the man who might in future years be the one to carry on his own political principles, but he had neither money nor family connections behind him, and marriage to Joan Scott would provide both. By the time Joan left Walmer, Canning for his part was probably wishing that Joan was not an heiress with a brother-in-law who would consider him a totally unsuitable match. When Titchfield and his father the Duke of Portland came to collect her from

Walmer, Mrs Crewe was with them, sensed what was afoot, and was all agog: 'to make bad worse', Canning told the Leighs, 'Mrs C began to form her little suspicions and to desire to communicate them to me'. Probably, though, Mrs Crewe's connection with the Duke was a help, for the course of true love (Joan had fallen in love with Canning just as he had with her) did not go smoothly. As both Joan's parents were dead, her brother-in-law, Titchfield, was head of her family and did all he could to prevent her from marrying an impecunious young man with no prospects. For six months the see-saw – will she, won't she – continued. The strain told on them both: Canning caught a bad cold in January and could not shake it off until April, when Joan fell quite dangerously ill. This brought matters to a head: Joan finally accepted Canning despite Titchfield's objections.

They were married by Canning's uncle William Leigh at 7.30 pm on 8 July 1800 at the Brook Street chapel. Frere was best man, and Pitt was there to sign the register, though when it came to the point, Frere told his brother, Pitt was 'so nervous that he could not sign as witness, and Canning whispered to me to sign without waiting for him'. Frere also recounted that on the way to the church:

> a fellow … peering into the coach recognized Pitt and saw Mr Leigh who was in full canonicals sitting opposite him and exclaimed 'What, Billy Pitt! and with a Parson too!' I said 'He thinks you are going to Tyburn, to be hanged privately', which was rather impudent of me; but Pitt was too much absorbed to be angry. He regarded the marriage as the one thing needed to give Canning the position necessary to lead a party, and this was the cause of his anxiety about it, which I would not have believed had I not witnessed it. … Had Canning been Pitt's own son, I do not think he could have been more interested in all that related to this marriage, though I knew how warm was the regard he had for Canning.[10]

At the age of 30, therefore, Canning seemed to have the world at his feet. Joan's fortune had given him the financial independence that an aspiring politician needed, on top of which Pitt, probably not wanting him to feel too dependent on his wife, appointed him that autumn to the lucrative post of Joint Paymaster-General, and made him a Privy Councillor. Canning's career was taking off, and his marriage was blissfully happy. In October Joan was well enough, despite a rather difficult early pregnancy, to visit the Leighs at Ashbourne, stopping a night with Charles Ellis on the way. Canning told Bess 'The curricle succeeded marvellously. … We travelled at the rate of 40 miles a day, from 20 to 30 of which we always went in the curricle [otherwise they rode]. The Leighs are, as you may suppose, delighted with Joan.' They spent

Christmas at Welbeck with the Titchfields, and in the New Year started packing up from their house in Spring Gardens to move into Canning's official residence – 'the best house in London' as he described it.

But in February disaster struck. The King, encouraged by the devious Lord Loughborough (who had started life as 'a snivelling Scotch attorney' and whom Pitt had appointed Lord Chancellor to replace the equally devious Lord Thurlow), had convinced himself that any measure of Catholic emancipation would be a violation of his Coronation Oath and would subvert the constitutional settlement of 1688 on which his own right to the throne was founded. Although Pitt had made no promise to follow up Irish Union by removing restrictions on Roman Catholics, he had let it be known, and told Cornwallis the Lord Lieutenant, that this was government policy. Thus faced with the King's adamant and very public refusal to countenance any such measure, Pitt felt he had no alternative but to resign, recommending Henry Addington, the Speaker, as his successor. Addington's father had been the great Lord Chatham's family doctor, and the son had been a friend of Pitt since boyhood.

There seems to have been a mutual understanding that Pitt was simply stepping temporarily to one side to give time for the dust to settle and for his health to have a much-needed chance to recover. Overwork and worry, lack of fresh air and exercise while parliament was sitting (often into the small hours) and not always having time for regular meals had taken a heavy toll. Increasingly Pitt had recourse to alcohol to provide the necessary stimulus, apart from sheer will-power, to keep him going, and unfortunately the alcohol was usually port, which brought on the gout to which, like his father, he was prone. When Pitt had been a delicate boy, copious and regular draughts of port wine had been prescribed for him by Dr Addington, and it is ironic that the resultant addiction was part of the reason why the doctor's son became Prime Minister. In 1801 Pitt, at the age of 42, was physically already a sick old man, and half of him clutched at the opportunity to lay down his office for what he thought would simply be a short interval that would give him a breather. As it turned out, Pitt was out of office for three years, and even that was not enough to restore his health. In 1805 his lifelong friend Wilberforce was dismayed by his appearance: 'His face anxious, diseased, reddened with wine, and soured and irritated by disappointments. Poor fellow, how unlike my youthful Pitt!'

Canning was very angry with Pitt for resigning. He told Lord Malmesbury that he had 'strongly advised Pitt *not* to yield on this occasion [as] so many concessions had been made, and so many important measures overruled, from the King's opposition to them, that Government had been weakened exceedingly; and if on this particular occasion a stand was not made, Pitt would retain only a nominal power'.[11] But as Lord Rosebery in his *Life of Pitt* pointed out, 'What more could he do? What war is to kings, resignation is to ministers; it is the *ultima ratio*. He was, perhaps, open to censure for not having himself prepared the king at an earlier stage for the projected policy. But a minister who had served George III for 17 years may be presumed to have understood the King's times and seasons better than any retrospective intelligence' – and much better than the 30-year-old Canning who had never served in cabinet let alone, like Rosebery, been Prime Minister. Pitt urged his friends not to resign, but Grenville, Dundas, Spencer and Windham did, as did Cornwallis and Castlereagh, who having understood that Catholic relief would follow the union felt honour bound to resign when it did not. Portland, who as Home Secretary had also been involved in the union, announced that he would resign but then delayed doing so, probably to give himself time to tidy up the secret service accounts that he had used with doubtful legality to ease the union through the Irish parliament.

Canning had no departmental responsibility for Ireland and was not in the cabinet, but despite Pitt's urgings he too resigned. Not only did he feel that an important constitutional principle was at stake, but he also felt passionately about the union. When it was first introduced he had told his cousin Bess (22 February 1799):

> I have been thinking of nothing else for these last two months, and luckily the winds and waves have been so good as to keep all foreign mails from coming in so that I have had plenty of time to think of it. ... And the result of my thoughts is that [the union] must succeed and will succeed, and that our poor Country will be saved, in spite of the folly and fury of some of its mistaken patriots, and all its self-interested ones. Next year I hope we shall be one People.

And as early as 1792 he had told Bootle Wilbraham that that 'if something be not done for [Irish Catholics], the consequences will probably be either war or massacre'. Events from the Rebellion of 1798 to the Omagh bombings of 1998 do indeed suggest that, sadly, the King's refusal to give Catholics a say in the government of their country poisoned the new United Kingdom at its birth. Canning was right, but he did no good by fussing and fuming, and his resignation did not help one little bit. Frere, writing after Canning's death, had no doubt that

> Pitt knew he must come in again soon ... and he wished, on his return, to find Canning in office, where he might have retained him without difficulty from his aristocratic supporters; but Canning would not let him. I was obliged

to remind him of it afterwards [when he was Prime Minister] and was crusty with Lord Dudley for much the same thing. I told him, 'Dudley is now doing to you what you did to Pitt – refusing to follow a lead the necessity of which you see, and he does not'.

Canning's resignation simply meant that less gifted contemporaries such as Castlereagh and Jenkinson would become cabinet ministers while he himself fretted on the back benches. To make matters worse (and possibly to make Canning more on edge than usual) Joan was soon due to give birth to their first son and giving some cause for anxiety. On Good Friday 1801 he wrote disconsolately to Bess:

> We are as well as people out of place can be – and not only out of place, but out of house too – for we cannot get a house of our own anywhere, and are therefore constrained to live and to litter (if that be a proper expression) in my Lord Glenbervie's. Joan suffers still, and will continue to until all is over. … She sends her love. And mine, to all.

Canning's successor, Lord Glenbervie, could hardly turn them out until Joan was well enough to move after the baby was born (on 25 April), but we need not be too sorry for him. Until January he had been plain Mr Sylvester Douglas, and had then agreed to go out to the Cape as governor on condition that he got a peerage; to Dundas's fury, no sooner did he get his peerage than he withdrew his acceptance of the post, only to be rewarded by Addington with the Paymaster's office that carried with it what Canning had called, with some truth, 'the best house in London', from which he, together with his wife and new-born son, had regretfully to move at the end of April 1801.

CHAPTER 6

Contrasting Fortunes

C anning hated being out of office. He had something other than politics to occupy his mind, however, as he had bought a small farm at South Hill, near Wokingham. He told Frere (7 July 1801):

I have bought a place – and a very pretty one – not very large, but large enough, in Windsor Forest – 28 miles from Town, 9 from Windsor – a good house, and a farm of 200 acres – with Cows, and pigs, and sheep (which I have just shorn and got 15 todd of wool – no, not 15, I forget exactly how many todd, but I shall get £15 for it).

Any attempt to reconcile himself to loss of office by pretending that he had settled down to a life of rural contentment was short lived, however. In August he was,

in the midst of my harvest ... [and] have the satisfaction of proving to myself that I shall lose about £100 annually by my farm (supposing it to prosper as it is now doing with every help of fine weather and high prices) in addition to the interest of the purchase money. ... I hope you find Foreign Ministering [Frere was Minister at Lisbon] a more profitable trade.[1]

The christening of their son, however, had been a boost for morale. Canning's uncle William Leigh officiated, and the godparents were the Princess of Wales, Dundas and Titchfield. He told Frere:

Dundas was present, Ld T. was not, but Sneyd was there to represent him, and Pitt was allowed to come to answer to Aunt Fanny. I cannot tell you how much I should have liked your being there. You would have found Pitt and Leigh as capable of being brought into collision at dinner that day as they were, some ten months before ... on the day of my marriage; but the Prss. being by, and understanding P. as well as she does, the effect was much more happy. It is very extraordinary, but P. with all that he has done, and thought, and seen, is such pure nature, that Leigh is himself scarcely more an ingénue than he.

Sadly, the little boy, named George after his father and Charles in honour of his godmother ('who very good-naturedly commanded that he should be called George'), did not long remain 'one of the finest boys that ever was seen; plump, goodhumoured, lively, full of health and vigour and spirit ... having been inoculated with the Cow Pox when he was but three weeks old, and having had the disease very favourably'. The South Hill cows may have had TB, since little George developed what sounds like a tubercular hip; he was always an invalid and died shortly before his 19th birthday. For George's sake his parents sold South Hill, which was conveniently near London (Canning's opponents called it 'the camp of observation on Bagshot Heath') and bought a house a hundred miles further north, at Hinckley, Leicestershire, so as to be near a specialist who, they vainly thought, might be able to help George. Joan spent much of the year at Hinckley with him while Canning was in London (they rented Gloucester Lodge, Brompton), an arrangement that gave posterity an invaluable series of letters between husband and wife, but deprived Canning of Joan's companionship and support – and since her political instincts were often sharper than his, her presence might have saved him from some of the blunders that were to set back his career.

The Cannings had three more children: William (named after his godfather, Pitt) who went into the Navy and was drowned off Madeira in 1829; Harriet, who married Lord Clanricarde; and Charles (Carlo) who became the first Viceroy of India – 'Clemency' Canning. Both Canning and Castlereagh were blessed with happy marriages, but each was tinged with sadness: the Castlereaghs were childless, and the Cannings had to bear the gradual deterioration and early death of their eldest son.

The years 1801 to 1804 were frustrating for Canning. Contemporaries who had been colleagues became cabinet ministers while he languished on the back benches – only unfortunately he did not languish. Until the 1802 general election, when he was elected for Tralee, he could not openly attack Addington in parliament because he owed his Wendover seat to Pitt who refused to go into opposition, but he made no secret of his contempt for 'the Doctor', as he called Addington. What made Canning's opposition so acerbic was not just that he felt sore and resentful, but that he was convinced that Addington and his government were simply not up to the task of leading Britain in time of war. Calling Addington 'the Doctor' was hurtful because it had the ring of truth: Lord Rosebery's *Pitt* describes him as having 'the indefinable air of a village apothecary inspecting the tongue of the state'. Nor were the members of Addington's government much more impressive. Its apologists have claimed that since it contained two future prime ministers it cannot have been all that weak, but Hawkesbury (the future Lord Liverpool) was a very weak Foreign Secretary, and Perceval had only recently and rather reluctantly entered politics as Solicitor-General. Glenbervie, who admittedly tended to run people down, described Hawkesbury as 'good-natured, and of great simplicity of manner, but ambitious beyond his years, having been pushed on by his father through his influence with the King, and [by his] university connection with Pitt's favourites, particularly Canning'.[2] As for Perceval, Glenbervie considered his appointment as Solicitor-General (promoted the following year to Attorney-General) as the result not so much of talent-spotting as of Addington's recognition of a kindred spirit who shared his pathological fear of 'the overgrowth of Popery'. These comments reflect general opinion at the time: it was only later that holding high political office brought out unexpected hidden talents; they both became prime ministers (Liverpool for a record 15 years).

Canning simply could not understand Pitt's support for Addington. He told Lord Malmesbury (10 February 1801) that Pitt had made him 'promise *not to laugh*' at him, but that 'this was all he could promise to undertake'. Years later, Canning told Granville how Addington (by then Lord Sidmouth) had taken him on one side after a meeting, and 'rather embarrassed, said "Mr C., will you allow me to avail myself of [this] chance to say to you very much I wish that the very unpleasant personal relations in which we have so long stood towards each other may cease?" I need not tell you that I took both the poor Doctor's hands, and shook and squeezed them with perfect cordiality. ... I have instigated Sheridan to ask him to dinner on Friday.'[3] But in 1801 Canning merely saw Addington's inadequacy, and failed to realize how hurtful his barbs were to a decent, kind, honest man who was doing his best, however inadequately, and was very wounded by such personal attacks.

Pitt had not wanted Canning to resign, and was exasperated to see him creating bad blood between those 'Pittites' who remained in office and those who had resigned. Lady Malmesbury told Canning's friend Sneyd:

> I have little doubt that his counsels were far from temperate ones, as his head has been much impaired by the weight of fortune and favours that have been showered upon it; besides, he had contrived to make himself so unpopular by that most horrid of vices, quizzing, that he has more enemies than any body living.[4]

It may well be that without Joan's money behind him Canning might have felt he must hold his nose and serve under Addington; but in justice to Canning, it must be remembered that personal attacks were by no means one-sided. Lady Stafford urged her son Granville to dissociate himself from Canning because he was telling everyone that Pitt 'holds this new Administration in great contempt ... and *a certain person* [the King] with [no] more respect'. Granville replied (20 February 1801): 'I am not surprised at very many malicious Reports being spread about Canning's conversation' (his mother was writing from Bath, a hotbed of gossip) and 'that Canning has to *anyone* talked disrespecturlly of HM I will answer for it is not true'. He was sure that this report 'had been spread by those who are anxious to hurt both him and the King and Mr Pitt, and I know from the best authority that there are no Lies (it is a strong word but such is the case) which Hawsbury [sic] and some of his near relations and friends have not propagated to hurt Canning. ... I must add that ... if I had followed his advice and not his example, I should have stayed in office.'

Meantime Castlereagh, who had also resigned, was no more enchanted than Canning with the new Prime Minister. He told Cooke on 16 March 1801, 'your [disparaging] comment about Addington I believe is all too true and if you knew how little reluctant he was to accept the charge [to be Prime Minister] it would not add to your confidence'. Castlereagh's old chief Lord Cornwallis resigned as well; he saw that failure to grant relief to the Catholics was a disaster. He wrote to Ross: 'It is too mortifying a reflection that the fatal blow [the royal veto] should be struck from the quarter most interested to avert it, and that Ireland is again to become a millstone about the neck of Britain and to be plunged into all its former horrors and miseries.'[5] He and Castlereagh would both have endorsed Lord Rosebery's verdict that union without the abolition of tithes, stipends for Catholic clergy and votes for Catholic electors was 'like cutting the face out of a portrait and leaving the picture in the frame'.[6] Castlereagh did, however, agree to continue to answer for Irish affairs and help tie up loose ends after he had handed in his resignation.

Not surprisingly, after two years of unremitting work on the Union Bill, followed by such bitter disappointment, Castlereagh's health was affected. On 22 April Cornwallis wrote that he had been 'for some days under great anxiety' about him, and a fortnight later was 'still very uneasy about Lord Castlereagh; he has had a return of his fever. They tell me there is no danger, but I have no idea of a fever of so long continuance without danger.'[7] The reason for the anxiety was that exhaustion and depression on their own could not account for the fever, yet the doctors could find no other cause for it; a mystery illness is always worrying. Castlereagh's illness kept him out of circulation for some three months. (A similar illness in 1807 after six months as Secretary of State for War would once more put him out of action for several weeks.)

Although Castlereagh's opinion of Addington was no more flattering than Canning's, he was prudent enough to keep it to himself. Meanwhile Adding-

ton himself was being lucky. On 2 April 1801 Nelson, by dint of disobey-
ing a signal to break off the engagement ('he put his glass to his sightless eye
and "I'm damned if I see it" he said') destroyed the Danish fleet off Copenhagen and with it the Armed Neutrality Pact with which the Baltic nations
had threatened Britain's naval supremacy. That victory was shortly followed
by news of Abercromby's defeat of the French army in Egypt. Pitt had left
Addington a stronger hand for negotiating terms for a peace settlement than
he himself had ever enjoyed, and talks were opened in October. Unfortunately, Hawkesbury as Foreign Secretary did not play his cards well – even
the King, who liked him, was very disparaging of his performance. Canning,
who, thanks to his involvement in the peace talks of 1797, knew far more
about the issues than 'Jenky' did (and was probably jealous of him), did not try
conceal his contempt for the way the negotiations were being handled. It was
one thing to return British conquests in the West Indies in order to gain peace
– Lord Malmesbury had been ready to make that sacrifice – but relinquishing
conquests in the Dutch East Indies, Goa and Pondicherry in India, Mauritius
and the Cape, let alone ceding Malta to France, seemed to Canning to show
a very misplaced trust in Napoleon's good faith. Luckily Napoleon invaded
Switzerland and restarted the war before the British had evacuated Malta, but
even so the Cape and other strategic possessions had to be recaptured all over
again when war resumed after all too short a period of peace.

However, when the peace treaty was signed at Amiens in March 1802 it
was greeted with relief and joy; after many years of war, the country was
ready for peace at any price, and Addington was able to introduce the first
peacetime budget for ten years. It has been argued that he was far more capable over finance than he has usually been given credit for, and that he, rather
than Pitt, should take the credit (or blame depending on your point of view)
for introducing income tax. True, Pitt, who first had the idea, did not get the
details right, so it was Addington who produced the first form of income tax
that actually worked, but Pitt had been consulted while the 1802 budget was
being prepared and had approved it. George Rose, who had been Secretary to
the Treasury, told Pitt's old tutor, the Bishop of Lincoln, that Pitt had prepared
'a great Plan of Finance which he has given to Mr. A but I fear the latter will
hardly be made to understand it'.[8]

Many of Pitt's erstwhile colleagues, notably Grenville, felt that by supporting Addington he was damaging both his own reputation and the interests of
the country. On 28 May 1802 Canning organized a dinner in honour of Pitt's
43rd birthday at the Merchant Taylors Hall, attended by nearly a thousand
people. They ended the evening by enthusiastically singing Pitt's praises in

verses Canning had written both to laud Pitt and to raise doubts about the wisdom of the terms of the peace treaty:

And O! if again the rude whirlwind should rise,
The dawning of peace should fresh darkness deform
The regrets of the good and the fears of the wise
Shall turn to the Pilot that weathered the storm.

Pitt did not attend that birthday dinner, and was rather cross with Canning for having organized it, since he still looked on Addington as his nominee who therefore deserved to be supported. But Canning's efforts had sown seeds of doubt in Pitt's mind.

Addington meanwhile, buoyed by the general mood of euphoria, called a general election in June, which gave him an increased majority. With Pitt's encouragement, Castlereagh agreed to join the government as President of the Board of Control (of India). According to Hobhouse's diary, before accepting office Castlereagh stipulated that the government must accept responsibility for some £18,000 worth of debts that he had incurred as Chief Secretary. If true, that is not as discreditable as it might sound, since both the Duke of Portland as Home Secretary and Castlereagh as Irish Secretary had used bribery on behalf of, and with the connivance of, government in order to get the Union Bill through the Irish parliament. Hobhouse's diary is usually based simply on gossip, but the fact that the story was current shows that Castlereagh at this period was not looked upon as the upright and honourable statesman that he later became. The methods he had been compelled to use as Irish Secretary had given him a reputation for sleaze, just as Canning's behaviour towards Addington had given him a reputation for factious and self-seeking opposition.

Castlereagh's new post as President of the Board of Control, like that of Chief Secretary of Ireland, was outside the mainstream of British politics, but this time he was in the cabinet, and that gave him general experience of government. The Board of Control was an ideal office for him: it required a conscientious and capable administrator who had the presence and manner to keep the members of the East India board reasonably happy while at the same time controlling their behaviour. There was need for such control: Englishmen went out to India to make their fortunes, and were not too particular as to how they did it – Canning's young cousin William declined to go out to India on leaving Cambridge since 'a fortune is seldom acquired without oppression and chicanery', and Thackeray's *Vanity Fair* suggests that his assessment was not far off the mark. The impeachment of Warren Hastings, though unfair, suggests that even governors were not above suspicion.

The Governor-General was Lord Wellesley. Imperious by nature, he had been made even more so by his years in India. Helped for much of the time by having his younger brother Arthur, the future Duke of Wellington, as one of his generals, Wellesley added more territory to the East India Company's possessions than even the great Clive had done. Castlereagh was lucky not to have taken office a few months earlier, when it would have fallen to him to order Wellesley to return the conquered French territories in accordance with the peace terms agreed at Amiens. As it was, it had been Hawkesbury who issued those orders, which Wellesley loftily ignored, saying, 'I really cannot crouch to young Jenky whom I have laughed at ever since I have known him.' By the time Wellesley's high-handed refusal to obey instructions had reached London, Britain was at war again, so the less said about it the better; and since in Wellesley's eyes anyone would have been an improvement on 'Jenky', Castlereagh got off to a good start. In any case, since it could take nine months for a report from Calcutta to reach London and another nine months for any reply to get back, Castlereagh could hardly be blamed if he failed to prevent Wellesley incurring yet more expense on the Company's and the taxpayer's behalf.

This was just as well, as a war between three Mahratta chiefs had just given Wellesley a pretext to crush their marauding cavalry and nip in the bud the threat posed by their French-trained and French-officered armies. He decided, regardless of the wishes of the 'cent per cent rascals of Leadenhall Street', to invade central India, making his brother Arthur commander-in-chief, and the operation proceeded on a scale which, in Lady Longford's words, 'would make the Mysore campaign look like an economy drive'.[9] Wellesley could see the strategic importance of India, while the East India Company directors in Leadenhall Street could see no further than their shareholders who would have to pay for the war. Castlereagh sided with the Company, whose aversion to spending money was fully shared by the government, but because of the time it took for despatches to pass between England and India the Mahratta campaign was brought to a triumphant conclusion before it could be countermanded. When the news of the victories in the Deccan reached London, parliament sent the victorious general thanks for his 'memorable service', and the future Duke of Wellington was awarded the Order of the Bath, thus becoming Sir Arthur, and was given a golden vase worth 2,000 guineas, a sword worth £1,000 and countless congratulatory addresses. But the cost in human lives as well as money had been heavy: Wellington later said that the battle of Assaye was 'the bloodiest for the numbers [involved] that I ever saw'.

Unfortunately Wellesley's next campaign was a failure. In 1804 he sent General Lake to try and capture Holkah, the last remaining Mahratta ruler. Lake's ruthlessness had been successful against the Irish peasantry, but unlike them the Mahrattas were properly armed, so Lake was ignominiously defeated and Wellesley was summoned home. Sir Arthur meanwhile had left India on health grounds and had arrived back in England in September 1805 to find that his elder brother had been recalled. He went to protest to the President of the Board of Control, but his interview, which might easily have been stormy, made a very good impression on Castlereagh, who was as a rule better at controlling his temper and remaining polite than Canning, who might have let his irritation show by making some acid remark that caused resentment. One result of Castlereagh's time at the Board of Control, therefore, was that whereas Lord Wellesley (by then a marquess, but to his fury only an Irish one – a 'gilt potato' as he indignantly called it) disliked Castlereagh for having recalled him, his younger brother, the future Duke, was favourably impressed by him. Castlereagh, in fact, was building a reputation as a dependable 'safe pair of hands', and although he was still a poor speaker and debater, he nonetheless added weight to the government front bench in the House of Commons.

His work at the Board of Control kept Castlereagh in or near London for most of the year, and his connection with Ireland became correspondingly more tenuous. In the general election of 1805 he failed to be returned for County Down; the dowager Lady Downshire had gone over to Ireland specially for the occasion and her unremitting efforts among her tenantry were successful. According to Lord Henry Petty, 'Castlereagh's defeat was received with acclamation by all classes here [in Dublin], and the city would have been illuminated if the Mayor had not prevented it, giving rather awkwardly as an excuse that he did not think the occasion of sufficient magnitude.' [10] Castlereagh's early abandonment of the Opposition Whigs, his ruthlessness during the rebellion and the methods he had had to use as Chief Secretary to force through the union and abolish the Dublin parliament, had combined to make him generally unpopular throughout Ireland. After losing his County Down seat he found another one that did not require any canvassing of constituents, and henceforth Ireland became no more than the place he went to, when he had the time, to visit his father (who lived on at Newtownards, in remarkably robust health, until 1821). The Castlereaghs took a London house on the north side of St James's Square, still easily identifiable by the blue plaque bearing his name, where Emily could entertain, and she soon became well known as a political hostess. They also bought a comfortable but unpretentious large farmhouse at St Mary Cray in Kent, which was completely rural but within easy reach of London.

To revert to the year 1803. On 18 March, barely 14 months after the Peace of Amiens, Britain once more declared war on France after Napoleon had ignored an ultimatum to withdraw from Holland and Switzerland. People were coming to realize, as they would do with Hitler over a century later, that there would be no limit to a dictator's territorial ambitions. Like a war-horse scenting battle, Pitt came up to London, and Creevey, a strong supporter of the peace party, complained that 'This damned fellow Pitt has taken his seat and is here, and, what is worse, it is certain that he and his fellows are to support the war; they are to say that the time for criticism [of the ministry] is suspended.' The next day, Creevey thought Pitt a spent force: 'I really think Pitt is done; his face is no longer red, but yellow; his looks are dejected … and every now and then he gives a hollow cough. Upon my soul, hating him as I do, I am almost moved to pity to see his fallen greatness.' But when the House debated whether to accept a Russian offer of mediation, and 'Lord Hawkesbury [in] a speech of two hours … [made] a fair and reasonable … justification of the war', Creevey had to revise his opinion: 'Then came the great fiend himself – Pitt. … Never, to be sure, was there such an exhibition; its effect was dreadful. He spoke nearly two hours – all for war, and war without end.'

Renewal of hostilities made Pitt start to chafe at his exclusion from office. Shortly before war was resumed Addington had, to his credit, offered to take a junior position in a government headed by Pitt, saying he would agree to serve with anyone Pitt might choose, even Canning, with the exception of Grenville. Pitt had refused that offer, partly because his poor health still made him reluctant to take up the burden again, but mainly because he knew that he could not lead an effective government unless he could appoint the best ministers he could find. But power is a potent drug, and soon Addington was rather enjoying being Prime Minister. Before long, relations between him and Pitt deteriorated. Addington no longer felt any deference to Pitt, let alone any inclination to step down in his favour, and although Pitt for his part was reluctant to do anything to undermine His Majesty's government in a time of war by attacking it, that did not stop him from being a thorn in Addington's side. He tabled a motion to renew conscription, which was clearly a matter for government, and not for a private member to propose. Tension steadily increased, but Pitt, despite being very strongly pressed by his cousin Grenville to do so, would make no move – with what proved the unfortunate result that Grenville allied himself with Fox who was at least an out-and-out opponent of the government.

Pitt's reluctance to go into opposition did not stop Canning from sniping at the government at every opportunity. He was not, as some irritably thought, simply being factious: after a year of war even Addington was beginning to realize that he was out of his depth. Faringdon's diary for 19 May 1803 reports that Addington 'though a temperate man now drinks perhaps twenty glasses of wine at his dinner before he goes into the House of Commons, to invigorate himself'. Meantime, with Napoleon preparing invasion barges at Boulogne, Pitt took his duty as Warden of the Cinque Ports to see to the coastal defences very seriously. He drew up detailed and intricate instructions for the Volunteers' cavalry drill, and rode long distances inspecting the various detachments and seeing the fortifications against invasion. All this was at least good for his health, although his friends, particularly Grenville (and, needless to say, Canning), urged him to come out into open opposition. They told him that it was his patriotic duty to try and take the helm once more now that war had resumed.

Canning's relationship with Pitt at this time was like that of a headstrong son irritated, and sometimes petulant, at his father's caution. In June 1801 he had told Frere that he felt Pitt had 'used me most unfairly' (though why, it is difficult for the impartial observer to see). 'I have really forgiven him too, but as to putting myself in his power again – I shall be not a little cautious.' It was as if Canning thought that Pitt had resigned for no other reason than to disappoint him, and Pitt's patience with Canning throughout this period was very striking; he often invited him to stay at Walmer and never resented his familiarity. Others, however, did resent Canning's closeness to Pitt, and jealousy may have been behind a good deal of the hostility that some of his colleagues bore towards Canning. Back in the mid-1790s there had been tut-tutting when, as a junior minister, he leant over in the House to tap Pitt on the shoulder to gain his attention; and after Pitt had become Prime Minister again in 1805 and Canning was in the government but not in the cabinet, Addington (by then Lord Sidmouth, President of the Council) complained to his brother Hiley of 'a certain person who is more impudent and obnoxious than ever ... and allowed to appear in the House of Commons as the prochain ami'.[11]

These years bring out an important difference between Canning and Castlereagh. Both men were very definitely Pittites, but whereas Canning was a personal friend of Pitt but not in his cabinet, Castlereagh was not a personal friend but was in his cabinet during his last ministry of 1804–06. And of course in 1802 Castlereagh had done what Pitt wanted and accepted office under Addington, whereas Canning had gone against Pitt's wishes and refused to do so. Bruce's *Life of General Sir Charles Napier*[12] tells of an episode that encapsulates the difference in the two men's relationship with Pitt. Napier was staying with Pitt at Putney together with Pitt's nephew and niece (Charles

Stanhope, and his sister Lady Hester who kept house for Pitt) and they were all indulging in horseplay. Pitt was trying to avoid having his face blackened with burnt cork, when Lords Castlereagh and Hawkesbury were announced. Napier told Bruce that '"Let them wait in the other room" was the answer; and the great minister instantly turned to the battle, catching up a cushion and belabouring us with it in glorious fun.' It was ten full minutes before Pitt (who had lost the battle and was having his face daubed) said 'Stop ... we must not keep these grandees waiting any longer.' Napier then describes how, after his face had been cleaned and the towel and basin hidden behind the sofa, 'a new phase of Mr Pitt's manner appeared. ... I had known Lord Castlereagh from my childhood, had often been engaged with him in athletic sports, pitching the stone or bar, and looked upon him as what indeed he was, a model of quiet grace and strength combined. What was my surprise to see both him and Lord Liverpool bending like spaniels on approaching the man we had just been maltreating with such successful insolence of fun!' Canning was not there on that occasion, but had been present at other times when Pitt was indulging in similar schoolboy behaviour – as when he joined in a game of Blind Man's Buff at the Princess of Wales's house at Blackheath, which, considering that Caroline was very highly sexed and had a colourful reputation, was a rash thing for a Prime Minister to do (but of course paparazzi were still a long way in the future). Castlereagh was never on such a familiar footing with Pitt as to see him behaving like that; Canning never served in one of Pitt's cabinets. Perhaps that may have sown seeds of jealousy in them both, for different reasons.

Addington's ministry managed to survive for a year after war had been declared. Canning took a prominent part in attacking it in the House of Commons, until in May 1804 Addington eventually resigned and Pitt became Prime Minister once more. Two years earlier, Pitt had declined Addington's offer to resign in his favour because of the stipulation against Grenville becoming a minister, and Pitt knew he must have a free hand to form an effective ministry. Unfortunately he still did not have a free hand: this time the veto came not from Addington but from the King, who refused point-blank to allow Fox to become a Secretary of State. As a result Grenville, who had become so exasperated with Pitt's refusal to go into opposition that he had joined forces with Fox, said he would not join the government either. The upshot was that in order to be sure of a parliamentary majority Pitt had to bring in Addington (who was given a peerage as Lord Sidmouth), and Pitt's last ministry in 1804 was a pale shadow of his first. Having to include some Addingtonians also made it impossible for Pitt to bring Canning into the cabinet; instead, he gave him the choice between Treasurer of the Navy or Secretary for War, neither of which was automatically a cabinet post, but either of which could become one, as it had with Windham in 1794. (Pitt did decide to bring Canning into the cabinet towards the end of 1805, but died before he could do so.)

Canning chose the Navy; the Treasurership was after all 'a plum job, with £4,000 a year and a house' – and there was an unexpected bonus, in that the housekeeper at the Navy Pay Office in Somerset House died, so Canning was able to appoint his aunt Hitty's unmarried sister Bess Patrick in her place – 'in which situation if she comports herself decently,' he wrote to his cousin 'there is no reason why she should [not] continue as long as the late Mrs Browne, some half a century. Harry tells me he is busy preparing patterns of the Mob Caps, Check Aprons, key-rings and girdles in which it will be right for her to appear henceforward. The present wig too, I think, must be exchanged for one of a more venerable and grizzly appearance, [and] there is no reason why her friends should not favour her with any suggestions of this sort which they may think advisable.' Like all politicians of the time, Canning never hesitated to use his influence and interest in a way that today would be thought positively corrupt. But unlike some politicians, he only did so if he thought the person concerned was right for the job; thus, he asked Wellington to take Hitty's son Charles as an honorary ADC, and, unlike most such ADCs, he ended up as a colonel on Wellington's staff; he started Charles's brother Stratford off on his Foreign Office career, and he ended up as Lord Stratford de Redcliffe KG, a very distinguished diplomat; while the gallant conduct of Hitty's nephew, Robert Patrick, whom he had likewise helped in his career, 'had no small influence on the fate of Soult's campaign' according to Oman's *History of the Peninsular War*. The 'old boy net' was unfair, but worked surprisingly well when not abused.

Canning's new office gave him the privilege of seeing Nelson off on his final voyage that ended at Trafalgar, but he had soon found that his duties were not, as he had supposed, mainly ceremonial. It was not surprising that he had thought so, as his predecessor had been Addington's brother-in-law, Bragge Bathurst, who was hardly a man to be entrusted with a responsible post, but in fact Canning found that he had considerable responsibilities: he had to make the case for naval expenditure, and to see that when the money was voted it was well spent. There was even more to do than usual, because Addington's most dangerous appointment had been to make Lord St Vincent First Lord of the Admiralty. As Sir John Jervis, he had been the admiral who gained a famous victory against the Spaniards in 1797 off Cape St Vincent, for which he was given his peerage (Nelson commanded a squadron in the battle, and made a decisive contribution by running his ship against one twice her own

size, boarding her, and using her as a bridge to board and capture the next
Spanish battleship as well – 'Nelson's Bridge' they called it). At the Admiralty,
St Vincent attacked the corruption and inefficiency of the naval dockyards so
virulently that he brought virtually all naval repairs and shipbuilding to a halt,
so Canning inherited a situation in which Napoleon was busily rebuilding the
French navy while the Royal Navy was in a run-down condition. St Vincent
had not been mistaken in believing that there was much corruption: a year
after Canning became Treasurer, Dundas (or Lord Melville as he had become)
was impeached for misusing naval funds; the guilty man was in fact Trotter,
the Paymaster of the Navy, but Dundas had been nominally responsible for
what occurred within his department. Canning had told Joan what a help it
was to have a capable man like Trotter at his side; little did he know.

There could indeed be a surprising naivety about Canning on occasions. No
sooner had he become a minister in Pitt's new government than, in a debate on
8 June, he attacked the record of the previous government, saying that he did
'not really think that an administration so constituted as the former [one] was
fit for the country in its present crisis'. He seemed to have forgotten that he was
now a colleague of the ministers he was criticizing – particularly the Foreign
Secretary, who had been his old friend Jenky (Lord Hawkesbury). It was not
surprising that *The Times* (in an article possibly planted by Bragge Bathurst)
stated that Canning's attack would make it impossible for him and Hawkesbury to serve in the same government, but it was surprising that Canning was
astonished to find that his speech had upset his old friend. 'Jenky' handed in
his resignation, and it took all Pitt's and Canning's persuasion to make him
change his mind; luckily, and to Hawkesbury's great credit, their friendship
was strong enough for him to forgive Canning and not hold it against him in
years to come. It is strange that a man as intelligent as Canning simply did not
realize how wounding his verbal assaults could be – especially after Jenkinson's reaction to that spoof recruiting poster ('Tis the bold Colonel Jenkinson
that calls you to arms') 11 years earlier. In his attack on ministerial incompetence it was not only Hawkesbury who had cause to take offence: Canning
had stated that ministers generally were 'not fit for the country in its present
crisis'. He was singularly inept at gaining the confidence and friendship of his
colleagues.

Castlereagh continued to serve as President of the Board of Control in the
new government, and after Sidmouth had resigned in 1805 Pitt asked him to
take on the War Department as well; three years as a cabinet minister had
confirmed his reputation, earned in Dublin, of being a thoroughly sound and
capable administrator. Castlereagh did not remain at the War Office long

enough to make much impression, but the few months he was Secretary of
State gave him the opportunity to learn how the War Department worked (or
didn't work). That experience helped him two years later, when he became
War Secretary once more, to devise and push through an effective method of
recruitment for the army that had eluded his predecessors.

Pitt's government only lasted 20 months, and was a pale shadow of his
previous administration. He himself was a sick man, and lacked the parliamentary support he had enjoyed when backed by men of the calibre of Grenville,
Dundas and Windham. Pitt had no supporters in the House of Commons of
the weight and calibre of Fox or Sheridan on the Opposition benches, and
because the King's support was at best lukewarm, the solid core of country
members who would support the King's government regardless of party could
not be relied on, and Pitt was constantly sniped at not only by the Opposition but by many Addingtonans who were nominally on the government side.
In April 1805 Pitt received a body-blow: a commission of inquiry had implicated Melville in Trotter's misappropriation of naval funds (referred to above),
and on 9 April the House of Commons passed a vote of censure on him. The
actual vote was a tie, and the Speaker, after ten minutes of agonized dithering,
used his casting vote against Melville. Pitt was devastated. Malmesbury's son
Fitzharris 'distinctly saw the tears trickling down his cheeks. ... A few young
ardent followers of Pitt, with myself, locked their arms together and made a
circle, in which he moved, I believe unconsciously, out of the House.' Sidmouth
had been particularly venomous against Melville, and when his nominee was
not appointed in Melville's place, resigned, and Pitt went down to Weymouth
to try and persuade the King to let him bring Fox and Grenville into the cabinet, but George III remained as pig-headedly obstinate as ever. During that
summer and autumn, however, things seemed to be looking up. Pitt managed
(by means of a large subsidy) to bring Austria back into the war against Napoleon, and in October the news of Trafalgar boosted the government's and the
country's morale. At the Lord Mayor's Banquet on 9 November Pitt made
what turned out to be almost his last and certainly his best-known speech. It
was very short, and ended with the words, 'England has saved herself by her
exertions, and will, as I trust, save Europe by her example.'

Almost immediately, however, gloomy news came in from the Continent:
the Austrians had been defeated at Ulm. Pitt's health at this time fluctuated
according to the news of the war, but he was steadily becoming weaker. At the
end of the session in December he went down to Bath to take the waters and
try to recover his strength. Canning spent a week with him – 'it was a great
comfort to have happened to contribute so much to his amusement' (such as

writing an ode to Trafalgar for Pitt and Mulgrave to exercise their minds on by making suggestions and critical comments). But on 3 January Castlereagh arrived with the official news from the War Office of the battle of Auster-litz. Austria was effectively knocked out of the war, and Prussia was signing a treaty with Napoleon. Pitt had to get back for the new session of parliament, and on 11 January he arrived at his house in Putney. Whether or not he actually said 'Roll up that map of Europe, it will not be wanted again for many a year' on his arrival, the news of Austerlitz had certainly dealt him a mortal blow. But he could not rest: the war was going on and ministers needed instructions. Castlereagh and Hawkesbury came to see him on government business on 13 January, but the effort proved too much. Pitt told his doctor, Farquhar, that 'when in conversation with persons upon important business, I felt suddenly as if I had been cut in two'. That same day he had asked Canning to visit him (not on business), but found that ten minutes was as long as he could manage; he asked Canning to stay in the house and come to his room again in the evening, but by then was too weak to see him. Doctor Farquar and the Bishop of Lincoln were the only people apart from family to see Pitt after that, and early in the morning of 23 January he died.

Canning felt Pitt's death dreadfully. Politically he had hitched his wagon to Pitt's star, and now that star was extinguished, he felt temporarily lost. At a personal level, too, this was a devastating blow: he had loved Pitt, who in many ways had filled the gap left by the death first of his father and then of his uncle Stratford.[13] Canning looked up to Pitt and in many ways seems to have treated him, subconsciously, as a father-substitute. He was relieved and glad that before Pitt died their disagreements had been set aside, and they were once more on the same easy terms of friendship as they had been before 1801. Their rapprochement was probably helped by their mutual anger and indigna-tion at Dundas's impeachment, when Canning had (according to Lady Bess-borough) 'stood forth alone, in defiance of public opinion'. For him, as for Pitt, Dundas was not only a staunch political ally but a personal friend as well; it was through him and his wife that Canning had met Joan, and he was godfather to their eldest son George.

Pitt's death meant the fall of his ministry, and both Canning and Castlereagh found themselves in opposition, which for Castlereagh was a new experience (apart from his early years in the Dublin parliament). Canning found opposi-tion this time far less irksome than it had been two years previously, when Pitt's refusal to oppose the government had made him feel uncomfortable and frustrated. This time Canning knew where he stood, and moreover he was once more on level terms with men like Hawkesbury and Castlereagh. The fact that they had been cabinet ministers and he had not no longer rankled, particularly since he was more effective in debate than either of them. Pitt's death had enabled him to grow up politically; 'what would Pitt have done?' always remained an important consideration for him, but now he had to answer that question for himself.

The King was forced to turn to Grenville to form a government, and this time he had to allow Fox to be in the cabinet. But although the new administration was called 'the Ministry of all the Talents', Pittites were excluded – not because Grenville did not want them but because in order to ensure the support of enough 'country' MPs he had to offer places to Sidmouth and his followers (prompting Canning to say that 'Mr. Fox has got the Doctor, as people must have the measles once in their life'). When Fox fell ill in the summer of 1806, Grenville asked Canning to join the government with a seat in the cabinet, offering places also, though not in the cabinet, for other Pittites including Castlereagh and Perceval. However, Canning stood out for at least one other Pittite to be in the cabinet with him, and nothing came of it. Fox's death in August threw everything into the melting pot, and without Fox's talents the ministry struggled to survive. Early in 1807 Grenville's government was eventually brought down, just as Pitt's government had been six years earlier, by the King's refusal to allow any measure of relief to be offered to Catholics. The government had decided it must allow Catholics to be promoted to senior ranks in the army and navy, and that provoked mutiny from Sidmouth and his supporters, who were almost as bigotedly anti-Catholic as the King himself. Grenville tried to save the government by turning to the Pittites; his brother Tom Grenville offered to give up the Admiralty to Canning,[14] and Grenville's nephew, Lord Temple, urged that 'the numbers we would lose by turning out Lord Sidmouth would be more than counterbalanced by the numbers who are ready to come to us with Canning'.[15] But by then it was too late. Once again, the King's fear of popery brought a government down – though the cackhanded way in which it had handled its measure for Catholic relief suggested that it was in terminal decline anyway. As Sheridan ruefully put it, he had 'heard of men beating their heads against a brick wall, but never before of their building the wall to beat them against'.

CHAPTER 7

Cabinet Colleagues

But in spite of all the world will say
My talents yet feel no decay
They're what they were before;
And now, at sixty-nine, I still
Can fold my paper, point my quill,
And when did I do more?

Then what's such idle talk about,
Think ye that age shall keep me out?
No! if so old I grow,
Less time to lose I thence infer;
And as to friends and character,
I lost them long ago.[1]

The King was glad to be rid of Grenville, whom he had never liked – 'he supports principles [i.e. Catholic emancipation] opposed to that Constitution which as a Peer and a servant of the public, it was his duty to support'. However, it was easier to get rid of him than find a replacement. Not until 18 March 1807 did Grenville learn that 'the general opinion is that the Duke of Portland will come here, with Perceval, who in that case will of course be the real [Prime] Minister'.[2] The Duke was 69 years old, suffered from gout and dropsy, and hated speaking in public, but having succeeded to his dukedom at the age of 24 he had learned how to wield political patronage from that master of the art, the Duke of Newcastle. David Wilkinson's biography of Portland[3] points out the immense prestige of an eighteenth-century duke, especially one who had been playing a leading part in English politics for over 40 years. It was not the first time that Portland had been asked to form a government: in 1782 he had been made Prime Minister, when the 'real Prime Minister' in the House of Commons had been Fox. That government had been short lived, and from 1784 to 1794 Portland had led the Opposition in the

Henry Bentinck, 3rd Duke of Portland. When Portland was Home Secretary, Lord Minto said of him, 'The Duke of Portland will look at his nails and raise his spectacles from his nose for a fortnight before he answers me.' His procrastination as Prime Minister was part of the reason for the duel of 1809.

House of Lords, exemplifying the Whig aristocracy whose power George III had been determined to break. But in 1794, when Britain was threatened by revolutionary France, Portland and some other Opposition peers joined the government – Pitt sardonically commenting that they feared their wealth and even their heads were in danger from the Jacobins – and as Home Secretary he created a very effective espionage and counter-insurgency network.[4] By 1807 Portland, in his 70th year, was a man that George III felt he could trust. One great merit in the King's eyes was that he had not resigned in 1801 in protest against the royal veto on Catholic emancipation; George III's anti-Catholic obsession which made him distrust Grenville also influenced him against many others, notably Canning (Castlereagh too had been under a cloud when he was Irish Secretary – 'Who is this young Lord?' the King had asked indignantly at a levee in January 1801).

But 'sound' though Portland might be in the King's eyes, that did not mean that he possessed the qualities needed to lead a wartime government. Lord Minto had complained that 'The Duke of Portland will look at his nails and raise his spectacles from his nose for a fortnight before he answers me.' However, when asked to form a government Portland did not hesitate: it would have been against nature for an eighteenth-century duke to refuse office, however bad his health. In any case, he had no intention of being a Prime Minister in the modern sense, but as First Lord of the Treasury he would administer government patronage while leaving the nation's finances to the Chancellor of the Exchequer, Spencer Perceval. And since Perceval was also Leader of the House of Commons, he was, as Grenville had predicted, 'the real Prime Minister'.

Perceval played a major part in the events that followed. A younger son of the second Earl of Egmont, he had built up a very successful practice at the Bar, earning £4,000 or £5,000 a year. He had entered parliament in 1797 at the behest of his eldest brother, and in 1801 became Solicitor-General and soon afterwards Attorney-General, first under Addington and then under Pitt. In opposition during Grenville's 'Ministry of All the Talents', he was an effective debater, but no orator (or writer – the Prince of Wales later remarked that 'it is a great misfortune to Mr Perceval to write in a style which would disgrace a respectable washerwoman'). When Portland invited him to join the government he wanted to become Attorney-General again, and only agreed to take the Exchequer on condition that he also received a sinecure to compensate him for his loss of income. A very small man, he did not exude an air of natural authority in the way that, say, the six-foot Castlereagh did. Temple thought him 'very weak' as Leader of the House, and that he 'proved that a chattering lawyer in Opposition does not necessarily make a good manager of

Spencer Perceval succeeded the Duke of Portland as Prime Minister in 1809 and became the only British prime minister to be assassinated (in April 1812).

the House of Commons'. Part of the trouble was that his wife had just had her 13th child – Wilberforce blamed her for 'fagging him and keeping him up all night' – and he had to cope with the double load of Leader of the Commons, which involved constant and often exhausting attendance well into the small hours, as well as being Chancellor of the Exchequer. In the latter post he was rather out of his depth, but he was alert, hard-working and, above all, very determined. Moreover, as a staunch and firmly Protestant churchman, the King was predisposed to like him. Lord Holland's *Further Memoirs of the Whig Party* sums up Perceval by saying, 'he had too much spirit to be intimidated, and too much bigotry to be convinced by argument'.

The other members of Portland's cabinet, who almost all contributed in one way or another to the rupture that would occur between Castlereagh and Canning, were as follows:

- **Lord Camden**, Castlereagh's uncle, was Lord President of the Council. A friend since Cambridge days of Pitt, he was amiable and intelligent and had considerable experience as a cabinet minister, but when faced with difficult problems as Lord Lieutenant of Ireland he had shown himself weak and indecisive (hence Canning's nickname for him – 'Chuckle').
- **Lord Eldon** (born 1751) was Lord Chancellor, a brilliant lawyer and the nearest the eighteenth century could get to a self-made lord. When Princess Charlotte was told he was to supervise her upbringing she protested at the idea of the granddaughter of the King of England having to answer to the grandson of a Newcastle coal-heaver (actually he had been a coal factor). At the age of 21 Eldon had eloped with the 16-year-old Miss Surtees, whose parents did not approve but came round when Eldon started to make good at the Newcastle Bar. He entered parliament in 1783, was Solicitor-General 1788, Attorney-General 1793, given a peerage in 1799 and became Lord Chancellor on Loughborough's retirement in 1801. Very conservative.
- **Lord Westmoreland** (10th earl, born 1759) had also known Pitt at Cambridge. He went to the Middle Temple, and eloped in 1782 with the daughter and heiress of the banker Robert Child. He was Lord Lieutenant of Ireland (conservative and very Protestant) between 1789 and 1794. His wife died in 1793 and he remarried in 1800, but would part from his wife in 1811. He became Lord Privy Seal in 1798, and clung to that office like a limpet until 1827. Lady Holland called him 'coarse in mind, manner and language'. Canning called him 'le sôt privé'.
- **Lord Hawkesbury** ('Jenky' of Christ Church days) was Home Secretary. He had been summoned to the House of Lords as Lord Hawkesbury in

1808, and became Earl of Liverpool on his father's death in 1808. He was still Canning's friend despite the latter's attacks on him as Foreign Secretary under Addington.

- **Lord Mulgrave** (born 1755). After Eton he joined the Middle Temple but in 1775 enlisted as an ensign and fought in the War of Independence. He was a close friend of Pitt, who sent him as a brigadier to report on the siege of Toulon in 1794, and brought him into the cabinet in 1804 as Chancellor of the Duchy of Lancaster and, temporarily, Foreign Secretary. In 1807 he became First Lord of the Admiralty and 'appears to have found [its] heavy administrative duties a strain and complained of the impossibility of meeting all the demands that were put upon the Navy'.[5]

- **The Earl of Chatham**, Pitt's elder brother, was Master-General of the Ordnance. Rosebery's *Pitt* calls him 'an underrated figure. He was, no doubt, indolent and extravagant; as a general, he was a conspicuous failure; he was useless as the head of a department, but in cabinet, he was of singular value.' Eldon, a shrewd judge, called him 'the ablest man I ever knew in the Cabinet; ... when his turn came to deliver his opinion, he *toppled* over all the others'; and Fortescue's *History of the British Army* says that at the Ordnance he 'brought the British Artillery up to a pitch of excellence unknown in his day'.

- **Lord Bathurst** (born 1762) was President of the Board of Trade. Grenville called him 'a very amiable man with a good understanding, though his talents were far from brilliant. A High Churchman and a High Tory greatly averse to changes, but acquiescing in many. Nervous and reserved, with a good deal of humour.'[6] He would prove himself a sound Secretary for War and the Colonies from 1812 to 1822, when he was usually consulted on foreign affairs.

- **Castlereagh** was Secretary for War and the Colonies.

- **Canning** was Foreign Secretary.

Thus Castlereagh, Canning and Perceval were the only cabinet ministers to sit in the House of Commons ('Viscount Castlereagh' was only a courtesy title). Castlereagh and Canning both had previous experience of their new departments: Castlereagh had been Secretary for War and the Colonies for a few months in 1805–06, and Canning had been Under-Secretary in the Foreign Office in the 1790s. During the last months of Grenville's government they seem to have agreed that Perceval should lead the House of Commons: Canning had never previously been a cabinet minister, and Castlereagh's necessary ruthlessness as Chief Secretary in Ireland had made him very unpopular in some quarters, nor was he, at this stage, a good speaker. But although Perceval was therefore the obvious choice to lead the Commons, he unfortunately lacked the authority that might have compensated for Portland's semi-detached style of leadership, and the result was 'a government of departments' with no overall control or strategic direction. A typical letter from Portland to Perceval gives a flavour of how government business was conducted: 'Lord Castlereagh was so good as to inform me of the result of the last cabinet. It has my entire concurrence. ... Had I been apprised of Lord Castlereagh's intention of summoning a meeting so early as Friday I would have remained in town.'[7]

This lack of coordination and leadership made friction between ministers almost inevitable, but to start with Castlereagh and Canning got on well. At a personal level, they shared an Irish background and had a family connection through Castlereagh's sister having married Canning's cousin – whom Castlereagh continued to treat as a brother-in-law despite his sister's early death. They were both disciples of Pitt, and in 1805 when Castlereagh had been Secretary for War and Canning had been Treasurer of the Navy they had collaborated in strategic planning. When Nelson first met Castlereagh in August 1805 he dismissed him as 'a man who has only sat one solitary day in his Office, and of course knows but little of what has passed', but later on he was pleasantly surprised when the minister seemed to agree that neutral shipping bound for Cadiz, where Villeneuve's combined fleet was sheltering, could be seized and sent to Gibraltar. Nelson's opinion of Canning was that that he was refreshingly able, 'a very clever, deep-headed man', but that he somehow seemed to arouse the baser competitive instincts.[8] The two men's planning in 1805 resulted in victory at Trafalgar, but in the 1807 government there was no Pitt to chair cabinet discussions. Usually Canning and Castlereagh agreed on war policy – we find Castlereagh writing to Canning, 'my view of the Turkish question accords entirely with yours' (cut their losses and pull out of the Dardanelles), but a fortnight later Canning, acting on Foreign Office intelligence, had wanted to support a hoped-for royalist rising in Brittany while Castlereagh demurred:

> If I was only to consult my own inclinations, I can assure you with perfect truth, I should most gladly accept your proposals but they must depend on military support [and] there are considerable objections to the foundations being laid with one department, whilst the ultimate execution must depend on another. ... There seems also some objection in principle to the official transfer of the business from a purely military to a diplomatic channel. I confess I am not myself at present impressed with any very sanguine hope that the game of the Royalists can be played with much military advantage.[9]

Canning, Castlereagh (and Mulgrave) pulling together harmoniously. The King
told Canning that seizing the Danish fleet was 'a very immoral act. So immoral
that I won't ask who originated it. I have determined not to ask that question'; but,
Canning told his wife, 'all in the most perfect good humour, laughing even at his
own difficulties'. ('British tars, towing the Danish fleet into harbour' by James Gillray, hand-coloured etching, published by Hannah Humphrey, 1 October 1807.)

Inter-departmental jealousy probably exacerbated disagreements between
ministers when there was no Prime Minister to act as umpire.

So long as things were going reasonably well, that did not matter, as
Canning and Castlereagh were of one mind in their conviction that Napoleon
must be defeated. When they acted in concert, the results were dramatic.
After Napoleon had defeated the Russians at Friedland in June 1807 Canning
received intelligence that made him at once inform the cabinet: 'There can be
no doubt that Buonaparte reckons upon the Danish fleet ... as an instrument
of hostility against Great Britain', adding that the Danes were 'in a state of
ill humour and irritation against this country which renders but too probable their compliance' with Napoleon's demands. With Castlereagh's energetic
support – and with Mulgrave working day and night at the Admiralty to draw

up the naval plan – for once in a way a British expedition was launched swiftly and effectively, and the Danish fleet was secured. High-handed though this action was, it saved England from losing control of the seas, and although the Opposition naturally condemned this attack on a neutral country, the King good-humouredly told Canning that he preferred not to know whose idea it was. Later that year, naval supremacy was again secured when the Portuguese Regent was persuaded to sail to Rio de Janeiro in the nick of time to save his navy from Napoleon's clutches. Although the ambassador, Lord Strangford, claimed the credit, it was in fact due to Canning's alertness.

Canning's most serious disagreement with his colleagues in 1807 was not with Castlereagh but with Perceval, who was determined to pass Orders in Council to restrict trade between neutrals and the Continent. Canning realized the harmful effect this would have on relations with the United States, which were already prickly. Cabinet ministers were asked to submit their views in writing (no proper discussion, apparently), and Portland and Bathurst were the only ones who shared Canning's concern. Canning was exasperated that Perceval could only see the issue on narrow legalistic grounds, and did not realize the effect the Orders would have on Anglo-American relations (the American author Bradford Perkins's *Prologue to War* calls them 'the Portland Ministry's greatest single contribution to eventual war' in 1812 with the United States). Canning held no brief for the Americans, who were behaving shabbily by taking advantage of the French embargo to build up their own trade at Britain's expense, and trying to persuade seamen in British warships to desert, while at the same time relying on the Royal Navy for protection, but he did not let his feelings control his foreign policy. (Bradford Perkins thinks Canning was 'more aware of the possibility of diplomatic controversy than his colleagues', but that his 'prevaricating letters and sophisticated expressions' were partly responsible for the war of 1812.)

Castlereagh had not been well while the Orders in Council were being discussed, and had merely submitted a brief memorandum agreeing with the majority. If he had taken a fuller part he would almost certainly have argued in favour – he had after all allowed Nelson to seize neutral ships bound for Cadiz – but his main preoccupation had been his reform of army recruitment (without which Wellington could not have succeeded in the Peninsula). Castlereagh introduced these measures on 22 July, after which – to quote *DNB* – he 'relapsed into a corpse-like appearance by internal haemorrhaging' (probably the 'corpse-like appearance' was the result of being bled by doctors rather than internal bleeding). As in 1801, there was no clear diagnosis of his illness, and not until the end of January 1808 was he fully back at work. His inability to give his full attention to the War Department had a paralysing effect on strategic decisions: as Napier's *Peninsular War* acidly puts it, some 15,000 troops had been literally as well as metaphorically at sea for two months while the Secretary of State for War was away from his desk.

During the summer of 1808 an unexpected opportunity arose for a 'second front'. The previous year Napoleon had cowed the Spanish government into allowing a French army to march through Spain to attack Portugal. Once there, the French showed no disposition to leave, and in the spring of 1808 Napoleon put his brother Joseph Buonaparte on the Spanish throne instead of King Ferdinand. That was too much for Spanish pride: popular uprisings occurred, and in June deputies from the Asturias came to London to ask for help. Despite the doubts of the King and of some of the more conservative members of the cabinet about supporting a popular uprising – after all, the French Revolution had started as a justified protest against bad government and look where that had led – public opinion in favour of the Spaniards was strong enough for Canning to declare unequivocally in the House of Commons on 15 June that 'any nation of Europe that starts up with a determination to oppose a Power which ... is the common enemy of all nations ... becomes instantly our essential ally'. Castlereagh, equally enthusiastic, sent a three-man military mission to prepare to receive arms and supplies from England even while Spain was still nominally at war with Britain, and by 4 July Canning was able to send official envoys from the Foreign Office – Stuart to Corunna with 'two hundred thousand pounds which His Majesty is pleased to advance by way of loan', Hunter to Asturias with a slightly smaller sum, and Duff back to his old post at Cadiz. These envoys were instructed to urge the provinces to unite under a central junta.[10]

There happened to be a small force at Cork, ready to embark for Venezuela to support Miranda's rebellion. It was decided to send it to the Peninsula instead, under the command of Sir Arthur Wellesley, despite the fact that he was, and remained, Chief Secretary of Ireland. Sir Arthur sailed on ahead, and finding that Galicia did not need any British troops, landed his force at Mondego Bay, south of Oporto (whose bishop agreed to supply commissariat and transport). The French army of occupation under Junot had been found to be stronger than first thought, so General Spencer was ordered to join Wellesley with 5,000 men from Gibraltar, and a force under Sir John Moore, which had been recalled from the Baltic, was to be sent straight on to Portugal. In the eyes of the Horse Guards and the King, Wellesley was far too junior a lieutenant-general to command this combined force, and on 30 July he was disgusted to receive a despatch from Castlereagh informing him that Sir Hew Dalrymple,

the governor of Gibraltar, would supersede him, with another elderly guards-
man, Sir Harry Burrard, as second in command. To us who know that Wellesley became by far Britain's most successful general, that seems the height of
folly, but in view of Sir Arthur's lack of seniority it was perfectly reasonable
to put Dalrymple in command. As governor of Gibraltar he had established a
good rapport with the Spanish general Castaños, although Britain was still at
war with Spain, and he understood the military and political situation in the
Peninsula better than anyone. Admittedly it was many years since he had seen
active service, but Burrard, who was appointed his second in command, had
been second in command the previous year at Copenhagen (where Wellesley
had commanded a division) and had often seen action before that. Wellesley
Pole thought that 'the appointment of Sir Hew was ... merely meant to parry
something of the kind much worse', presumably meaning the Duke of York,
who was known to long for a command in the field. The Duke had been a
failure as commander of the British Expeditionary Force in the Low Countries
in 1794, and had done little better during the Helder Expedition of 1799, but
since he was commander-in-chief the Duke could reasonably have insisted that
in view of Wellesley's lack of seniority, he should himself take over. Dalrymple
and Burrard, however, were too senior for that argument to work.

But Castlereagh may have had another reason for deciding that Wellesley
could not remain in command. Sir John Moore was senior to Wellesley, so
would automatically have taken over command from him, whereas Dalrymple and Burrard were Moore's seniors. Considering that Moore had seen
action in Corsica, the West Indies, Holland, Egypt and Italy, had revolution-
ized army training (he introduced light infantry) and was idolized by his men,
Castlereagh's reluctance to let him take over the command may seem perverse,
but it was shared by most of his colleagues. Not only was Moore a partisan
Opposition Whig who had freely criticized the government, but much more
seriously he had shown a constant tendency to think he knew better than the
civil authorities to whom he had been subordinate. During the British occupation of Corsica in 1795 the British Resident, Gilbert Eliot (later Lord Minto),
had actually sent him home for stirring up discord: he had behaved gallantly
during the capture of the island (admittedly Nelson, who lost an eye there,
complained that Moore had been slow and uncooperative at the siege of Calvi,
but then Nelson seldom had much time for the army), but after the fighting
was over Moore supported the Corsican leader Paoli against Minto's wishes.
Twelve years later in Sicily much the same thing happened. Moore wanted
Drummond, the British minister, to force reforms on the Neapolitan Court;
Drummond judged that this would only make things worse, so Moore quar-

relled with him. Canning had been at the Foreign Office on each occasion (in 1795 as Under-Secretary responsible for the Mediterranean), so would twice have had a complaint about Moore land on his desk. Finally in 1808 Moore had been sent to the Baltic with 10,000 men to help Sweden against Russia, and had so angered King Gustavus that he was put in prison and had to escape in a laundry cart. This time it was not entirely Moore's fault, as Gustavus was mad, and Moore's instructions had been ambivalent – to support Gustavus but not let his troops be deployed as Gustavus had wanted them (in Denmark). Moore thought his instructions had been deliberately ambiguous so that, whatever went wrong, he could be said to have disobeyed orders. When he returned to England on 15 July, he was summoned to London while his troop transports were made ready to sail straight on to Portugal, and saw Castlereagh on 18 July. He was relieved that his conduct in Sweden was approved, but nothing was said about this next mission except that he was asked how soon his troops would be ready to proceed to the Peninsula. The next day Moore was summoned again, and told that he was to take his troops to Portugal but that he would then come under the command of Dalrymple and Burrard, neither of whom had half his military experience. Moore angrily told Castlereagh exactly what he thought of him ('thank God I have got *that* off my stomach', he told his military secretary the next day), and just before he sailed he received a stiff letter from Castlereagh saying that his remarks had been reported to the Duke of York and the King, and that 'had not the arrangements for the army been so far advanced ... there would have been every disposition on [the government's] part to ... relieve you from a situation in which you appear to consider yourself to have been placed without a due attention to your feeling as an officer'. If Castlereagh hoped this letter would provoke Moore to refuse to go to Portugal at all, he was mistaken, and on 31 July, after several days of foul winds, Moore and his 10,000 men left the shores of England behind. It was not a propitious start to the campaign.

Although Castlereagh had to tell Wellesley that he was to be superseded, he realized that he was far more competent than either Dalrymple or Burrard, so enclosed a private letter with his official despatch, urging Wellesley to press on as quickly as possible and try to defeat the French before the other two generals arrived. Wellesley did just that, and a skirmish at Rolica drove Junot's army back to Vimeiro, less than 25 miles from Lisbon. But at that point Burrard arrived and forbade Wellesley to attack. Luckily, Burrard then went back on board his ship for the night, and to Wellesley's delight the French attacked early the next morning. Burrard to his credit did not attempt to interfere in the battle, and Junot's army was trounced, but Burrard then forbade the pursuit that would have routed it. Wellesley, disgusted, told his staff, 'Well then, we have nothing to do, but to go and shoot red-legged partridges.'

Burrard's refusal to allow Wellesley to follow up his victory seems inexplicable until we realize that the idea of a British army actually winning a battle was quite outside his experience. He had been in the American war which Britain lost, in the Low Countries where the Duke of York had 'marched his men to the top of the hill and marched them down again', and with the Helder Expedition which had only managed to re-embark safely because the French had not realized how parlous their situation was and offered an armistice. True, Copenhagen had been a success, but that had been a naval rather than a military victory. All Burrard's military experience would therefore have led him to suppose that Junot's retreat from the battlefield was a feint designed to lure the British to destruction.

Worse was to follow. Dalrymple arrived, and before he had decided what to do, Junot sent General Kellerman to offer an armistice. The two amiable guardsmen were no match in negotiations for one of Napoleon's canniest generals, and the terms of the armistice that came to be known as the Convention of Cintra allowed Junot to take his army, their arms and equipment and baggage back to France in British ships. It also allowed the French to take with them any Portuguese traitors who might otherwise stand trial for treachery, *and* any Portuguese prisoners of war they had captured. (There was also a clause allowing the Russian fleet in the Tagus to sail for Brest, but luckily the British admiral flatly refused to be bound by a military treaty.)

The one-sided arrangements for Portuguese quislings and prisoners of war were bad enough; almost worse, there was no stipulation that the personal possessions the French were allowed to take with them back to France must not include their loot, of which there was a great deal since gold from the mines of Brazil had adorned many Lisbon churches and affluent private houses. When news of Cintra first reached Britain on 4 September in the form of an indignant letter from the Portuguese minister Souza, Canning replied that he must have been mistaken. The King, too, 'could hardly bring himself to believe that any British officer could, under the circumstances, think of agreeing to such a Convention. The King could never sanction such a proceeding, if unfortunately it should have any existence.' Castlereagh thought the same. On 4 September he wrote to his brother Charles, who was serving in Portugal, 'our joy on Wellesley's glorious conduct and successes has been cruelly disturbed by a communication from Souza of a supposed Convention, to which ..., however, W's name appears affixed. ... [It] would secure to the French advantages beyond their reach ... whilst their 16,000 men are now press'd upon by not less than 50,000 men British and Portuguese.' He pointed out that the Convention recognized Buonaparte as Emperor, granted safe return to the French together with their plunder, gave them the right to protect Portuguese traitors but not release Portuguese prisoners of war, and 'give France the Russian fleet' (though thanks to the Admiral this did not happen).

The fact that the Convention was signed by Wellesley and not by Dalrymple or Burrard was embarrassing. Later Wellesley would defend its terms, saying he was 'convinced that if we had not allowed [Junot] to evacuate [Portugal] in August, we should have been glad to do so in November or December, after we should have lost many men in the operations which we must have carried on against them, in a most unhealthy country in the worst season of the year'.[11] But at the time, he told his brother:

> Matters have got worse. ... Sir Hew has agreed to a suspension of hostilities which he made me sign. ... I wish I was away from this Army. Things will not flourish as we are situated, and organised; & I am much afraid that my friends in England will consider me responsible for many things over which I have no power.[12]

To say he 'had no power' over the terms of the Convention is nonsense. Since he had been in command during the battle, it was for him to agree the terms of any armistice. Had he wished to insist on different terms he could have refused to sign, but he seems to have left the negotiations to Dalrymple and Burrard and signed the armistice without demur. One can only conclude that the reason he acquiesced so easily was that he was having a fit of the sulks. Dalrymple and Burrard had robbed him of the fruits of his victory, so let them stew in their own juice. Junot was relieved and delighted at the terms he was given, allegedly telling the captain of the British ship taking him back to France that his army 'were not only beat, but their minds subdued ... they feared to retreat to Lisbon, as the inhabitants would have butchered them. ... What could have induced the [British] officers to make [those terms] was a matter of astonishment to him.'[13]

When it became clear that the Convention was indeed as Souza had described, the British public was dismayed. There were even dark mutterings of treason (Canning's aunt wrote to her son in Constantinople, 'there must have been sad mismanagement somewhere or other, this is not treason I hope'.[14]) Treason there was not: it was simply that the two gallant old generals, Dalrymple and Burrard, were outwitted by Kellerman. Nor does Wellesley come out of the affair well. He told Lord Temple, 'I signed notwithstanding my objection to it, because I would not, in the face of the whole army, set myself up in opposition to the commander of the forces. ... My refusal to sign ... would only have tended to raise my character at the expense of others,' and he told Castlereagh that 'although my name is affixed to this instrument I beg that you will not believe that I negotiated it, that I approve of it, or that I have had any hand in wording it.' But as we have seen, the fact remains that Wellesley need not have signed the Convention but did sign it, and without making any formal note of protest.

Canning meanwhile had gone to join his family at Hinckley for a much-needed break (part of the reason why Cintra made so much bad blood within the cabinet was that the news came at a time when ministers were exhausted by a long, hard-working summer, and being dispersed could not consult one another). Details of the victory at Vimeiro did not reach Canning until 16 September, and he at once dashed off a note to Perceval: 'There can be no doubt that we ought to take this as a great event and accordingly I am about to make the bellringers here drunk – they cannot ring worse after that encouragement than they have been doing of their own account.' But when he had had time to read Perceval's letter properly he realized that it put a very different complexion on things, and the next day Canning wrote to Perceval again:

> The news as reported *by the guard* [of the Mail Coach] was all glorious. ... [But] when your note came ... a few hours' reflection has shown me all the disgrace and disaster of this transaction. ... I yet think you did right to fire the [victory] guns. ... But, having said this, I think there is not the least chance or probability of the transaction turning out to be such as we can approve. Portugal must hate us for the article giving up their plunder. Instead of hailing us as deliverers, they must consider us as having interfered only to sanction and secure French robbers. ... And then poor Castlereagh who has been working night and day to get transports to convey our troops to the scene of action ... is all at once to find tonnage for this precious freight [of Junot's men with their arms and plunder], for which I suppose our own expeditions must stand still.

Perceval's marginal comments on that letter are revealing. Against 'plunder' he wrote 'Surely this cannot be, if capable of proof'; his lawyer's mind failed to grasp that a Portuguese citizen might find it difficult to stop a French soldier with a loaded musket from carrying off his gold plate, even if he could prove that it was loot. He did at least agree that Canning's question 'What right had the British army to stipulate for the impunity of traitors?' (i.e. allow safe conduct for Portuguese citizens who had helped Junot) 'might well be one of the points on which the King should be satisfied'.

Canning evidently assumed that Castlereagh would agree that the Convention was unacceptable. He wrote to him, saying that if Perceval was right to suggest 'that plunder, identified to be such, is *not* to be taken away', then Dalrymple must be made to say so clearly, and,

> As for the [other] Articles ... what business had [Dalrymple] to stipulate impunity for civil traitors ... and the giving up of civil persons [i.e. Portuguese 'Patriots']? ... I will be in town time enough to attend a Cabinet in the evening of Monday [19th] and I cannot help anxiously wishing that no despatches, without a strong intimation of disapprobation, should go till after a full declaration.

However, the cabinet met before Canning could return to London, and decided that a convention made by a general could not be repudiated even if he had acted ultra vires, citing (not entirely relevant) precedents in Egypt and Malta. Canning was extremely angry that this was agreed in his absence, though probably his plea had not actually been ignored but had simply not been received in time. It also seems that Castlereagh asked that the cabinet's decision should not be ratified until Canning had had a chance to put his point of view. What is not clear is why both Castlereagh and the King (who had originally said he 'could never sanction' the Convention as it stood) changed their minds. True, on 30 September Castlereagh wrote to thank his brother Charles for sending him a copy of a Proclamation issued by the British authorities saying that the French might not take their plunder home with them: 'A thousand thanks for your Intelligence – Dalrymple tells us nothing,' he replied. But Stewart's letter from Portugal must have come after the cabinet had already agreed the Convention, and in any case such a proclamation would in practice be meaningless except as a face-saver. Perhaps both Castlereagh and the King decided they must accept the Convention on the grounds that it would be wrong for politicians in England to disown their generals in the field, especially as the general whose name was on the Convention was Wellesley's.

The government's handling of the Convention of Cintra was the catalyst that made Canning lose confidence in his colleagues, not least Castlereagh; and knowing how sharp Canning's tongue could be, he probably made some fairly scathing comments that would not have endeared him to those colleagues. Military historians have tended to praise Castlereagh for backing up his generals, and condemn Canning as a typical politician trying to shift the blame for anything that went wrong on to the generals. Canning for his part could not see why, if a diplomat could be repudiated if he had exceeded his instructions (as had just happened with Erskine in Washington), the same principle should not apply to generals. He saw that the Convention would make the Portuguese – and indeed their Spanish neighbours – feel that Britain could not be trusted not to let down her allies. He was probably right, and probably it was not only Britain's diplomacy that suffered but also her military campaigns: would the Spanish general Cuesta have been so uncooperative towards Wellington at Talavera, one wonders, if he had had less reason to mistrust the British? Canning's objections to the terms of the Convention were so strong that he insisted on circulating his dissenting opinion and sending a copy to the King. Apart from the likely effect on any British campaign in the Peninsula, Canning protested that by endorsing the notion that a British general could 'take upon himself to act, to the best of his judgment, for and on behalf of the Prince Regent [of Portugal]', the cabinet had implied that, with the Regent absent in Brazil, Portugal had become a British protectorate.

Cintra had soured relations within the government. Problems that would have been resolved amicably now became irritants. When in August military and civilian agents in Spain were getting their wires crossed, and Canning told Castlereagh that this was making it difficult to 'manage the Juntas' because they could 'appeal from Stuart and Hunter to Doyle and Patrick', there was no ill feeling; Castlereagh had agreed and promptly rebuked Doyle. But when, six months later, Frere (our ambassador) arrived in Cadiz to try and persuade the Junta to use it as a military base, only to find a British squadron sent by an officious colonel from Lisbon anchored offshore, so that the Junta, fearing a second Gibraltar, refused us permission to use Cadiz, Canning was furious, and saw it as deliberate War Office interference in Foreign Office affairs.

As for public opinion about Cintra, it was well expressed in a popular rhyme:

This is the city of Lisbon
This is the gold that lay in the city of Lisbon
These are the French, which took the gold, which lay in the city of Lisbon.
This is Sir Arthur (whose valour and skill
Began so well but ended so ill)
Who beat the French, who took the gold, that lay in the city of Lisbon.

This is Sir Hew, whom nobody knew,
Who made the Convention that nobody owns,
That saved old Junot's baggage and bones,
Altho' Sir Arthur, whose valour and skill &c.

These are the ships that conveyed the spoil
That the French had plundered with so much toil

Because Sir Hew, whom nobody knew, &c.

This is John Bull in great dismay
At the sight of the ships that conveyed away
The gold and the silver, and all of the spoil,
That the French had plundered with so much toil,
Because Sir Hew, whom nobody knew, &c.

The army in Portugal seems to have felt the same: Captain Bowles of the Cold-stream Guards wrote home approvingly from Abrantes in October 1811 of that 'squib that had come out from England'.

Public opinion forced the government to recall Dalrymple and Burrard to face a board of inquiry. Wellesley prudently asked permission to return before he was summoned, which Castlereagh granted, telling his brother (30 September), 'I have written to Wellesley to make it easy for him to come home if he feels it advisable. I do however hope he will take the high line of serving with good humour under Moore.' But Wellesley did return to England, though before he did so he went to see Moore, and in a long and friendly conversation said that Moore ought to be made commander-in-chief, and undertook to speak for him to Castlereagh. That did not prove necessary: before Wellesley reached England the cabinet had already, though with great reluctance, decided that there was no alternative to Moore. They had tried Chatham, but he could not go at once; Canning would have liked Lord Moira (which judging by his later success in India might have been a better idea than it seemed at the time), and so the cabinet made their 'disagreeable but necessary decision ... the ministers still did not like or trust him, but they had little choice'.[15]

It was believed by many – including Lady Hester Stanhope who was infatuated with Moore – that the duel between Canning and Castlereagh was really caused by Castlereagh having given Moore the command. Stapleton's *Life of Canning* avers that Canning expostulated to Castlereagh, 'Good God, and do you really mean to say that you allowed a man, entertaining such feelings with regard to an expedition [predicting its failure] to assume the command of it?', and that this was the cause of their dispute. As Canning's personal secretary, Stapleton was very close to Canning, but this reminiscence is clearly muddled: the incident is meant to have taken place in July, which was when Castlereagh, much to Moore's annoyance, did *not* give him the command. It may well be that when things started to go wrong with Moore's campaign Castlereagh might have told Canning about Moore's earlier doubts, and received that somewhat tetchy reply; certainly Canning had only acquiesced very reluctantly to Moore's appointment as commander-in-chief; but that was true of the cabinet as a whole. They could see no alternative.

Unfortunately the cabinet's doubts about Moore were all too justified. Before Dalrymple left Portugal he had shown Moore his instructions from London (which would also be his successor's), and they had both agreed that, as Moore wrote in his diary, 'As usual, it was plausible nonsense ... the sort of gibberish which men in office use and fancy themselves military men.' That jaundiced comment reflected Moore's opinion of his orders for the Baltic Expedition earlier that year which had indeed had been 'plausible nonsense', but this time his orders made sound sense. He was to proceed to Galicia to join up with a force of 10,000 men being sent out to Corunna under General Baird. Admittedly, those orders show that the government had no idea how bad Portuguese roads were: while leaving it to Moore's discretion to decide how much of the army to send round by sea, they added, 'the cavalry and artillery will of course' travel overland, not realizing the roads would have been impassable for gun carriages. But that was a detail. Moore was after all given the discretion to decide how to move his army up to the north coast, and could have used the available ships to send his guns round by sea while the main body marched overland. Instead he told Castlereagh that the sea passage would be hazardous so late in the season, that he did not think Galicia could supply both his men and Baird's and that in any case Lord William Bentinck, the military attaché to Spain, had told him the Spanish generals would like him to advance towards Salamanca. So, despite his orders, that was what Moore was going to do, and for him then to complain, as he did, that 'they' (the politicians) 'talked of going into Spain as of going into Hyde Park' when no supplies had been arranged, no route reconnoitred and when autumn rains would soon make movement difficult, was disingenuous. What 'they', the government, had wanted was for Moore and Baird to join forces with the Marquis de la Romaña's 10,000 regular troops that had been brought back from Denmark, and advance eastward along the Biscay coast to support the Spanish general Blake's 'army of the north'. That plan would enable Moore to be supplied from the sea, and if the worst came to the worst to be evacuated by the Royal Navy.

It is doubtful if a combined force of Moore's, Baird's and La Romaña's armies could have won any great victory, for the simple reason that the French moved very much faster than the British, and the Spaniards were disorganized. Before Moore had even crossed the Tagus into Spain, Blake's army had been forced back despite strong resistance, and on 10 November Blake and Romaña (who had not even had time to procure horses for his cavalry) were faced by the combined armies of Lefebvre and Victor. Despite fighting bravely they had to retire, only to be attacked in the flank by the army of Marshal Soult. Moore, meanwhile, reached Salamanca on 13 November and realized he was in a precarious position. He had sent his cavalry and artillery round by a wide detour to the south, since the direct route was unsuitable for guns, and was dangerously exposed in the middle of a flat plain without cavalry or guns for protection. He also found that the Spaniards were far less keen to help him than he had expected, and food supplies were not forthcoming. He told Castlereagh on 24 November: 'We are here on our own ... in complete ignorance of the plans and wishes of the Spanish government ... the Junta ... are incapable of forming any plan or coming to any fixed determination.' Baird meanwhile was not best pleased to find that he had to march 200 miles south-wards to join Moore, who tried to placate him by writing (28 November): 'I know that you should have landed at Cadiz, and that I should have met you at Seville, where the army should have been united and equipped. But it was ordered otherwise, and it is our business to make every effort ... to obey our orders [and] aid the Spaniards as far as lies within our power.' Again Moore was being disingenuous; 'they' had told him to do nothing of the kind. He was 'in a scrape' that was largely of his own making.

On 28 November Moore heard that the Spanish army of the centre, under General Castaños, had been utterly defeated at Tudela. That decided him, despite the pleas of the new British minister to the Central Junta (John Hookham Frere, who was a friend of Canning), to retreat to Lisbon and send Baird back to Corunna as he had previously decided. But then Moore heard that Romaña had rallied his forces at Leon, and that Madrid was in arms against the French. At last, the Spaniards were making an effort to save themselves. Moore therefore countermanded his order for Baird to retreat and told him to come on to join him as soon as possible. The cavalry and guns also at last arrived. So spurred on by an intercepted French despatch telling him that Soult was not far away to the northwest while the other French armies were near Madrid, Moore advanced on Soult. He knew that he could be putting his head into the lion's mouth, but to stand by and do nothing would make the Spaniards lose all faith in the British. Thus he advanced cautiously – 'bridle in hand'. A brisk cavalry skirmish at Sahagun on 21 December routed Soult's advance guard, but Moore then waited two days while oxen were killed and roasted to give his men a hot meal before advancing to make a night attack on Soult's main army. At that very moment he learned that a French army commanded by Napoleon in person had, by forced marches through the moun-tains north of Madrid, got dangerously close. Moore at once ordered his army to turn about, and managed by skilful manoeuvring to pull his army back out of the plain. Unfortunately Romaña had also had to fall back on Astorga, which was his supply base. Moore knew it was, but decided that his own need was greater, and the resultant chaos in Astorga did nothing for British morale, already at a low ebb by the order to retreat instead of having a go at the French. The free-for-all scrimmage at Romaña's food depots did nothing to improve Anglo-Spanish relations, especially as many of Romaña's men had typhus and his army had lost most of its equipment.

Once clear of Astorga, Moore made a half-hearted attempt to make a stand at Lugo (by then Napoleon, feeling there were few further laurels to be won and anxious about rumours of disaffection in Paris, had gone back over the Pyrenees), but decided it was safer to retreat. By now his men had marched hundreds of miles and, apart from the cavalry action at Sahagun, had not struck a single blow against the enemy. Moore's rearguard were brilliant, but the same could not be said for the rest of the army. The artist Sir Robert Ker Porter depicted the route: mule tracks winding round precipitous snow-covered mountains reminiscent of the Himalayas. But in fact it was a perfectly good road and Porter's near-vertical mountain sides were no more than roll-ing hills. Moore's army certainly had a cold and cheerless march to the coast in mid-winter; if it was not freezing they had rain, mud and slush to contend with, but the real trouble was not the terrain, nor even the enemy at their heels, but the barrels of wine stored in some villages which were broken into by the retreating troops. We read of soldiers and camp followers seen lying on the ground dead drunk and having to be left behind to the mercy of the pursuing French; Moore had perhaps not taken into account how demoralizing it was for men to go on and on retreating and never turning to make a stand. When the army reached Corunna and simply had to fight off the pursuing French in order to cover the evacuation, Moore showed himself a fine leader and his men fought well. Moore himself was mortally wounded, and buried on the field: 'not a drum was heard, not a funeral note, as his corse to the rampart we hurried. ... We carved not a line, and we raised not a stone, but we left him alone in his glory.' It was a heroic death that gave him an imperishable reputa-tion for courage and self-sacrifice.

But a retreat is not a victory. Casualties had been heavy, all the horses and guns and much other equipment had been lost (including some invaluable specie that was on its way from Corunna for Moore's use when the cart carry-ing it was pushed off the road). To make matters worse some of the transports were shipwrecked on the way home and a great many soldiers were drowned. The sight of the ragged, half-starved, filthy survivors landing at ports along the south coast caused shock and dismay: as Rifleman Harris put it, 'They must have been a good deal surprised at the spectacle we presented. Our beards were long and ragged; almost all were without shoes and stockings; many had their clothes and accoutrements in fragments, with their heads swathed in old rags, and our weapons were covered with rust; whilst not a few had now, from toil and fatigue, become quite blind.'

Had Moore lived to return to England he would undoubtedly have faced a court martial. He had disobeyed orders by marching into central Spain instead of joining Baird in Galicia; had waited a whole month at Salamanca – and in war, he who hesitates is lost – and, despite brilliant tactical handling, had lost the best part of Britain's only army. But his gallant death put Moore beyond criticism, so the government was blamed instead. Castlereagh and Canning took the brunt of the public anger, the former because he was War Minister and Canning because Frere was being blamed for having persuaded Moore to advance on Madrid against his better judgement, and Frere was Canning's appointee and friend. As we have seen, Moore kept a diary that could be used as a means of self-exculpation, and he also wrote frequent letters to friends at home, including Pitt's niece, Lady Hester Stanhope, who had been passionately fond of Moore and was distraught at his death – all the more so because her favourite brother had been killed at Corunna. Understandably she wanted to be able to blame someone other than Moore himself for what had gone wrong, and Frere was the obvious target, but in fact Frere seems to have had better judgement than Moore. As ambassador in Madrid in 1804 he had got to know the country well, General Romaña had been a personal friend and it was largely thanks to Frere that he and his army were brought back to Spain from garrison duties in Denmark. Crabb Robinson of *The Times* saw the two men land at Corunna on 20 October and lead a triumphant procession through the town, and thought Frere was later treated very unfairly; he would have known before he left England that Moore had been ordered north to meet Baird, with a view to joining forces with Romaña and if possible with Blake. While waiting at Salamanca, Moore wrote (27 November) to ask Frere whether he advised advancing to help the Spanish patriots in Madrid, despite the danger, or retreating to Lisbon to embark and take his army round to southern Spain. Frere, who was with the Central Junta, had no more idea than Moore what the Spanish armies were up to – the fog of war was thick – but was hearing glowing accounts of their feats of arms. He replied (30 November):

> Considerations both of policy and generosity call upon us for immediate effort. ... I would venture to recommend [holding] Astorga whence a retreat to Corunna would (so far as an unmilitary man may be allowed to judge of a country which he has travelled over) be less difficult than through Portugal

to Lisbon; we ought, in that place [Astorga] to wait for reinforcements. ... I mention this however merely as in my humble opinion the least objectionable of the two modes of retreat. ... The covering of Madrid is surely a point of great moment for its effect in Spain. ... The people of Madrid ... ought surely to be encouraged by some show of support.

In other words, Frere suggested that Moore should belatedly try and carry out his original orders and go north to join Baird. Moore hesitated and stayed at Salamanca, so on 3 December Frere wrote again urging him to support 'the determination of the Spanish people ... by all means in his power'. By the time Moore received that letter he had at last decided to march northward to join Baird; and if it was indeed Frere's advice that decided him not to retreat to Lisbon, then Frere deserves credit. Napoleon had expected Moore to retreat through Portugal once he realized his danger, and had sent a force to cut him off or harry his retreat.[16] Had Moore retired to Lisbon as he had planned, the result, along a road far worse than the one to Corunna, would have been an even greater disaster than in fact occurred.

Unfortunately Frere was so exasperated with Moore's dilatoriness that he sent a separate sealed note with that second letter. The note was only to be handed over if Moore had decided to retreat to Lisbon after all, and since Moore had in the end not so decided, it should never have been delivered. However, its bearer, a swaggering and unreliable French royalist named Charmilly, revealed that he had it, and when Moore demanded to see it, handed it over. That note proved fatal for Frere. It said:

> In the event which I do not wish to presuppose, of your continuing the determination already announced to me of retiring with the army under your command, I have to request that Colonel Charmilly, who is the bearer of this, and whose intelligence [about the Madrid rising] has already been referred to, may be previously examined before a Council of War

That was a threat to call a court of inquiry if Moore retreated to Lisbon, and Frere had no business to question a general's military judgement like that, especially as it implied cowardice on the general's part. Moore was extremely angry and did not keep his feelings to himself. It is to Canning's credit that he did not seek to counter the virulent attacks on Frere made by Moore's friends by pointing out Moore's errors; instead, when the Commons debated the campaign he declared that Moore had 'acted as a statesman no less than as a soldier; because even though he might fail he must have gained an advantage for Spain ... by drawing off the French army'.

CHAPTER 8

The Year of the Duel

During the opening weeks of 1809 Canning was feeling increasingly frustrated. The Peninsular campaign that had started so gloriously had quickly slid towards disaster; first, two bumbling generals had thrown away the fruits of Wellesley's victory at Vimeiro, and then another general, acclaimed in military circles as Britain's finest tactical commander, had succeeded in destroying Britain's only army. It was not just the campaign's failure that Canning minded; after all, his whole political life from 1794 onwards had seen a series of defeats and he had learned from Pitt not to be dismayed but to try again. What Canning found frustrating was that the government was blamed for the shortcomings and failures of generals – all the more so because he personally had wished to repudiate the terms of Cintra but had been over-ruled, and then had not thought Moore the right choice as commander-in-chief (he wanted Moira) although he had reluctantly acquiesced in the appointment. Canning also felt bitter because he had been obliged to recall his friend Frere and let him become the scapegoat for Sir John Moore, whose gallant death had put him above criticism.

Moore's shortcomings apart, Britain's whole military organization was chaotic. Armaments came under the Master of the Ordnance, the Secretary for War was in charge of soldiers' pay and the deployment of the home forces, the Horse Guards under the commander-in-chief decided promotions and appointments, while the Commissariat came under the Chancellor of the Exchequer – in the words of the military historian General Maurice, 'the Treasury is the most important war power of England'. The Secretary of State for War was meant to be in overall charge, but to confuse matters yet further, Castlereagh was Secretary of State for War *and the Colonies*, a combination that had made sense when the West Indies had been the main theatre of war, but by 1809 made no sense at all. As Foreign Secretary, Canning could not help being very much aware of all this muddle and inefficiency, and saw the consequences all too clearly. During December, he had discussed the Peninsular campaign with Portland, who had agreed that Moore's appointment had been a mistake: 'if you are willing to *take your full share* of the blame in our Ministerial capacities by having trusted Moore with the command of the Army in Spain, how much more ought I to be to plead Guilty'. He would have liked to recall Moore, but by then it was too late.

Canning was convinced that the British military effort should be concentrated on the Peninsula, and early in 1809 reinforcements had actually been embarked, but when it became plain that Moore's army would have to be evacuated, they had to be disembarked so that the empty transports could be sent to Corunna and Vigo to take off Moore's and Baird's men. Canning hoped that they could be sent round to Cadiz, to continue the war from there, instead of which they came back to England in a very bad state, so that the only British military force left in the Peninsula was the Lisbon garrison under General Cradock. To rub salt into the wound, the meddling of Castlereagh's agent Sir George Smith (already described) frustrated Frere's efforts to obtain Cadiz as a base for any future campaign. Canning told Frere on 15 January that without Cadiz 'there is an end to the war in Spain – of the British operations there I mean'. The whole situation was frustrating beyond belief, and to cap it all Canning was forced (as we have seen) to recall Frere – an act of injustice to one who was not only one of his ambassadors but also a personal friend.

Meanwhile the armies of Spain had collapsed, and on the other hand Austria was showing signs of being ready to rejoin the war in return for a subsidy of £2.5 million down and £5 million a year thereafter. Subsidies had been Pitt's favoured method of waging war on the Continent, and after some haggling the government agreed, and even before Moore's death at Corunna, Castlereagh was hatching plans for a British invasion of northern France or Holland to support an Austrian campaign by drawing troops away from central Europe. The distance to the coast of Holland was far less than to Portugal or Spain, and there was a Treasury argument that it would be easier to provide specie in the shape of Dutch guilders than in Portuguese or Spanish coinage, although after the Dutch expedition was launched Castlereagh told its commander (17 August) that no specie was available. The argument against an expedition to northern Europe was that previous ones had shown that any belief that the local people might rise up and join the invaders was a triumph of hope over experience. Canning feared that any such expedition would draw off troops from the Peninsula where, he believed, there was much more hope of success, and so far as helping Austria was concerned Moore had at least shown that a Peninsular campaign could draw French troops away from other theatres.

Canning's belief in a Peninsular campaign had been strengthened in December 1808 by a report from Villiers, the British envoy, that the Portuguese would like Wellesley to come and command their forces. Wellesley was very willing to go, but Castlereagh vetoed it and Canning had to tell Villiers, 'Sir Arthur Wellesley is thought too good for the Portuguese. Will Doyle do?' (It was lucky that the invitation to Doyle went astray, since he was senior to Wellesley who could therefore never have been given the command in the Peninsula if Doyle had been there.) Villiers's enthusiasm and Canning's persistence did at least persuade the cabinet to send out General Beresford to train the Portuguese levies, and in due course he turned the Portuguese army into a fine fighting force. He was a 40-year-old Irishman with a glass eye and a total lack of charm, but had served in Madeira and could speak some Portuguese. But for the time being the British position was tenuous as Cradock's force consisted mainly of men who had been, or become, unfit to serve with Moore. Canning strongly supported Villiers's plea for reinforcements, and on 14 February sent a memorandum to the cabinet urging that the British army in Portugal should be increased to 15,000 men and that Sir Arthur Wellesley should be appointed to command it.

Castlereagh demurred and no action was taken – not for 'want of urgency on my part, or of willingness on Sir A. Wellesley's', Canning told Villiers – adding 'I am persuaded, as sincerely and as strongly as you could wish me to be, that Sir A. Wellesley at the head of a large combined force in Portugal, is the first necessary element of success.' [1] Canning's pertinacity, so often irritating to his colleagues, gradually paid off. On 27 February Castlereagh ordered what British forces there were in Spain and Gibraltar to concentrate on Lisbon, and on 7 March Wellesley submitted a memorandum supporting Canning's arguments for not abandoning Portugal. Eventually on 26 March Castlereagh recommended that Sir Arthur Wellesley should be sent out with three regiments of cavalry to command the forces in Portugal. The King grumbled at 'so young a Lieutenant-General holding so distinguished a command while his seniors remain unemployed', but reluctantly acquiesced even though it meant Cradock being passed over in favour of a junior general (he was offered the lieutenant-governorship of Gibraltar as a consolation prize, but refused it).

It is generally believed that Castlereagh deserves the credit for having appointed Wellesley, but this is a myth – promulgated mainly by Fortescue, whose *History of the British Army*, while highly critical of politicians generally, especially Canning, is surprisingly favourable to Castlereagh. In fact, Castlereagh opposed Wellesley's appointment, while Canning urged it on him. To quote Rory Muir: 'The old myth that Castlereagh deserves the credit for Britain's commitment to Portugal is completely fallacious, being based on his constant friendship with Wellesley. Ironically it was Canning, whom Fortescue so disliked, who had the "desperate struggle to prevail with the Cabinet", not Castlereagh, his hero among politicians.'[2] Canning's insistence that the Peninsular campaign must be renewed had prevailed, but only just, and Castlereagh continued planning what became known as the Walcheren Expedition (to Holland) rather than concentrating on reinforcing Wellesley's campaign in the Peninsula.

Arguments over the conduct of the war were not the only cause of friction within the cabinet. A contumacious Opposition MP, Colonel Wardle, had accused the Duke of York of conspiring with one of his mistresses, Mrs Clark, to sell army commissions. Mrs Clark had certainly done so, and the Opposition was demanding an inquiry to find out if the Duke himself had been implicated. Perceval handled the matter ineptly. Canning wanted the Duke to be persuaded to 'retire *till he was cleared*' which 'would have driven Parliament to the alternative of either proceeding to trial, or of abandoning the charge silently', but Perceval instead defended the Duke in what Wilberforce described as a 'capital speech softening, yet not quite convincing me', which merely served to give the impression of an attempted government cover-up. Although nothing was proved against the Duke, enough mud had been thrown to force him to retire for the time being as commander-in-chief. The government had 'got into a scrape' and Canning felt that if it had followed the line he had suggested, it need not have done. (At least the Duke's predicament probably made it easier for Wellesley, despite his lack of seniority, to be given the Peninsular command.)

Perceval's mishandling of the Duke of York's inquiry seems to have been the last straw for Canning. On 24 March he told the Duke of Portland that no one 'can shut his eyes to the plain fact that the Government has sunk in public esteem'. Its handling of Cintra and of 'the failure in Spain' had made it 'responsible in public opinion for transactions of which the blame did not, in fact, rest with ourselves', and unless changes in the government were made, Canning said, he must himself resign:

> I feel it my duty to your Grace, as well as to myself, fairly to avow to your
> Grace that the Government, as at present constituted, does not appear to me
> equal to the great task which it has to perform.

Portland's response was to invite Canning to Bulstrode, his Buckinghamshire seat, during the Easter recess. We know (from Lord Colchester's *Diaries and Memoirs*) that Dr Jackson, the Dean of Christ Church, an old friend of Portland, had tried the previous year to persuade the Duke to resign, and Canning too said at their meeting at Bulstrode that he thought the Duke should resign on health grounds.[3] Portland evidently agreed, because a month later he submitted his resignation, but the King refused to accept it. Canning suggested to Portland that Lord Chatham might be a suitable successor, since the King liked him, and as the son of the great Earl of Chatham his appointment would not provoke jealousy: 'I did not disguise from myself his defects,' Canning added, 'but some of those defects might be said to point him out for the first place rather than a subordinate one – he is too *big* for a Department in a Government so constituted as this – the Treasury *as it is*, cannot cope with the Ordnance under Lord Chatham.' (Inability to control his department's expenditure does not seem a very cogent argument for promoting a minister to be First Lord of the Treasury, but may explain why Fortescue believed Chatham had 'brought the British artillery up to a pitch of excellence unknown in his day'.)

Canning's belief that Chatham would make a good Prime Minister has often been derided, but he would have known from discussions within cabinet that Chatham was an intelligent man with good judgement. He would also have naturally tended to look up to Chatham as Pitt's elder brother who had always been friendly toward him and had shown kindness to his family.[4] Canning may have been starry-eyed in thinking that Chatham would take a firmer grip of government than Portland, but he was realistic in thinking that if Chatham were Prime Minister he would bring Lord Wellesley, Sir Arthur's eldest brother, into the government, probably as Secretary for War and the Colonies. That would bring a political supporter of Canning into the cabinet and at the same time remove Castlereagh to another post less crucial to the war effort; but any idea that Canning wanted to get rid of Castlereagh because he saw him as a possible rival is absurd. Castlereagh's reputation was at a very low ebb: as Napier's *Peninsular War* acidly points out, in 1807 some 15,000 troops had been at sea for two months, and the following year, 'the Troops were dispersed without meaning – 10,000 soldiers exiled to Sweden, as many more idly kept in Sicily; Gibraltar was unnecessarily filled with fighting men; and Spencer wandered between Ceuta, Lisbon, and Cadiz, seeking, like the Knight of La Mancha, for a foe to combat!' Napier was unjust to blame all the disasters of 1808 on the Secretary of State for War, since the government as a whole was responsible, but the lack of grip had been largely the result of Castlereagh having been away from his desk, ill, for several months. Nor had Castlereagh yet mastered the art of parliamentary debate or public speaking. Even by 1814 when Canning's cousin Stratford met Castlereagh in Paris (and found to his surprise that he liked him) he noted Castlereagh's 'habit of using the first word that came to hand without much regard to its signification, and an involved method of composition when speaking in the House of Commons, [that] had exposed him to criticism and even to ridicule'.[5]

When Canning went to see Portland during that Easter recess of 1809 it was in fact not personal ambition that drove him to demand changes in the government but a sense of frustration because, with the country engaged in a life-or-death struggle, he could see from inside that the war was going badly because government policy was uncoordinated and ineffective. After their talk, Portland pledged Canning to silence, but told Bathurst what had transpired. Bathurst agreed that Castlereagh must be moved from the War Office but persuaded Canning to hold his hand for the moment. This was because there was to be a censure debate accusing Castlereagh of 'corrupt and criminal practices' in having procured Lord Clancarty's election to parliament. By the standards of the time that was nothing out of the ordinary, but Castlereagh had made many enemies during his time as Irish Secretary, and the Opposition, feeling that after Cintra, Corunna and the scandal over the Duke of York's mistress they had the government on the run, saw their chance at striking a further blow. It seemed quite likely that the censure debate planned for 25 April would cause Castlereagh's resignation anyway and leave the way clear for a complete cabinet reshuffle. However, the call for an inquiry was defeated by just 47 votes – it was particularly galling for Canning that his own speech in defence of his colleague had probably tipped the balance. Three days later Portland told Lord Camden, who (so the Duke told Canning) 'is decidedly of opinion that nothing will be so desirable as Lord C's removal [to the House of Lords] and that a change of office would be equally so provided it could be reconciled to his Feeling'. But Camden never mentioned any of this to his nephew. On 30 April Canning had a long talk with the Speaker, Abbot (during which he expressed his opinion of some of his colleagues very freely), and also told the ever-dependable George Rose what was going on. By 5 May Canning's patience had worn thin, and he told Portland that he intended to resign after the debate on the conduct of the war in Spain that was due to take place the following week.

That galvanized Portland to ask for an audience with the King on 10 May at which he offered his resignation, suggesting Chatham as his successor, and Wellesley to become Secretary for War. The King refused to accept Portland's resignation and asked for time to consider, and on 24 May Portland got round to putting Lord Chancellor Eldon in the picture. On 2 June Canning went to see the King and submitted his resignation, but the King (as he had done with Portland) insisted that he must stay in office until he (the King) had thought of a solution. When the royal plan was hatched, it proposed that Castlereagh should remain in his current office but hand over responsibility for the European theatre to Canning, and take over the Board of Control (of India) instead. One only need ask whether, for example, Gibraltar was to be a colony or part of Europe, to see how fatuous the King's suggestion was, and in any case he made it meaningless by stipulating that Castlereagh should retain control of any operations already under way, meaning Wellington's Peninsular campaign and the planned invasion of Holland.

At this point, Canning really ought to have insisted on resigning, as it was clear that the King was simply stringing him along. Why didn't he? Partly because it was a very drastic step to take. The King could not actually prevent a minister from handing back his seals of office, but if Canning had done so against George III's wishes then he could not expect to regain office during his reign – and no one could have predicted that this would effectively end within 18 months. It could well be argued that, feeling as strongly as he did about the need to reform the government, Canning ought to have made that personal sacrifice for his country's good, and that perhaps the price he had paid for resigning over a matter of principle in 1801 may have made him shrink from doing so again. But there could have been another reason why Canning held back from resigning. He had known Portland ever since his undergraduate days and must have heard his uncle Stratford talking about him with respect long before that. Portland had offered him a parliamentary seat in 1792, and when the Duke was installed as Chancellor of Oxford University in 1793 Canning had composed and delivered the Ode in honour of the occasion. The Duke was therefore someone that Canning had always looked up to and who had always been kind to him (just as had been the case with Lord Chatham). And although for two years Canning had been in Portland's cabinet, he might not have had enough official correspondence from the Duke to open his eyes to his woolly-mindedness. Aspinall's *Later Correspondence of George III* shows that Portland was a man who found it extremely difficult to tell anyone what they might not wish to hear. For instance, this is how he told the King that Lord Harrowby had refused office on health grounds:

> It is with sincere concern that the Duke of Portland humbly requests your Majesty's permission to lay before your Majesty the answer he has received from Lord Harrowby to the gracious offer of the Presidency of the Board of Control for the Affairs of India which your Majesty commanded the D of Portland to make to him, by which Lord Harrowby desires him to make the most favourable representation to your Majesty of the sincerest gratitude that he has always felt for your Majesty's service, a sentiment which would

necessarily urge him to pay the most implicit obedience to your Majesty's commands, did not the state of his health remind him that such an exertion would only prevent him from rendering that occasional service in Parliament which he has been able to perform from time to time & wholly disappoint those expectations which your Majesty's great goodness & condescension may have induced your Majesty to form, & therefore to lay his humble but anxious hopes at your Majesty's feet that he may be excused by your Majesty from undertaking the employment proposed to him.

Anyone who (like the King) had received letters like that would realize that Portland was unlikely to be firm, resolute and consistent, or to keep a promise if it became difficult to do so. Portland was not the man to insist on resigning against the King's wishes, or to wield the knife and carry out a cabinet reshuffle. Canning was blinded by Portland's reputation as a great Whig leader and by having always looked up to him from his youth. But by June his eyes were starting to be opened. Portland tried to pacify him by appointing his friend Granville Leveson-Gower Secretary for War with a seat in the cabinet, but Canning, far from being pacified, was furious. He told Granville that he should not have 'fallen for such a trick' which was clearly just a sop to keep Canning quiet, whereas it would do more harm than good by irritating Perceval without adding any real weight in cabinet to Canning.

On 18 June Canning asked Portland what was happening, saying, 'I must know by tomorrow or I resign.' Portland assured him that he was asking Castlereagh to 'accept the government of India' (part of the King's unrealistic plan) and urged Canning to hold his hand, as his resignation would break up the government. Three days later, at the end of the parliamentary session, Portland at last brought himself to tell Perceval of Canning's ultimatum. Perceval told Canning that he 'at once expressed surprise, both at the transaction itself, and at its concealment', and had said that no changes could now take place since the cabinet had just approved a plan for an expeditionary force to the Scheldt, which Castlereagh as Secretary for War must see through.

Perceval had every right to feel angry that Portland had not told him, as Leader of the House, what was afoot before discussing it with nearly half the cabinet; he also probably felt that, since the government had managed to weather the parliamentary session, the heat was now off and there was no need for any reshuffle. But Canning's reply to Perceval was chilly: he told him that the King had insisted on secrecy but that Portland had, weeks ago, asked Camden to put to Castlereagh a plan to move him to another post – 'if Lord Camden has not done this, I dare say he has good reason for it. But [this concealment] is no fault of mine, and I cannot believe it to be any fault of the Duke of Portland.' It was now becoming clear that both the King and Perceval wanted Canning's influence curbed, not increased, and to that end they wanted to keep Lord Wellesley out of the cabinet. By putting a block on any reshuffle until the Walcheren Expedition had sailed, Perceval made sure that Wellesley would be safely out of the way when any changes did take place, since he was about to go out to Spain as ambassador in place of Frere. Perceval's and the King's blocking tactics, and the shifty evasiveness of Camden who continued to intimate that he had told, or was just about to tell, Castlereagh of the plan to move him while never doing so, combined with Portland's chronic procrastination, were steadily undermining Canning's position without him fully realizing it; and this despite the fact that almost all the cabinet, even those like Eldon who disliked him, thought it essential to retain Canning and were suggesting various ways of moving Castlereagh to another post. Liverpool (as Hawkesbury had now become), although feeling he had 'some right to complain of this want of confidence on the part of His Grace' for not telling him about Canning's démarche and thought Castlereagh was a perfectly good Secretary for War, was clear that 'the decision on public grounds must be made in favour of Mr Canning'. He even offered to give up the Home Office to Castlereagh if that would help, and Camden offered to give up *his* office to his nephew, albeit reluctantly and with conditions attached (in the end he retained his office for some years, until eventually he received the marquessate which he had craved).

Camden's reluctance to upset his nephew explains why, incredible though it seems, no one said anything to Castlereagh himself about the matter that almost all his colleagues were discussing. Back in May Portland had asked Camden to speak to him; Camden didn't, but let Portland think he had, and in mid-July Canning learned with some consternation that Castlereagh had still not been told. He pointed out to Portland with some force that this concealment would be seen 'as an act of injustice against Lord Castlereagh', and told Joan that he 'doubted not' that he would be blamed for the Duke's procrastination. How right he was.

Behind all the negotiations and intrigues lay the King's determination to prevent Canning from becoming Leader of the House of Commons, let alone Prime Minister. He did not trust Canning, whose support of Catholic emancipation was in his eyes little short of treason. Also Canning was not, in Margaret Thatcher's phrase, 'one of us'. The fact that he was the only member of the cabinet who was neither a lord or the son of a lord counted for a great deal in those days, not least with the King, who saw Canning as a man too useful to lose but who needed to be kept in his place. Probably most of the cabinet felt the same, apart from Liverpool, an old friend, Chatham, who approved of him as his brother's protégé, and Granville Leveson-Gower, who was too junior to count. They recognized that Canning was the most able member of the cabinet but did not want to serve under him. Canning had to contend with a glass ceiling: how could one whose mother was an actress get to the top?

After Perceval's insistence that no reshuffle could take place until the Walcheren Expedition had been launched, Canning again offered his resignation and the King again refused to accept it. To make matters worse he forbade Portland to say anything to Castlereagh until the Walcheren campaign was actually over. On 5 July Canning complained to Joan of 'the old D's apparent twaddling and shuffling' (only 'apparent' – did he still not realize Portland was a broken reed?), and told her:

> Yesterday the old D desired to see me. ... They had resolved upon getting
> Ld. Camden *out* – and then Cast. might give up the seals intirely & go to Ld
> Camd's place – & then Wellesley, if I liked it, might have the seals – but still
> have to go to Spain & I do the duties of his office for the summer. Would this
> content me? Or did I insist on Cast. going out intirely? ... I feel that I could
> not without great *savageness* visit upon Cghr's intire removal – so I think I shall
> say yes today – & I shall like getting Chuckle [Camden] out prodigiously.

A week later Canning had hopes that Portland might at long last act: 'At last things begin to move a little forward. ... Ld Camden ... is to go to the K. today. I daresay he will endeavour to do some mischief too, but I do not fear him.' How wrong he was. He had no idea of the King's enmity towards him, writing to Joan on 28 July, 'Yes dearest love I think it is all settled upon the whole. Poor old Kn [Knobbs] has behaved perfectly throughout. It is true that he doesn't like Wellesley at all – but there is nothing dishonest in that.'

The Walcheren Expedition sailed on 28 July, and at long last Portland screwed up his courage to ask the King that 'your Majesty will graciously condescend, I hope, to forbear from deferring the intimation to Lord Castlereagh'. The King grudgingly consented, though telling the Duke that he 'must be aware that many of his colleagues are against the measure and that it has been pressed forward much earlier than the King had expected'. But alas, the prospect of actually telling Castlereagh that he must leave the War Office was too much for the old Duke's constitution. On 11 August, while on his way to Bulstrode in his carriage, he had a stroke. Four days later he told the King that he was 'sufficiently recovered to execute any command which Your Majesty may think proper to lay on him', but it was clear that the end of the Portland ministry was near.

Castlereagh meanwhile had been busy with the final arrangements for the Walcheren Expedition. Ever since Austria had shown signs of re-entering the war, he had been making tentative plans for some kind of expedition to northern Europe, perhaps a landing at Ostend or Dunkirk, that had gradually crystallized into an attempt to land on Walcheren Island at the mouth of the Scheldt, capture the fortified port of Flushing and destroy any shipping there, and then press on to Antwerp to capture or destroy the French fleet and disable the harbour installations, and, if there was little resistance, go on to establish a bridgehead on the mainland. But there were many ifs and buts: a landing could only be attempted if the wind was easterly, so if weather conditions were bad could they sail round to the Elbe instead? The answer was no; Canning reported that the Prussians would not support a landing, and specie there would be too expensive.

The thinking behind the Walcheren Expedition was that any operation would divert French troops from the Austrian front, but that with a bit of luck those troops would arrive too late to prevent the British from achieving their objective. The flaw in that thinking was that there was no single, clear objective. As Napoleon later remarked, the British force was either too big or too small: too small to obtain a firm bridgehead that could present a real threat to northern France, too big for a *coup de main* (i.e. a large-scale commando raid) whose success would depend on surprise.

At all events, by 18 May Castlereagh decided to mount a combined operation on the Scheldt estuary. He offered the command to Chatham, whose military experience was limited to commanding a brigade in the much smaller Helder Expedition of 1799. Chatham hesitated before accepting, perhaps realizing that generalship was not his forte, but he saw that this could be an opportunity to show himself a worthy son and heir of the great Lord Chatham, and may even have hoped, as Canning certainly did, that a successful campaign might help him to succeed Portland as Prime Minister. But the more Chatham learned about the naval and military staff appreciations, the less enthusiastic he became. War Office briefings had been discouraging. Colonel Gordon warned that 'a very large proportion of our naval and military means would be put to imminent hazard', General Hope opined that there would be 'great risk without, perhaps, an adequate security for the attainment of its object', while Sir David Dundas, the new commander-in-chief, pointed out that any attempt would have to be made quickly before the new defences at Antwerp were complete, and would be 'of very great risk ... the safe return of the army employed may be very hazardous'. Furthermore General Brownrigg said flatly that he thought Antwerp was an unrealistic aim, though 'possibly 15,000 men might' be enough to capture the island of Walcheren 'and 10,000 to hold it'. The Admiralty, on the other hand, very much liked the idea of destroying French ships at anchor, although they were doubtful about a combined operation under military control ('the obstacles to carrying the army up the Scheldt appear to be very material'), and Admiral Home Popham on 16 June emphasized the need for speed: 'I see the season advancing fast and if we are imperceptibly led on till the midsummer fine weather is past, we shall have the most dreadful of all difficulties, the weather, to encounter.' Perhaps because of all these uncertainties, the joint military and naval planning was chaotic. Chatham thought he 'should get on faster if I could communicate directly with Popham but I do not know where he is to be found' and asked if Castlereagh could perhaps tell him. Not until 19 June did the Admiralty unearth two naval officers who had visited those parts 15 years earlier and thought 'to the best of their recollection' that it should be feasible to land troops 'between the point of Sandfleet and Lillo', only about 15 miles from Antwerp. (It is worth noting that in 1802 Nelson ruled out a raid on Walcheren as impracticable; he had taken advice from an ex-smuggler named Yawkins ('a knowing one') who knew the shoals and currents in the Scheldt estuary, and preferred his opinion to that of an over-enthusiastic Royal Navy officer, Captain Owen.) On the strength of this advice the cabinet agreed on 21 June to a plan 'to capture and destroy all the shipping and port installations at Flushing and Antwerp, reduce the island of Walcheren' and 'if possible make the Scheldt unnavigable'. The only minister at the cabinet meeting to demur was Chatham, who was the only one other than Castlereagh to have actually seen the War Office and Admiralty briefings. The whole cabinet, including Canning, were thus complicit in launching a disastrous campaign.

Walcheren was an utterly predictable disaster. By the time the expedition sailed at the end of July surprise had been lost and most of the favourable summer weather was over. Inter-service cooperation was poor, so that it was easy to blame Chatham, the army commander, and Sir Richard Strachan, the admiral, for all that went wrong:

> Lord Chatham, with his sabre drawn
> Stood waiting for Sir Richard Strachan
> Sir Richard, longing to be at 'em
> Stood waiting for the Earl of Chatham.

Those lines, though helpful in diverting blame from the politicians, are not entirely fair. True, Chatham was as slow-moving as the turtles for his dinners that formed the most precious part of his wagon train, but how far this was because he soon realized that any landing at Antwerp was impracticable, and how far it was sheer laziness, is difficult to say. Strachan was a very fine naval commander, but was as ignorant of military requirements as Chatham was of naval limitations: the Admiral could not see why it was necessary to land a whole brigade on Cadsand, opposite Flushing, in one go rather than in penny packets (which the enemy could attack in detail), nor could Chatham see any reason why the fleet should shelter uselessly at anchor for three days just because there happened to be an onshore gale. Had the winds been favourable (which they weren't), and had Chatham been a Wellington and Strachan a Nelson (which they certainly weren't), then they might have reached Antwerp and held it long enough to make it unusable as a port, and given more luck with the weather and unusual tardiness on the part of the French, they might also have managed to extricate their force without too heavy casualties. As it was, not until 15 August did Flushing surrender, and already on 5 August Strachan had feared 'it will not be practicable to get to Antwerp' before French reinforcements arrived in strength. At the beginning of August it could have been taken with a comparatively small force, but that chance had been missed. And even with superb leadership and good weather, the low-lying islands of South Beveland and Walcheren would still have been malarial (as Castlereagh had been warned), and once the French had opened the dykes to defend Flushing, dysentery, typhus and typhoid combined with malaria would have produced the deadly disease known as Walcheren Fever.

By 27 August a council of war finally decided that a siege of Antwerp was impossible. Strachan wrote that 'the army is so sickly and the Enemy gaining strength that Lord Chatham has given up the object of the expedition notwithstanding the differences of opinion in regard to that measure with the Navy', and reluctantly agreed to evacuate the troops in South Beveland (the springboard for an attack on Antwerp) straight away, without first sinking ships to block the Scheldt at that point. On 10 September Chatham was given permission to return home and leave Sir Eyre Coote in command of a garrison on Walcheren, whence 10,948 sick had already been evacuated, and a week later Coote reported 7,853 sick and 309 deaths.[6] 'Walcheren Fever' was responsible for more casualties in the British army than the bloodiest of campaigns; the only cavalry to disembark, drawn from the 9th Light Dragoons, were never engaged but suffered 200 casualties, and over two years later when the regiment was serving in the Peninsula so many men were still going sick from 'Walcheren Fever' that it had to hand over its horses to another regiment and be sent home.

By the time that the House of Commons held its post-mortem on the campaign Portland was dead, Castlereagh and Canning were out of office and there was a new government. A vote of censure was rejected by 275 votes to 227, but that reflected the politics of the day rather than the facts of the case.

୧୬

While Lord Chatham was making his stately progress up the Scheldt, Castlereagh and Mulgrave sent the King a fulsome report (19 August) of 'the cordial emulation of the Navy and Your Majesty's land forces in the display of dutiful zeal for your Majesty's service'. But it was already difficult to pretend that things had gone according to plan, and since Castlereagh had been the main proponent of the Scheldt Expedition his position was becoming precarious. Perceval realized this, and buttonholed Canning at a levee at the end of August to suggest that he should sound out Portland about his intentions. Canning agreed, although, as he said, to do so would be 'more likely to hasten than retard' Portland's departure, which was of course the reason why Perceval had suggested it. By this time the news from Walcheren was dire, and Perceval wanted at all costs to make sure that Portland resigned before he could keep his long-deferred promise to move Castlereagh from the War Department. When Canning saw Portland, he gave his own opinion that 'a [Prime] Minister ... in the Commons, is essentially necessary. On this principle, the easiest arrangement would be the devolution of your Grace's office on Mr Perceval.' Canning would then resign, but would continue to support the government, and assured Portland that despite what 'personal ambition might be supposed to recommend, my sincere wish is to retire, at the same time with your Grace's and His Majesty's gracious approbation'. This disclaimer seems to have been genuine, as he told Joan (who was in Hinckley so that they had to communicate by letter) how much he would welcome a chance to be free from the burdens of office for a spell. He was badly in need of a break and felt sure he would not be out of office for long, as he did not think Perceval would be able to form a government.

But Canning badly underestimated Perceval, whose limitations over the last two years had been only too obvious, but who was a far more ruthless political in-fighter and far more ambitious than he seemed. On 3 September Perceval told his brother, Lord Arden, 'I think I am ready for the King's service to sacrifice every feeling of personal pride or vanity which might be wounded by [ceasing to be Leader]. But ... I fear ... such a sacrifice would be felt by my friends and the public as a degradation which I ought not to submit to ... [as] it might much abridge my means of future service to the King and the Country' – in other words, he was really not at all willing to 'sacrifice every personal feeling of pride and vanity', and was certainly not going to play second fiddle. He tricked Canning into what was meant to be an informal and private discussion about the future, pointing out that if he became First Lord of the Treasury, then Canning could continue as Foreign Secretary, whereas if Canning became First Lord, Perceval would lose his position as Leader of the House of Commons – 'this, I own', Canning told Joan, 'I could not bear. It would *hurt me for him*. It would be a great humiliation.' Canning suggested that Perceval might go to the House of Lords as Lord President or Lord Privy Seal, but Perceval said he could not afford to 'maintain the honour and dignity' of a peer.

It is generally assumed that Canning insisted all along that a new Prime Minister must be in the Commons, and that if Perceval would not go to the Lords, he (Canning) would have to resign. The Wellesley papers suggest that it is not as simple as that. When Wellesley had (after protracted delay because he wanted to take his mistress with him) gone to Madrid as ambassador, he left Benjamin Sydenham in charge of his private affairs in England. Sydenham had hero-worshipped Wellesley ever since he served him in India, but was tactless and gullible.[7] When it became clear that Portland would be resigning, Canning wrote a despatch to Wellesley asking him to return to England so that he would be available to take office in a new administration, but Perceval got to hear of this and forbade Canning to send it. After Portland had resigned and when Perceval was trying to form a government, Sydenham wrote to Wellesley saying that he would have been asked to be first minister, but that Canning had refused to serve under him; so when Perceval then wrote inviting Wellesley to be Foreign Secretary, he accepted since he no longer felt in any way bound to Canning. Once Canning knew what had happened, he wrote to assure Wellesley that what Sydenham had told him was untrue; he pointed out that the allegation made no sense anyway, for 'if the Cabinet had advised the King, and the King had approved the advice, to make you First Minister, in God's name why were you not so? If my single opposition was the sole impediment, that impediment was removed by my resignation.'[8] Sydenham had been told that Canning had refused to serve under Wellesley by Wellesley Pole, Wellesley's younger brother, who had just accepted Perceval's invitation to become Chief Secretary of Ireland. Presumably Pole would not have accepted office unless Perceval had assured him that his eldest brother was no longer bound to Canning. George Rose later wrote that Perceval had 'played a lawyer's trick', and Canning's letter to Wellesley of 28 October seems to confirm his verdict.

Canning in 1809, shortly before the duel. Lawrence, the artist, thought he seemed pensive and preoccupied.

Canning also corrected the impression conveyed to Wellesley by Sydenham that it was he who had brought about Portland's resignation in September. On the contrary, Canning said, it,

> was *precipitated* when I least expected it – Perceval, on 28 August, seeing the time approaching when I could claim the execution of the promise respecting the War Department, began the correspondence which led to the confession of my opinions upon the arrangement most advisable *whenever* the Duke should retire. Of that retirement there was then no question. On the 2nd September I wrote to the Duke of Portland reminding him that the time was come for writing to you [to ask him to return from Spain and take over from Castlereagh]. On the 4th Perceval, having heard of my letter, wrote to the Duke urging him to resign, for the avowed purpose of covering Castlereagh's retreat in a general arrangement; but with the further object, if one may judge from the uses which have been made of it, of being able to attribute *my* resignation to the cause to which, by the representations sent to you, I find you have been led to attribute it.

Once he had read Canning's letter Wellesley realized he had been misled, but too late; by then he had accepted office as Foreign Secretary in Perceval's government, and Canning was out of office.

Canning had offered his resignation at the end of the first week of September, at the same time as Portland did so, and this time the King was happy to accept it. On 16 September the King sent for Perceval to ask him about forming a new government, and then sent for Canning, who went away under the impression that his audience had gone well. He told Joan, 'I think it is secure that *if* I go out, I go out without quarrelling with Knobbs & that was the grand point of all'. Two days later he wrote:

> Do you know my dearest love, I very much doubt whether the result which will leave me at liberty for Hinckley will not be the best in every way, supposing, I mean … that Kn[obbs] lets me go in good humour. That is the result which I rather suspect. But the suspense is most certainly very nervous.

But Canning had misjudged George III as completely as he had been taken in by Perceval. The King had listened attentively to all he had to say, drawing him out by comments and questions, but inwardly seething with indignation. He told Perceval that it had been 'the most extraordinary speech he had ever heard'. Possibly Perceval had set a trap for him by telling him that the King *wanted* his absolutely candid opinion and advice, but Canning should have been on guard. He had utterly failed to realize the depth of the King's hostility.

Canning continued to do the work of Foreign Secretary until a successor was appointed – the war did not stop while domestic political wrangling took its course – but since he no longer considered himself a member of the cabinet he did not attend a cabinet meeting on 9 September. Castlereagh asked his uncle Lord Camden why Canning had not been there, and for the first time was told of the manoeuvres that had been going on behind his back for the last five months. The fuse was lit.

CHAPTER 9

The Duel

By the early nineteenth century duels were becoming less common, but they still occurred. In 1798 the Opposition leader Tierney had challenged Pitt over a careless remark made during a debate that he refused to withdraw. Wilberforce was horrified at the consequent duel. Not only did he strongly disapprove of duels on moral grounds (especially one that took place on Putney Heath in mid-afternoon on Whitsunday, with no attempt at secrecy and several onlookers), but he thought it reprehensible for the Prime Minister in time of war to expose himself to such risk. The King, too, strongly disapproved, and 'the political world was surprised and dismayed',[1] but Pitt knew that if he refused a challenge his ascendancy in the House of Commons would evaporate. The *Morning Post* of 18 May, the day after the duel, reported that after the seconds had made 'some ineffectual efforts ... to prevent further proceedings, the parties took their ground at a distance of twelve paces [and] fired at the same moment without effect; a second case was also fired in the same manner, Mr Pitt firing his pistol into the air; the seconds then jointly interfered and insisted that the matter should be no further'. Fifteen years earlier, when Fox had been 'called out' by a political opponent, he was wounded by the first shot, yet Adam fired again (this time missing) while Fox fired in the air. In 1829 Lord Winchelsea challenged the Duke of Wellington (the last duel of this kind), and Lord Falmouth only agreed to act as Winchelsea's second on condition that he did not take aim; and both men fired into the air. Duels had been slowly becoming less murderous.

Officers in the armed services seem to have been particularly touchy about their honour, and it was harder to stop duelling in the services than among civilians. But as Britain became more embroiled in war, the military and naval authorities, and the King, did their best to discourage the practice, as they did not want officers killing one another instead of killing Frenchmen. But duels did happen. In 1802 a naval captain (for whom Nelson appeared as a character

witness) killed an army colonel in a duel sparked off by angry words over a
dog fight in Hyde Park, and as late as 1808 we find an officer serving in India
being court martialled for 'scandalous and infamous behaviour unbecoming to
a gentleman in having suffered abusive language to be applied to him' without
'taking measures appropriate to the vindication of his insulted honour' [i.e.
issuing a challenge]. The officer pointed out that the fellow-officer who had
insulted him had been too drunk to control his language, and was acquitted,
but his general sent him home under a cloud for *not* fighting a duel.[2] (But that
was in India.)

In 1809, therefore, no one would have thought it extraordinary if Castlereagh
had challenged Canning to a duel as soon as he had learned what had been going
on behind his back. Public opinion would not have approved of two Secretaries
of State shooting at one another in the middle of a war for national survival,
but nor would people have been surprised. What was surprising, however, was
that it took nine full days after he learned of the plans to remove him from his
office for Castlereagh to decide that honour required him to demand satisfaction – not until 19 September did he challenge Canning. Yet there could have
been no aggravating circumstance that Castlereagh could have learned by then
that he had not already learned on 10 September, since Camden had then with-
held the fact that Portland had asked him to tell his nephew what was proposed,
had agreed to do so, and had even led Portland, and through him Canning, to
think he had done so. Camden's selective account of events would therefore
have had to suggest that Canning had been guilty of deliberate concealment.
Nor did Camden reveal that after Portland had found out that Castlereagh had
been kept in the dark, the King then stepped in and insisted that he must not
be told until after the Walcheren Expedition had sailed (at which point, as we
know, Portland had his stroke so that Castlereagh was still kept in ignorance).
Camden's version of events as given to his nephew on 10 September would in
fact have been just as damning to Canning as anything else that Castlereagh
could have been told in the nine days that followed. Why on earth, then, did
he wait so long before demanding satisfaction from Canning for the injury he
believed had been done to his honour?

Possibly Edward Cooke may have stoked up the heat of Castlereagh's anger.
Cooke had been Castlereagh's Under-Secretary both in Ireland and at the
War Department, and liked and admired him greatly, while he considered
Canning an untrustworthy liberal. Indeed, Cooke's dislike of Canning seems
to have been almost pathological: he condemned Canning's speech defending
Castlereagh over the Clancarty affair in April as proof of his 'extreme duplic-
ity – he acted openly to Lord C. as a friend, behind his back as an enemy',[3]

Castlereagh in 1809, by Lawrence. Mrs Arbuthnot spoke of his 'remarkably fine commanding figure ... smile sweeter than it is possible to describe ... benevolent and amiable countenance ... an air of dignity and nobleness', but to political enemies Castlereagh was a figure of hate. What Hazlitt saw in this portrait was 'the prim, smirking smile of a haberdasher'.

whereas in fact Canning's speech helped save Castlereagh from censure – curious conduct for an 'enemy'. That implacable dislike of Canning would have made Cooke's arguments against issuing a challenge somewhat unpersuasive – he admits they were 'against my judgment'. Nor would Perceval's visit to Castlereagh on 11 September have done anything to soothe Castlereagh's sense of injury. Unlike Cooke, Perceval would with all his heart have wished to avert a duel, but, according to George Rose, 'not until Lord Castlereagh was shown all the correspondence by Mr Perceval [did] he express any resentment or uncomfortable feeling on the subject'.[4] Nothing in that correspondence could have shown Canning in a worse light than Camden had done the previous day, but it would have revealed something much more wounding to Castlereagh's pride than anything Canning could have done, namely, that virtually all Castlereagh's colleagues agreed that he ought to be moved from his current office. It is clear both from the wording of his challenge to Canning, and from the letter he wrote after the duel to his father, that this is what really angered Castlereagh – learning that his colleagues did not think him up to his job would have been a bitter blow to his pride. He had to hit out at someone, and in view of his uncle's selective account, Canning was the obvious choice. Even so, that still does not explain why he brooded for so long. Eight days elapsed after Perceval had seen him before, in Cooke's words, 'at length he sent for Lord Yarmouth. … I looked upon his decision with complacency and satisfaction. … I think your Brother's mind is now relieved and at ease.'

Lord Yarmouth, who agreed to act as Castlereagh's second, was his cousin on his mother's side. The son and heir of Lord Hertford, he was a notoriously vicious character (he was the model for Thackeray's Marquis of Steyne in *Vanity Fair*), and would have been the last man to dissuade anyone from fighting a duel – indeed, according to Cooke, he 'coincided completely' with his cousin's wish to do so. To Yarmouth's credit, though, once Canning's second had explained the true state of affairs he did his best to act as a conciliator, but to no avail.

Castlereagh's challenge is a remarkable document. It was rather unusual to send a written challenge; the more usual procedure was to send a friend to 'ask for satisfaction', as when Tierney had sent his second, General Walpole, to call on Pitt with a challenge to a duel (which he accepted at once). But to send a long and convoluted description of one's grievances, rather than a brief note asking for 'satisfaction', was extraordinary. Castlereagh's 'challenge' is too long to print in full, but these extracts may help the reader to gauge the state of mind of the writer.

Dated 'St. James's Square. Septr. 19th 1809', the letter starts by saying 'Sir,

It is unnecessary for me to enter into any detailed statement of the Circumstances which preceded the recent Resignations', but then goes on to do just that:

> It appears a Proposition had been agitated, without any Communication with me, for my Removal from the War Department, and that you towards the close of the session having re-urged a decision upon this Question, with the alternative of your seceding from the Government, procured a positive promise from the Duke of Portland (the execution of which you afterwards considered yourself entitled to enforce) that such Removal should be carried into effect.
>
> Notwithstanding this promise, by which I consider that you pronounced it unfit that I should remain charged with the conduct of the War, and by which my situation as a Minister of the Crown was made dependent upon your Will and Pleasure, you continued to sit in the same Cabinet with me, and to leave me, not only in the persuasion that I possessed your Confidence and Support as a Colleague, but ... to originate and proceed in the Execution of a new Enterprize of the most arduous and important nature [the Walcheren Expedition], with your apparent concurrence and ostensible approbation.
>
> You were fully aware, that if my situation in the Government had been disclosed to me, I could not have submitted to remain one moment in Office without the entire abandonment of my private Honor and publick Duty – You knew I was deceived and you continued to deceive me.
>
> I ... am ready to acknowledge, that when you press'd for decision for my Removal, you also press'd for its disclosure, and that it was resisted by the Duke of Portland, and some Members of the Government, supposed to be my Friends; – but I can never admit that you have a Right to make use of such a Plea in justification of an Act affecting my honor. ... Nor can I admit, that the Head of any Administration, or any supposed Private Friend ... can authorize or sanction any Man in such a course of long and persevering Deception, for were I to admit such a Principle, my Honor and Character would be from that moment at the Discretion of Persons wholly unauthorized ... to act for me in such a case – It was therefore your Act and your Conduct which deceived me, and it is impossible for me to acquiesce in being placed in a situation by you, which no Man of Honor could knowingly submit into, without forfeiting that Character.
>
> I have no Right as a Public Man to resent your demanding upon publick grounds my removal from the particular office I have held ... but I have a distinct Right to expect that a Proposition justifiable in itself shall not be executed in an unjustifiable manner, and at the expence of my Honor and Reputation, and I consider that you were bound, at least to avail yourself of the same alternative, namely your own Resignation to take yourself out of the Predicament of practising such a Deceit towards me, which you did exercise

in demanding a decision for my Removal.

Under these circumstances I must require that Satisfaction from you, to which I feel myself entitled to lay claim.

I have the honor to be, Sir, Your obedient, and humble Servant,
Castlereagh.

The complete 'challenge' is half as long again. Wilberforce later called it 'a cold-blooded measure of deliberate revenge'. It was worded in a way that left no room for Canning to make any explanation, even though it was clear that Castlereagh was not aware that Camden had promised to tell him about the proposed reshuffle, and that Canning had for some time thought that this had been done. Nor, of course, could Castlereagh know that when it transpired that Camden had never told him anything, the King had stepped in and forbidden Portland to do so. But Castlereagh's challenge suggests that he was not interested in finding out any facts – his pride had been hurt, his reputation damaged and he wanted revenge. Although his letter states that he cannot object 'on public grounds' to Canning's demands for a cabinet reshuffle, he goes on to object on the grounds that these demands were made 'at the expence of my Honor and Reputation'. It was the fact that *most of the cabinet* had thought he should be moved from the War Department that really hurt, and challenging the man who had been the first to query his competence was a way of assuaging his injured pride and, with luck, helping to restore his reputation. Explanations were not what Castlereagh wanted, and Canning had no choice but to accept the challenge:

Gloucester Lodge Septr. 20. 1809. 1/2 p. 10 A.M.
My Lord, The Tone and the Purport of your Lordship's letter (which I have this moment received), of course preclude any other answer, on my part, to the Misapprehensions and Misrepresentations with which it abounds, than that I will cheerfully give to your Lordship, the Satisfaction which you require.

I have the honour to be, My Lord
Your Lordship's most obedient humble servant, Geo. Canning

Canning would probably have asked Lord Wellesley to act as his second if he had not been in Spain. Instead, he asked Henry Wellesley, who declined, saying that he was commanded to go to Windsor, although the real reason was probably that he did not want to get involved – his brother Wellesley Pole had just accepted office from Perceval, so public support for Canning would have been embarrassing. Charles Ellis, a close friend of Canning, then agreed to act as second, and Wellesley went with him to see Lord Yarmouth, hoping that by putting the record straight a duel could be avoided even at this late stage.

Immediately after their visit Ellis wrote the following Memorandum 'at Mr. Henry Wellesley's, immediately after his conversation with Lord Yarmouth on Wednesday Night September 20th 1809':

> Lord Castlereagh's Letter was such as to put it out of Mr. Canning's Power to offer any Explanation, but that I felt it my duty to state to Lord Y. that I had been informed by Mr. Canning confidentially of every step which he took in this Business, and that it did not at any time occur to me that Lord Castlereagh had cause for offence, nor do I think that Lord C. had a case which could justify the step he had taken. I stated this without Mr. Canning's knowledge (in confirmation of which I referred to Mr. Henry Wellesley who had been present), but that as Lord Y. had expressed a desire for an explanation of any misunderstandings or misrepresentations (alluded to in Mr. Canning's Letter) I would state to him the course of the Transaction. ...
>
> [I explained that the] arrangement of a change of a War Department did not originate on the part of Mr. Canning, but was the consequence of the Expression of his Dissatisfaction at the general state of the Government [and] the time of carrying it into Execution was not left at his option. It was postponed till the issue of the [Walcheren] Expedition at the desire of Lord Castlereagh's Friends, notwithstanding Mr. Canning's having pointed out and warned them against the Possibility of the result of the Expedition being such as to render the Execution of the Arrangement at that time still more unpleasant to Lord Castlereagh's feelings. ... It was agreed by Lord Castlereagh's Friends that the interval might be employed in breaking the arrangement to Lord Castlereagh, and Mr. Canning did not know that the Interval had not been so employed. This arrangement was throughout treated by Lord Castlereagh's Friends as an amicable one, which need not lead to his Retirement from the administration.
>
> I made this statement not in the expectation of its producing any alteration in Lord Castlereagh's Determination ... but because I felt it right to give Lord Y. the opportunity of laying before Lord Castlereagh a correct statement of the Facts. Lord Yarmouth desired me to wait till he had reported our conversation to Lord Castlereagh, and returned saying that what he had stated had produced no alteration in Lord Castlereagh's Feelings.

Canning, meanwhile, was spending the evening and most of the night clearing his desk at the Foreign Office, and then writing a letter to Joan. It is far too long to give in full; the original in the Harewood MSS is written in remarkably clear handwriting on copious small sheets of paper, and is a very moving document.

> The poor old Duke's procrastination & Ld Camden's malice or mismanagement have led to [these] consequences. If anything happens to me, dearest love, be

comforted with the assurance that I could do no otherwise than I have done, & that the publication that I leave in charge to Charles Bagot of all that has passed between me and the D of P since Easter, will clear my name to the world. ... God bless you, my own, best and dearest love! A better and dearer never did God give to man. But yet, my own beloved Joan, do you know I derive some comfort from reflecting upon the sort of widowhood in which you have been living for the last two or three years. I think – I <u>hope</u> – you will feel my loss less than if we had been in habits of constant and uninterrupted society.

The letter continues, from Gloucester Lodge and not the Foreign Office:

I should have liked to see my poor little George. He is a good little boy. He may be a scholar I hope – & it will be for his happiness to be so, if his lameness continues – but lame or not, do not breed him [i.e. bring him up as] a statesman. He would feel, & fret, & lament, & hate, & despise, as much as his father. ... I know not what to say of William, I am afraid he is unamiable. But then he certainly is not loved like his brother & sister. ... George's health & Harriet's exquisite delightfulness have perhaps been in his way. ... What shall I say of dear little Toddles [Harriet]? Let her think of papa – as if we only were absent, and love him always. George will conceive what death is, but neither of the others need ever know a pang on my account.

[Instructions about money follow] ... £8,800 from the Alienation Office must be repaid instantly [the custom, which today would be criminal, was for ministers to use their own accounts to bank official funds] – £6,000 of it is in Exchequer Bills in Drummond's custody, about £800 with Drummond, £800 with Hal [his cousin, a banker], and a quarter's salary and dividends due 10th Oct. will produce nearly £2000. But it is so very important that this sum be paid immediately that I shall ask Charles Ellis to advance £2000 for the purpose, giving him as security 1 small snuff box and 2 pictures set in diamonds, and my own love will redeem them as soon as the dividends are paid.

[He leaves everything, which wasn't much, to Joan, but] ... please give my mother £300 a year. I do not make it an absolute <u>bequest</u>, because I owe my own love all. But I am sure it will be as effectual as if I did so.

And now, my own best, and dearest, & most beloved love, I think I have said nearly all that is necessary to say. ... I hope I have made you happy; & if I leave you a happy mother and a <u>proud</u> widow, I am content. Adieu, Adieu.

Canning was not being unduly pessimistic in assuming that he would be killed. Atkinson's treatise, *The British Duelling Pistol*, states that 'if a gentleman practised diligently with a pistol which was well made mechanically, was nicely balanced, suited the size and strength of his hand, and "came up" easily, he would acquire sufficient accuracy in quick snap-shooting to be sure of hitting a man-sized target at any distance up to twenty paces'. Castlereagh was known to have 'practised with pistols' during his time as Irish Secretary, and it was generally understood that he had 'taken the field' at least once.[5] When during the Union debates Carew, the MP for Waterford, had threatened to report Castlereagh's attempt to bribe him to the Speaker, he had replied, 'Do, and I'll deny every word point-blank.' Carew said that in that case he would 'meet him on Parson's Green' but prudently withdrew his challenge after being warned that the Irish Secretary was a very good shot. It would be reasonable for Canning to assume that once Castlereagh had decided on a duel he would polish up his skill, perhaps in his cellars in St James's Square – he had his own pair of duelling pistols, and knew enough about duelling to realize that it was not to be undertaken lightly. A duel was often lethal.

At five o'clock on Thursday morning, 21 September, Castlereagh and Yarmouth set out in a curricle from St James's Square. On their way to Putney, Castlereagh is said to have discoursed on the latest opera and hummed some of its tunes, which could either mean that he felt no anxiety about what lay ahead, or that, like his fellow-Irishman Wellington, he believed in keeping a stiff upper lip. Canning meanwhile set out with Charles Ellis from Brompton, and all four men arrived at Putney Heath well before seven o'clock. Ellis described the ensuing duel in a *Statement ... of what passed at Putney* written that same day:

> Thursday Morning Sept 21st
>
> On my arrival with Mr. Canning at Putney, Lord Yarmouth took me aside and proposed that we should load the Pistols together. – After loading them he asked me whether <u>I denied the Offence?</u> I replied that I did, and that I thought on my conscience, Lord Castlereagh had no case whatever against Mr. Canning. Lord Y. then said, 'In such case it is most usual to fire together'. – I answered, 'Canning has no pretension whatever to the first fire' – He replied, 'Perhaps it may be rather conceding a point, but I think they had better fire at the same moment' – Lord Yarmouth next asked what should be the distance, and added, 'I conclude it is not your wish to render this Business more desperate than is necessary' – I replied, – 'I certainly can have no such wish.' – He then proposed twelve Paces, as the longest distance of which there was any precedent,[6] to which I assented.
>
> I then told Lord Y. that I would now mention to him, what I had omitted the night before, the name of one of the Persons who most strongly pressed for the delay in the Execution of the arrangement of a change in the War Department, and who had undertaken to break it to Lord Castlereagh at the proper moment – namely Lord Castlereagh's intimate friend & relation Lord Camden. [and] that there was now in Mr Perceval's possession a letter from

Mr Canning to the Duke of Portland in which he requested the Duke to bear in mind, in case Mr. Canning should ever be blamed for the concealment of this arrangement from Lord Castlereagh, that he (Mr. Canning) had objected to the concealment and up to a late period had been ignorant of its having been acted upon. – I added that the concealment had been acquiesced in by Mr. Canning, upon its being represented by the Duke of Portland as the King's desire.

Lord Yarmouth said this last circumstance might possibly be important, and regretted its not having been communicated the Evening before. – I replied that I had not at that time been aware of it. – That I now communicated it to him in confidence, to be reported to Lord Castlereagh only if he thought it would produce a good effect – and relying upon his honour to make use of it in no way which could cast any imputation upon Mr. Canning. – He then took Lord Castlereagh aside, and on his return merely proposed that 'we should walk'. – We then went out upon the Heath. Lord Y. first measured the ground and desired me to step it after him. He then proposed to toss up to decide which of us should give the word – it fell to him.

When I was about to deliver the Pistol to Mr. Canning I said to Lord Yarmouth 'I must cock it for him, for I cannot trust him to do it himself – He has never fired a Pistol in his Life'. After the first shot Lord Y. expressed a wish that the Business might, if possible, be prevented from going further; and desired me to speak to Mr. Canning and to see whether any explanation could take place. I went to Mr. Canning, and Lord Yarmouth at the same time took Lord Castlereagh aside – Mr. Canning's answer to me was that he could give no explanation; that he came there to give Lord Castlereagh satisfaction, and that he was the best judge when he had got enough.

I reported to Lord Yarmouth that Mr. Canning had no grievance against Lord Castlereagh, and that Lord C. must decide when he was satisfied. On this Lord Y. said 'It is a pity then, as no mischief is yet done, that Mr. Canning did not fire in the air, the Business might then have stopped here. I fear now they must fire another shot, but I hope you will agree with me, whatever may be the result of this shot, not to allow the Business to proceed further'. I answered – 'It can on no account be allowed to proceed further' – He then said aloud, 'After this shot we walk off the ground' – He then gave the word again.

On perceiving a Rent in Mr. Canning's Pantaloons I immediately ran up to him and assisted him in walking away, – after a few paces Mr. Canning stopped and said to me – 'but perhaps I ought to remain' – and then louder, 'Are you sure we have done'? Lord Yarmouth said 'certainly', and then Lord Castlereagh came up, and, together with myself, assisted Mr. Canning in walking to Lord Yarmouth's House.

As I was about to go away, Lord Yarmouth asked me whether I thought it would be proper for us to draw up a Statement. – I replied that I thought it would not. He then added – 'It is not our Business to write for the Newspapers' – This is the substance of what passed to the best of my Recollection.

Yarmouth's remark ('It is a pity, as no mischief is yet done, that Mr Canning did not fire in the air') cannot have meant that Castlereagh's first shot had been deliberately wide and that he only insisted on a second shot *because* Canning had not fired into the air, since both men had agreed to fire 'at the same moment'. With hindsight, we know that Canning should indeed have fired into the air, as Castlereagh's first shot did no damage and he could not honourably have asked for a second shot if his opponent had fired into the air. But Canning could not have banked on Castlereagh's first shot missing. Knowing that his opponent had the reputation of being a very good shot, Canning probably felt that his best hope of survival was to aim at his opponent in the hope of putting him off his stroke. There was – and still is – no reason to suppose that Castlereagh did not want to hurt Canning; his second shot went through the thigh only a few millimetres from the femoral artery. If he had simply been trying to teach his opponent a lesson by winging him, Castlereagh would have aimed much lower.

There is, in fact, more than one puzzle about this duel. Unless *The British Duelling Pistol* (see above) is completely wrong, a man using his own tailor-made pistol could reckon to hit a man with a snap-shot at 20 paces, and this was at 12 paces; yet Castlereagh's first shot missed completely. Why? His second shot, also, is puzzling. A good shot who wanted to maim but not kill would not have aimed at the thigh – far too dangerous. None of it makes sense, but paradoxically this is in a way to Castlereagh's credit, for if the duel had been a cold-blooded attempt to restore his damaged political reputation, then what he needed to do was to show his superiority (and, as a bonus, put a political rival *hors de combat* for a spell) not by trying to kill him, but by shooting him, literally and metaphorically, in the foot. Killing Canning would have ruined Castlereagh for life: he might have managed to escape a conviction for wilful murder, but this was England and not Dublin, and he would have been utterly disgraced. The shots fired that morning on Putney Heath seem to rule out the idea that the duel was a calculated act to restore his reputation; despite Castlereagh's icy calm exterior, the duel was a hot-blooded act, an emotional response to his feeling that his honour had been insulted. So, why on earth did he wait for nine days before he did anything, when it was normal to issue a challenge straight away?

One possible explanation for Castlereagh's first shot going wide and his second shot being very nearly fatal could be based on a belief that Canning managed to put a bullet through the lapel of Castlereagh's overcoat.[7] If he had done so, and with his first shot, perhaps that could have angered Castlereagh so that he decided to take aim with his second shot after deliberately sparing his opponent with his first. But the story of Canning's near miss is very unlikely to be correct. The *Courier* of 22 September, under the headline 'Narrow Escape for Lord Castlereagh', reported, 'It is said that Lord Castlereagh had a narrow escape, the button of the right lapel of his coat being shot through.' The *Courier* was a fairly colourful evening newspaper; it also reported that 'the parties went into Lord Yarmouth's house on Putney Heath and remained in consultation for half an hour' (certainly untrue), that they had arrived at the ground at 6 am (wrong again; it was about 6:40 am), that Yarmouth's servants were told to go away so that they should not know what was happening (obviously), that both carriages were turned round to give the impression that they were about to return straight away to London, and that after the duel both men threw their pistols on the ground and Canning's was retrieved by a servant (highly improbable, especially as the servants had been told to go away). The *Courier* presumably obtained these juicy titbits from one of Lord Yarmouth's servants, who could not have been an eyewitness but would have claimed to be – an early example of cheque-book journalism, perhaps. The story of Canning hitting the lapel of his opponent's coat evidently came from the same source as the other stories which are known to be untrue, and in any case it is most unlikely that a man who 'had not the slightest idea of taking aim' (in the words of a private letter at the end of this chapter) could have got anywhere near his target; pistol shooting requires practice. *The Times* of 23 September copied the report in the *Courier*, saying specifically that its report was unsubstantiated, and bracketing it (following the *Courier*) with the report that 'the whole party went into Lord Yarmouth's house before the duel', together with a report that 'a bit of cloth had entered [Canning's leg] with the ball' which is, again, untrue. Probably *The Times*, anxious to gain a reputation as a newspaper of record, decided to get the best of both worlds by repeating some juicy gossip but at the same time disclaiming any responsibility for its truth (*plus ça change*). The evidence for any theory that Castlereagh failed to score with his first shot because he was put off his aim by being winged in his coat collar, and that he aimed so lethally with his second shot because Canning's near miss had angered him, simply is not there. The course of the duel remains an enigma, and the more closely it is examined the more puzzling it becomes.

After Canning had been helped back to his carriage, Charles Ellis took him home to Gloucester Lodge. Canning lost no time in writing (or, rather, dictating – for he was lying on a sofa) a letter to reassure his mother and aunts, of which there are at least three contemporary copies – he had no lack of aunts.

Gloucester Lodge

<u>Copy</u> Sept. 21st 1809

Pray, young women, had either of you ever a Ball pass through the fleshy part of your thigh? If not you can hardly conceive how slight a matter it is – provided (that is) that is passes through quite & clean, carrying only a little bit of your nankeen breeches so big **O** with it, and comes out on the other side without turning to the right or the left to any of the arteries, & bones &c &c which lie thereabouts.

If you have a mind to try the experiment, I would recommend Lord Castlereagh as the Operator. For here am I just as well as if I had not undergone the operation two hours ago – without pain, without fever, & with only two little holes which I dare say you could see through, if you were here, & would put your heads down; & Charles Ellis nursing me & nothing to do but to lie quiet on a sofa for a fortnight & then be up & about again.

So God bless you all & do not be frightened – at anything you hear – for seriously, soberly, upon my word of honour there is not the slightest danger, pain or inconvenience in my wound. Adieu.

The Times's account of the duel (23 September) tallies with those of Ellis and Castlereagh, apart from the three hearsay items already discussed. When it next mentions the duel, on 26 September, it simply lists previous political duels (Wilkes v. Lord Talbot and Mr Martin; Fox v. William Adam; the Duke of York v. Colonel Lennox; Pitt v. Tierney), and adds 'we believe this is the second time of Lord Castlereagh entering the field. Mr Canning had never fought a duel before.'

The *Courier*, as we have already seen, reported the duel more sensationally, and, being an evening paper, did so the day after the duel. It also told its readers that 'Mr Canning was in considerable pain yesterday afternoon from his wound, but he obtained a few hours rest during the night', and the next day, in response to 'the numerous enquiries about Mr Canning's health', the *Courier* assured its readers that 'we understand that Mr Canning's wound continues free from danger'.

The *Morning Chronicle* also reported the duel on Friday the 22nd, but less sensationally than the *Courier*. Its account claims to be 'by authority' (whose, it does not specify), and says simply that 'after taking ground they fired by signal, and missed; and no explanation then taking place, they fired a second time when the ball from Lord Castlereagh's pistol went through Mr Canning's breeches'. It also makes the mistake of saying that the duel took place at six o'clock (when it would have been still too dark to see properly) and not seven o'clock.

The *Observer* did not report the duel until Saturday the 24th, when it gave a brief factual account of what occurred (though stating incorrectly that the distance was ten yards). It also says that 'the answer to the numerous enquiries respecting Mr Canning is that he is as well as can be expected. We understand that he walks about his room to prevent any contraction of the muscles about the wounded part; but he has not been out.' It adds that his private secretary was in constant attendance.

More reliable than any press report is a manuscript letter (in the author's possession) to 'William Erskine Esq Advocate Edinburgh'. It is franked 'Geo: Canning', postmarked 'London September Thirtieth 1809' and signed 'G. Ellis'.

> Sunning Hill, Staines 29th Septr 1809
>
> Dear Sir, I have this moment received yours, dated Edinburgh 24th, & inclose this to town that it may be forwarded by my cousin, who (not I) was Canning's second in the late extraordinary duel. Extraordinary it certainly was, and, as you justly observe, 'the most foolish & ridiculous of all conceivable things', but it certainly was, on the part of Canning, absolutely unavoidable. It appears (and it is not the least curious part of this whole curious proceeding that a letter intended to convey a challenge should contain four pages of writing & be moulded into a historical document) that Canning, some months ago, disgusted with the whole political conduct of his colleagues, wished to retire from the ministry; that he actually tendered his resignation; that, to avert this evil, his colleagues proposed to him the removal of Ld Castlereagh and the substitution of another war-minister; that Canning accepted this compromise, and at the same time earnestly pressed the immediate communication of this arrangement to Lord C. ... [And because Canning did not resign when this was not done] his Lordship formally demanded 'that satisfaction to which he had a right to lay claim'.
>
> Canning is doing as well as possible. The ball passed through the upper part of his thigh without wounding the muscles or touching the bone, so that he will not be lame. Charles Ellis did all that it was possible to do to prevent the duel, and Ld Yarmouth (who was Ld C's second and behaved with admirable temper & judgment) assisted him most zealously, but ineffectually; for although the first shot on both sides was harmless, Ld C was resolved to try a second, & was then successful. Canning had never fired a pistol before, & had not the slightest idea of taking aim. As there is no mode by which one

gentleman can, consistently with his character, <u>refuse</u> to fight another, and as a <u>challenge</u> renders explanation absolutely impossible, I trust that you will not consider Canning as <u>imprudent</u> or <u>in any other respect</u> deserving of blame. What will be the ultimate result I cannot even guess, but it certainly was, on the part of Canning, absolutely unavoidable.

The simmering anger behind Castlereagh's challenge reveals his pent-up feelings, and there is no mystery as to why he challenged Canning to a duel. He felt humiliated and angry, and Canning was the man who had been insisting that the government needed to be changed. The mystery is the delay in issuing his challenge, with a subsidiary mystery about the way he aimed, or failed to aim, his two shots. It is strange.

Cartoon depicting the duel between Lord Castlereagh and George Canning on 21 September 1809 entitled 'Killing No Murder, or A New Ministerial Way of Settling the Affairs of the Nation'.

CHAPTER 10

The Aftermath

To start with, public opinion was strongly critical of the duel. First off the mark was the editor of the *Morning Chronicle*, who accompanied the paper's report of the duel the day after it happened (Friday 22nd) with a strong attack on both protagonists for their irresponsibility in indulging in a private quarrel at a time of national crisis when they should have been attending to affairs of state:

> The distractions of the Cabinet have at last burst into open and public violence. It will scarcely be credited by posterity, that two of His Majesty's principal Secretaries of State should so far forget the duty that they owed to their Sovereign and the example they ought to give to the country in obedience to its laws, to fight a duel. Yet the fact is actually so. ... [It is] most serious that His Majesty should have committed the affairs of State to persons whose intemperate passions were so little under the controul [sic] of reason.

That was written while it was generally assumed that the grounds for Castlereagh's challenge had been that Canning had attacked him for his misman-agement of the Walcheren Expedition. The *Morning Chronicle*, an Opposition newspaper, saw the duel as a chance to attack the government in general and the Secretary for War in particular for a succession of recent military failures: not only had Walcheren clearly been a disaster, but Wellington was in full retreat in the Peninsula despite his earlier victory at Talavera. Besides using the duel to highlight government incompetence, the *Morning Chronicle* saw its chance to press for a completely new administration and not simply a reshuffle of existing ministers:

> Out of evil we prophesy that good will come [in the shape of a government led by Grey or Grenville]. The nation should consider themselves under obligation to the services that [Canning] intended to his country [by pressing for Castlereagh's removal from the War Office]. What gratitude indeed

would they not have owed to him, if he had thereby succeeded in preventing
the mischiefs that have issued from that department [during the summer].

What's this pother all about?
Canning and Castlereagh *gone out?*
What! Castlereagh from places sever?
'Tis strange – but better late than never.
Oh! That our stars contrived it so
That both had gone out long ago.

On the following Monday the *Courier*, more supportive of the government than
the *Morning Chronicle*, complained that 'the Opposition [is trying] to fix upon
Lord Castlereagh the whole blame of the [Walcheren] Expedition, and praise
is lavished upon Mr Canning'. But then, as it became clear that the duel had
not been about the Walcheren campaign but about Castlereagh's anger at the
proposals to remove him from the War Department, public opinion swung
towards Canning, especially as the challenge had been worded in such a way
that Canning had no choice but to accept it. The Whig Lord Holland, despite
disliking Canning (having taken offence when he was told not to meddle in
Spanish politics – 'I did not conceive a Secretary of State, in granting a pass-
port to an English gentleman, had any authority or occasion to read him a
lecture as to his intercourse with foreigners,' he had complained[1]), nonetheless
condemned 'the conduct of Lord Castlereagh, who was an excellent marks-
man and had practised with pistols to qualify himself for the Irish House of
Commons'. Holland agreed with Wilberforce that 'if the concealment constituted the offence, then with the Duke of Portland and Lord Camden, not
Mr Canning, rested the guilt of the concealment'. Windham remarked that
'a gentleman does not fight to avenge his political wrongs, but to vindicate
his character', and Malmesbury pronounced that Canning's protest against
the secrecy imposed by Portland 'fully exculpates Canning as to the concealment, and shows that he has been fighting the poor old Duke's duel, or Lord
Camden's, or Hawkesbury's, or almost anybody's but his own'.

As news of the duel trickled slowly across Europe, most Englishmen probably shared the opinion of Wellington, who told his brother William that 'the
Duel which I suppose was the result of the preceding squabbles about places
... is v. unfortunate ... [and] will confirm the despicable opinions which all ...
have had of the public services of the State'.[2] Wellington also complained that
the duel enabled the French and their allies to crow over the dissensions and
incompetence of the British government. For Canning's close friends, relief
that he had not been killed seems to have prevailed over any other feeling – his
aunt Hitty, when telling her son Stratford (in Constantinople) about the duel,

said nothing about the rights and wrongs of the matter, but was simply thankful that the outcome had not been worse: 'he received a wound in the thigh, not dangerous thank God! Now, although the danger be over, yet I doubt not your mind will be agitated by the thoughts of what might have been the consequences of this duel ... had it not pleased a good Providence to avert the evil, by sparing so valuable a life.'

Castlereagh's friends naturally defended him. Edward Cooke told Charles Stewart that 'Probably the D of P's conduct was as bad, if not worse, than Mr C's; but he was secure in age and infirmity and Mr C's taking advantage of the Duke's failings ... was an aggravation of his conduct.' But that was a minority view: most people agreed with Wilberforce's description of Castlereagh's challenge as 'a cold-blooded measure of deliberate revenge' worded in such a way that Canning had no choice but to accept it. The well-informed and dependable George Rose, a fairly neutral observer who was a friend of Canning but had agreed to serve under Perceval, read all the relevant correspondence and concluded that it confirmed that Canning 'had long, and repeatedly, urged a communication of all that was in agitation' to Castlereagh, and that 'no delay respecting it could fairly be imputed to him'. He also concluded that Castlereagh's real grievance was that after being 'shown all the correspondence by Mr Perceval', he saw that most of his colleagues thought he ought to be removed from the War Department. Perceval was basically a decent and honourable man, even if he was capable of 'playing lawyer's tricks' when under pressure; he would never knowingly have provoked a duel. Unfortunately, though, his efforts to prove that Canning had not been to blame for the 'concealment' by showing Castlereagh 'all the correspondence', far from calming him down, had the opposite effect and had simply stoked his anger. Learning what a low opinion his colleagues seemed to have of his ability must have been extremely hurtful to a proud and ambitious man; it made Castlereagh want to hit back somehow, and the obvious target for his anger was Canning, who had set the whole matter off in the first place with his assertion that 'the Government, as at present constituted, does not appear to me equal to the great task which it has to perform'.

Immediately after the duel Castlereagh sat down to write to his father. The letter confirms his sense of betrayal and disgust with 'his colleagues, his friends, his private connexion Lord Camden', for having been ready to 'sacrifice' him to Canning:

> It has been painful to me to leave you so long in suspense, after the intimation I gave you some days since.[3] The outline of the case, which I then described to

you as a most painful one, you will collect from the enclosed correspondence which led to a meeting this morning between Mr Canning and myself. We each fired two pistols, my second shot took effect, but happily only passed through the fleshy part of the thigh. Mr Canning's conduct was very proper on the ground.

You will feel deeply I am sure the cruel situation in which long and unsuspectedly I have been placed, sacrificed to a colleague, as it turns out without even securing to the King's government the support from him of which my dismissal from the War Department was intended to be the price, and after thus surrendering me, I was by the infatuation and folly of those who call'd themselves my friends, allow'd to remain in total ignorance of my situation, to plunge into even heavier responsibility after my death warrant was sign'd, and further I was to be kept in profound ignorance of this, until the moment should arrive, namely, the close of the [Walcheren] expedition, when I was to be equally dismissed in the event of failure or success, unless Mr C in his mercy should be disposed to spare his victim, being made absolute master of my fate.

I hope my publick and private character will survive the peril to which it has been exposed, but you may imagine what would have been the impression had I submitted to be duped and practised upon, and how small a proportion of the world would have believed I was not privy to my own disgrace, it being more generally credible that a publick man should be guilty of a shabby act to keep himself in office, than that his colleagues, his friends, his private connexion Lord Camden, should presume without any authority from him, without even his knowledge, to place himself in a situation so full of danger and so full of dishonour. I must give them credit for good intentions, but I can only say in that case, preserve me from my friends and I shall not fear my enemies.

In other words, Castlereagh felt he had to fight a duel for the sake of his reputation, to show he did not accept the verdict of his colleagues that he was not up to his job. In a way he was right, for as Canning put it to Joan shortly before the duel, Castlereagh had 'disappeared as through a trapdoor'. But that letter to his father does not explain why Castlereagh delayed so long before he acted. When in 1798 Tierney took offence at a remark Pitt made in debate, he 'sent a note to the Minister on Friday, as soon as he left the House of Commons',[4] and Tierney's second, Colonel Walpole, delivered the note by hand to Pitt, who then appointed the time and place for a 'meeting'. Yet Castlereagh waited well over a week before deciding that his 'honor and character' required him to demand satisfaction. Why?

It almost seems as if Castlereagh had become slightly unhinged as he brooded over what Camden and Perceval had told him, and when he came to

Lord Camden, 2nd Earl and 1st Marquess, was Castlereagh's uncle. Canning called him 'Chuckle', and after the duel Castlereagh was bitter about his failure to tell him what his colleagues had been saying.

his senses after the duel was abashed at what he had done. *The Times* reported[5] that he had gone 'several times on Thursday and Friday to enquire after Mr Canning's health'; convention might have required one visit, but 'several times' suggests that he felt genuine concern . Immediately after the duel he told his father that '*happily* [my italics] the shot had only passed through the fleshy part of the thigh'; but there was still of course a risk of infection, though luckily the ball had passed right through the leg, and no cloth had lodged inside it. Castlereagh seems to have realized in the cold light of day how serious the consequences might be for himself if the wound he had inflicted went septic. Canning's death would have spelt the end of Castlereagh's career, for this was England, not Dublin. Moreover, by the time he wrote to his father his anger was directed more at Camden than at Canning, since it was clear that Canning had not been trying to act behind his back, but had thought that Camden had kept his nephew informed of what was being discussed.

Realizing that he was being blamed for his part – or rather failure to play his part – in the events that had led up to the duel, Camden decided to publish his own version of events. In a long apologia, he asserted that when Portland had first told him about a plan to move Castlereagh from the War Department, far from asking Camden to tell his nephew about it he had actually put him 'under the most solemn injunction of secresy [sic]'. Camden also asserted that this injunction to secrecy had made him 'so uneasy, that on 26th June [he] wrote to the Duke of Portland to know whether he was in any mistake about that, to which the Duke answered ... that he was not ... his Grace taking upon himself, in the clearest terms, whatever blame might attach to the concealment'. (In fairness to Camden, he may not have known that by this time the King had stepped in and forbidden Portland to tell Castlereagh of the plan to remove him from the War Department.) All this was presumably what Camden had told his nephew originally, but after the duel Castlereagh realized what damage his uncle's anxiety to absolve himself of any blame had done. He told his father (3 October):

> I return Ld Camden's letter, which, like every other part in this business is an attempt by colouring, and inaccurate representation, to extricate himself for the Embarrassment, in which he has involved himself. After the duel he came to my house ... and broke into my room in tears, condemning himself and stating his wretchedness. I told him I must acquit him of any Motives deliberately unkind to me, but that I could never forget the political injury he had exposed me to. ... Perceval has been authorised by the K to make a Govt. ... I do not consider that I can have anything to do with them [i.e. his late colleagues] after so recent and mark'd an Injury.

The other person besides his father to whom Castlereagh lost no time in explaining what had happened was his half-brother Charles Stewart, serving as Adjutant-General in Spain (to his chagrin he had not been entrusted with any command). Castlereagh clearly meant his letter to be shown to Wellington who, he feared, would not think much of his behaviour. It was a sensible move on Castlereagh's part to get his word in first before Wellington could hear about the duel from any other source, and, as we have seen, Wellington's natural reaction was to deprecate the 'squabbles about places' which 'will confirm the despicable opinions which [we] all have had of the public services of the State'. Later on, however, he came down on Castlereagh's side – a verdict that may have been helped by Castlereagh having said, in his letter to Charles, that the only reason he had hesitated to send Wellington out to Portugal in the spring, as Canning had been urging, was that he had first wanted to find out 'whether there was a reasonable prospect of finding the British Army in possession of Portugal'.

By the end of September public opinion was running against Castlereagh, so on 3 October he published his own version of events. This swayed public opinion back in his favour, as people naturally felt sympathy for a man whose colleagues had been plotting against him behind his back, but it would not have impressed those who knew that Canning had not been to blame for the 'concealment' and that his complaint about the ineffectiveness of the government 'as at present constituted' had not been specifically directed against Castlereagh. All that Canning needed to do, therefore, was to preserve a dignified silence and let the facts trickle out in their own good time. However, Canning's great weakness was that he could never keep quiet, even when silence would have been golden. Thus when Camden published his apologia in October (denying that he had let Portland think he had spoken to his nephew) Canning was provoked to publish his own reply on 27 November:

> It is to be regretted that your Lordship [Camden] was not party to the assurances given to me [that Castlereagh had been told of the plan to remove him from his office]; had I been made acquainted with those circumstances, I should then have resigned. ... [He then went on to say, in a long 'Statement of the cause of that Transaction upon a misapprehension of the leading facts of which Lord Castlereagh's Letter appears to have been founded' that] Mr Canning [wrote] to the Duke of Portland in the month of July that 'in justice to himself, it may be remembered, whenever hereafter this concealment shall be alledged (as he doubts not it will) against him, as an act of injustice towards Lord Castlereagh, that it did not originate in his suggestion; that so far from desiring it, he conceived, however erroneously, Lord Camden to be the sure

channel of communication to have been actually made. ... It is not true that
he was party in consenting to the concealment of that intended change from
Lord Castlereagh.

Unfortunately, this long and involved attempt to blame Camden for the
'concealment' did not help Canning but simply produced the reaction *'qui
s'excuse, s'accuse'*. It was, after all, only one man's word against another's.
Canning should have realized that there were only three people who actually
knew that he, not Camden, was speaking the truth: Camden himself, Portland and the King. Camden had flatly denied it, Portland could not confirm it
(because he was dead), and that left the King. If George III had let it be known
that Canning's 'Statement' was true (as he knew it was), then public opinion
would have remained firmly on Canning's side. As it was, the King deliberately kept quiet and let him swing in the wind, and Castlereagh to his relief was
able to tell his brother that Canning's apologia 'seems to have accomplished
every purpose of mine ... he has made but little way in justifying himself. ... I
have every reason to be satisfied with the course I have pursued and the recep-
tion it has met with from the world in general.'

In an article in the *Cambridge Historical Journal*, 1929–31, two eminent historians argued the rights and wrongs of the duel. Professor Webster defended
Castlereagh (quoting Cooke's letters), and Professor Temperley championed
Canning. Temperley admits that Canning should have insisted on resigning in
July when he had learned about the King's delaying tactics, even though resigning against the King's express wishes would have had serious consequences
for Canning personally, and from a patriotic point of view, with the war at a
critical point, it was not a good moment for a foreign secretary to resign. But
far more culpable was the conduct of the King. Temperley prints Portland's
letter to Canning of 18 July, in which he says that the King had laid it down
that Castlereagh must not be told what was in contemplation until after the
Walcheren Expedition had sailed. Temperley's verdict is clear:

> There are not many occasions in which even George III's personal influence
> was more important than this. And the exertion of it has even yet [1929] been
> hardly realised by historians. That Canning would have been wise to resign
> rather than submit to this 'progressive' delay, is quite clear. But it is also clear
> that he ... was given an assurance on the 28th June ... that the concealment
> would in all probability cease 'in one fortnight more at the latest'.

A year after the duel, a final onset of porphyria consigned George III to
ten years of unspeakable torment, held prisoner at Kew under conditions
that today would be described as a criminal violation of human rights, so he

deserves sympathy, not condemnation. George III genuinely had the interests of his country at heart, but unfortunately he was often a poor judge of what those interests were. His obstinacy had lost Britain the American colonies, and at a critical point of the war against Napoleon his personal prejudices lost for the nation the services of the most able of his 'confidential servants'.

The short-term result of the duel, in fact, was that both Castlereagh and Canning went down in popular estimation – two cabinet ministers fighting one another was not an edifying spectacle – but that most of the blame was attached to Canning. The long-term consequences were profound.

Two days before the duel, the cabinet had decided that Perceval would have either to recommend the King to send for Canning or invite the Opposition leaders, Grey and Grenville, to join the government; but then the duel put Canning temporarily *hors de combat*. Grenville showed some sign of being willing to serve, but Grey refused even to leave his Northumberland acres and come to London. That left Perceval free to form a government as best he could, without the complication, or the advantage, of having to think about Canning or the Opposition leaders, and through sheer grit and determination he succeeded, against all expectation, in forming a ministry that survived until his death in 1812. Wellesley became Foreign Secretary (under the impression that Canning had betrayed him), although his contempt for his colleagues (including Perceval and 'that ridiculous animal Jenky') made him a somewhat semi-detached member of the government, and he sat very light to the duties of his office. Matrimonial troubles (he was divorcing his wife) and philandering did not help; his brother (Wellington) had 'wish[ed] that Wellesley was *castrated*; or that he would like other people attend to his business and perform too. It is lamentable to see his Talents and Character and advantages … thrown away on whoring.' One can only speculate how well a government with Wellesley as First Lord of the Treasury in the Lords and Canning as Leader of the Commons might have worked. Early in 1812 Wellesley decided he had had enough of serving under Perceval and resigned, hoping that the Prince of Wales, by then Regent, would make him Prime Minister. But he should have heeded the advice of the Psalmist, 'Put not your trust in Princes'; all that happened was that Perceval asked Castlereagh to succeed Wellesley. It was thanks to the duel that Castlereagh, not Canning, was Foreign Secretary when the future of Europe was decided after the Napoleonic Wars. Creevey, writing in 1818, was convinced 'that Castlereagh would have expired politically in the year 1809 – that all the world by common consent had had enough of him – had it not been for the piece of perfidy [sic] by Canning, and that this, and this alone, had raised him from the dead'.

Because the duel enabled Castlereagh to achieve the fame that would otherwise have been Canning's, a cynic might suggest that his challenge was a deliberate act of cold, calculating ambition; but that idea will not wash. We know, with hindsight, how events unfolded in the years following the duel, but it would have been quite impossible to predict the outcome of the confused political manoeuvring that took place after Portland resigned. Hardly anyone thought Perceval would manage to form a government, let alone remain in office until his death. In any case, for Castlereagh to have issued his challenge as a deliberate, calculated move would been utterly foreign to his character. It was one thing to have wanted to assert his superiority, to erase any impression that he held his office only at Canning's pleasure, and to wreak vengeance on Canning for thinking that it was in his power to have him moved from that office – even to have been angry enough to kill his opponent if he felt his honour was at stake. But to set out cold-bloodedly to fight a duel in order to promote his own career would have been dishonourable, and Castlereagh's honour was important to him. A duel could be (especially if a woman was involved) a means of getting away with murder, but Castlereagh was no cold-blooded murderer.

A few weeks after asking Castlereagh to be Foreign Secretary, in May 1812 Perceval was assassinated in the lobby of the House of Commons by a bankrupt and possibly deranged merchant by the name of Bellingham, who blamed the Orders in Council for his ruin. After feverish manoeuvring, Canning's old friend Jenky, Lord Liverpool, became Prime Minister. He wanted to have Canning back as Foreign Secretary, and Castlereagh generously offered to stand down, but Canning, in what he later realized was the biggest mistake of his life, refused office unless he also became Leader of the Commons, which was too much to expect Castlereagh to concede. Canning's refusal has been put down to overweening conceit and ambition (Wendy Hinde's *Castlereagh* says it was 'compounded of false pride, ambition and jealousy'). That may well have played its part, but he probably felt, albeit subconsciously, reluctant to serve under the man who three years earlier had taken two shots at him with apparently lethal intent. Not for another three years did Canning, by then back in the cabinet at the Board of Control, seem to have recovered fully from any psychological scars left by the duel. His vigorous defence of Castlereagh against allegations of corruption (again!) in 1816 showed that he had let bygones be bygones – though whether Joan ever forgave the man who had tried to kill her husband is a different matter. (Nor, indeed, did Emily Castlereagh ever forgive Canning; when in 1827 he was trying to form a government she congratulated her brother-in-law Charles for refusing to serve under him: 'Your letter to the

K. [King] is <u>perfection</u>, Canning must be <u>gloriously</u> mortified to find himself deserted by almost all the Aristocracy', and a few days later she was mortified when Canning, having 'bamboozled the K', became Prime Minister.[6])

For Castlereagh, the memory of Putney Heath would have been less traumatic. Two revealing incidents, though, suggest that he may have come to regret what he had done. In April 1814 Stratford Canning, having returned the previous year from being chargé d'affaires in Constantinople, paid a courtesy call on the Foreign Secretary when visiting Paris, and to his surprise Castlereagh offered him the post of Envoy Extraordinary and Minister Plenipotentiary to Switzerland. Later that same year Stratford's brother William, who had been chaplain to Sir Gore Ouseley's embassy in Tehran, arrived in Vienna with despatches for Castlereagh. He was 'received with open arms at Lord C's by Planta and Morier. ... Lord C did not make his appearance at breakfast, but as soon as Planta announced my arrival to him, his Lordship was good enough to invite me to dinner, and received me in the most gractious manner and told me to my inexpressible delight (and which was the more agreeable as coming from him) that he had sent for Stratford and expected him in the course of three or four days.' Both these two cousins of Canning thought, rightly or wrongly, that Castlereagh was wanting to make amends for the duel by being kind to them.

The fact that Castlereagh and not Canning was Foreign Secretary from 1812 to 1822, and thus helped shape the future of Europe after the Napoleonic Wars, was therefore a consequence of that duel on Putney Heath. True, Canning refused Lord Liverpool's offer of the Foreign Office in August 1812, and always regretted that decision; but even if that refusal had nothing to do with memories of the duel, it is unlikely that Perceval would have chosen Castlereagh rather than Canning in the first place – the duel had largely effaced the memory of Castlereagh's shortcomings as Secretary of State for War. Once he found himself both Foreign Secretary and Leader of the House of Commons, he was soon confounding his critics with his mastery of the House. The Duke of Buckingham affirmed that 'Lord Castlereagh as Leader of the House never lets fall an indiscreet word for his opponents to use against him. It was a different matter with Mr Canning, and I am told that very often he did harm solely by his desire to make an effect by some brilliant remark.'[7] Having been Leader of the Irish House of Commons during a very turbulent time, Castlereagh knew how to handle awkward and recalcitrant members. How good a Foreign Secretary he was, and whether Canning would or would not have been a better one, deserves a chapter to itself. What is certain is that the influence of Great Britain in the world was greater in the period immediately after the defeat of Napoleon than at any other time before or since. And it is arguable, if not certain, that the duel between Canning and Castlereagh determined which of them would wield that influence as the British Foreign Secretary, and therefore what the post-war settlement of Europe would be like.

CHAPTER 11

Long-Term Consequences: The Two Foreign Secretaries

How much difference would it have made if the duel had not happened and if Castlereagh had not been Foreign Secretary when the peace settlement was being thrashed out at the Congress of Vienna?

Whoever had represented Britain at the end of the Napoleonic Wars would have held a far stronger hand than any other Foreign Secretary before or since. British sea power had been the one invariable factor during 20 years of war, and when Napoleon had eventually overreached himself by invading Russia and was being driven back across the Rhine, a British army had already invaded France across the Pyrenees. Castlereagh was far sighted enough to see that Britain's interest lay not in retaining all her captured French and Dutch colonies, but in being free to develop her worldwide trade without having to worry about interference from the Continent. The only major acquisition that Britain retained was the Cape (which had been taken from the Dutch twice, before and after the Peace of Amiens), and in return she helped pay for new forts along the Dutch frontier. Castlereagh's only Continental demand was that Antwerp must not be controlled by France, as that would make it, as he put it, 'a dagger pointed at the heart of England'. He told his ambassador in Vienna, Lord Aberdeen, that 'to leave it in the hands of France is little short of imposing on Great Britain the charge of a permanent war establishment'.

With such limited aims, Castlereagh could happily go along with the policy of the Austrian chancellor Metternich. That was to make the principle of legitimacy govern any peace settlement, a policy that helped keep the peace of Europe for just on a hundred years (there were localized conflicts like the Crimean, Prusso-Austrian and Prusso-Franco wars, but there was no general European war between 1815 and 1914). The Congress of Vienna did not make the same mistake as the 1919 Treaty of Versailles, of punishing the defeated aggressor so harshly that war broke out again within 20 years. If Canning had been Foreign Secretary, he would have taken much the same line as Castlereagh. Both men were disciples of Pitt and realized that Britain's war aim had been to get rid of a French government that was a disturber of the peace, not to punish the French people. But Canning would not have supported the Congress system that Castlereagh helped initiate. Castlereagh believed that half a dozen leaders sitting round the table and talking face to face could come to agreement on issues that could otherwise lead to conflict. Canning distrusted that method and did much to persuade Castlereagh eventually to abandon it; in present-day terms, he was a Eurosceptic whereas Castlereagh was a Europhile (although the autocrats of 1814 would be mortified to be likened to the Eurocrats of today).

Castlereagh's pre-eminence as a post-war European statesman came about largely by chance. When Napoleon's army after its retreat from Moscow was being pursued by vengeful Russians, Prussia and Austria were still hedging their bets but were open to persuasion to re-enter the war against France. Lord Aberdeen was sent to Vienna as British ambassador, while Lord Cathcart was attached to Tsar Alexander's headquarters, but a third British representative was needed for Berlin, both to urge Prussia to join the war and also to coordinate the British diplomatic effort. After the battle of Leipzig in October 1813 had brought victory within sight, there was an even more pressing need – to make sure that any peace terms offered by the Allies were acceptable to Britain. Cathcart was a general and not a diplomat, and Aberdeen was a rather callow 29-year-old who had succeeded to his title while still a young boy and had an exaggerated sense of his own importance (partly, perhaps, because Pitt had been his guardian after his father died). Aberdeen had been asked to be ambassador at Constantinople in 1810 but had declined the post because he thought Turkey might declare war and he felt his rank entitled him to a less precarious appointment.

The man Castlereagh chose for a British representative to coordinate the British diplomatic efforts of Cathcart and Aberdeen was his own brother, Charles Stewart. Charles was a dashing cavalryman (too dashing, Wellington thought, to be entrusted with any command) whose courage was proverbial. As a schoolboy he had risked his life trying, alas unsuccessfully, to rescue the ten-year-old Lord Waldegrave from drowning in the Thames.[1] He had fought with verve in the Low Countries, where he received the head wound that may have exacerbated his hot-headedness, and had also fought gallantly in the Peninsula under Sir John Moore; but he was no diplomat. Wellington commented, 'Castlereagh had a real respect for Charles's understanding, and a high opinion of his good sense and discretion. This appears incomprehensible to us who knew the two men', and Charles himself soon realized that he was getting out of his depth, telling his brother, 'If things come to a Congress pray send a very able man. ... You will want a devilish clever man there' (which at least suggests that Charles could read human nature better than Aberdeen, who said Metternich was 'not a very clever man'). Cathcart, older and wiser than Aberdeen, managed to get on good terms with the mercurial Tsar Alexander, but he too was a soldier rather than a diplomat. When Aberdeen blithely agreed that in a post-war settlement France should retain its conquered territories on the left bank of the Rhine including Antwerp, and for good measure allowed Britain's maritime rights to be up for negotiation, Castlereagh saw that a more competent representative than his brother Charles was needed to oversee the British diplomatic effort. After much discussion, the cabinet decided on 20 December 1813 that the only solution was for Castlereagh himself to go out as British representative at the Allied headquarters. The fact that he was Foreign Secretary and not a mere envoy put him on equal terms with the Austrian Chancellor, while, as the eldest son of a marquess, tall, good looking, with polished manners and great personal charm, he had all the attributes to impress the crowned heads of Prussia and Russia.

Castlereagh immediately felt a rapport with Metternich. Perhaps his own experience of trying to hold together two very different peoples – the Irish and the English – made him sympathetic with Metternich's desire to hold together the vast, polyglot Austrian Empire, with no common language or sense of national identity, nothing to hold it together except an all-pervasive and cumbersome bureaucracy. Metternich saw that such an empire, at the centre of Europe and with no defensible frontiers, could only survive if other nations agreed that 'legitimacy' must be the basis for any European settlement – in other words, back to the status quo before 1789. That suited Britain, who wanted to be left in peace to develop her trade – after all, the reason why Britain had reluctantly gone to war originally was that the Jacobins in France were stirring up unrest and threatening established governments.

Castlereagh's presence at Allied headquarters may have enabled Metternich to influence him towards a more conservative policy, but the most important result of his presence there was that for the first time in his life he saw war for what it really was. Before the days of photography or television, politicians had little conception of the horrors of war; they might be excited by news of victories or depressed by news of defeats, but they never saw or smelt the consequences of a battle. But in March 1814 Castlereagh did just that.

Napoleon, instead of accepting some remarkably lenient peace terms, counter-attacked the Allied armies pressing towards Paris, and the Allied headquarters unexpectedly found itself in a war zone. Castlereagh told Lord Liverpool, 'It is a most distressing sight to traverse repeatedly as we have done this wasted district in which for a space of 20 miles from [Bar-sur-Aube] to Troyes ... I saw more human bodies dead than alive.'[2] Service with the Volunteers could have given Castlereagh a glamourized idea of what war was like; what he saw in France must have disabused him of any such notions. It may well have turned him into what we would call a 'Europhile', just as politicians who had served in the Second World War worked for a European union in order to stop the nations of Europe tearing themselves apart once more in war. Had Canning been Foreign Secretary, he would have appointed a better representative than Stewart to Allied headquarters and would never have had that personal experience of the aftermath of battle. Would he perhaps have been less Eurosceptic if he had?

Despite Castlereagh's initial rapport with Metternich, he soon found that the Allied war aims were not the same as Britain's. The Tsar wanted to avenge Napoleon's invasion of Russia by invading France; Prussia wanted to avenge its defeats at Jena and Auerstadt, but also wanted to keep Russia from restoring the puppet kingdom of Poland and thus encroaching on Eastern Europe; Metternich too was wary of Russia and was in no hurry to help her overrun France – Napoleon was, after all, the Austrian Emperor's son-in-law. Accordingly, Metternich used delaying tactics and did not join the fight against France until 1814; he was not going to make the same mistake a third time of coming out openly against France until it was quite safe to do so. To Castlereagh, this seemed yet further proof of Austrian unreliability – time and again she had taken subsidies from England only to pull out of the war as soon as her armies suffered a reverse – but he was careful not to fall out with Metternich. Indeed, Castlereagh's greatest service to his country, and to Europe, was that amid all the bickering among the Allies he kept his head and his temper. It was his personal charm and flattery that in 1813 dissuaded the hot-headed Tsar from forging ahead without waiting for Prussia or Austria, and in 1814 saved him from panicking and asking for a truce when Napoleon counter-attacked. The Russians did not, however, march into Paris as conquerors, which would have provoked undying hostility and resentment; instead, Napoleon's old ministers Talleyrand and Fouché had time to engineer a coup and persuade Napoleon to abdicate. Germany's humiliation at the end of the 1914–18 war left a sullen defeated people to nurse revenge, and it was largely thanks to Castlereagh that this did not happen in 1814. (Unfortunately, though, the mercurial Tsar swung so violently from vengeance to magnanimity that he insisted that Napoleon, despite Castlereagh's doubts, be allowed to go and govern Elba.)

With Napoleon's defeat in April 1814, and the Allies welcoming a Bourbon king back to Paris, Castlereagh's reputation was immense. When Lord Liverpool wanted him to come home to manage the House of Commons, Castlereagh loftily replied (13 April 1814), 'It may appear presumptuous in me to say so, but my remaining [in Paris] is beyond comparison more important than my original mission'; Liverpool 'must therefore manage' without him, and after a brief sojourn in England, helping to entertain the Allied sovereigns, Castlereagh left for the Congress of Vienna. This time, however, Liverpool did insist that he must come back and manage the House of Commons, and asked Wellington to go to Vienna in his place. Malicious gossip said that Castlereagh was recalled because Emily had been arousing comment by such gaffes as wearing her husband's Garter as a tiara and wearing dresses that were far more décolleté than her figure any longer warranted (a habit which, with her propensity for making tactless remarks, had prompted Lady Errol to call her, unkindly, 'the naked truth'). But the truth is that the Prime Minister really needed Castlereagh to return home to lead the House of Commons, and if Liverpool had really been worried about Britain's image abroad, he would have complained not about Castlereagh's wife but about his brother, Charles Stewart, who when drunk (as he frequently was) made embarrassing advances to any lady within reach. (He is also alleged to have thrown a coachman into the Danube; but none of that stopped him from remaining British Minister at Vienna so long as Castlereagh was Foreign Secretary.)

Mingling with reactionary Continental monarchs and statesmen probably influenced Castlereagh's own outlook, but his reputation as a reactionary in home affairs was not entirely justified. Government measures such as the infamous 'Six Acts' were the brainchild of the Home Secretary, Lord Sidmouth, and as he was a peer the measures were introduced and first debated in the House of Lords. Only then were they debated in the Commons, where Castlereagh as Leader had to try and pilot them through. Castlereagh cannot therefore escape cabinet responsibility for the repressive acts of Lord Liverpool's government such as the notorious Six Acts aimed to repress riots and suppress 'seditious' speech or writings, or the vicious penal laws that meant a man could be hanged for sheep-stealing or transported to Australia for petty crimes; but in fairness to him, they were not measures that he would himself necessarily have put forward – and in any case, his concern was for foreign affairs. For all that, the couplet in Shelley's bitter diatribe against the government – 'I met murder by the way; he wore a mask like Castlereagh' – was not entirely undeserved;

perhaps Canning may after all have been right to refuse the Foreign Secretary-ship in 1812 unless he had also had the lead in the Commons and thus had been in a position to have a restraining influence on ministers like Sidmouth and Eldon.

Castlereagh's plan for a conference system, by which the leaders of the great powers could meet together periodically and settle any differences amicably, was warmly backed by Metternich, though for rather different reasons: he saw it more as a device for putting off change of any sort. At the Congress of Vienna Talleyrand observed that 'Le congrès danse, il ne marche pas'; he saw that Metternich's various flirtations and the constant balls and entertainments were not simply a natural wish to celebrate the end of so many years of war, but a device for delaying any decisions that might be prejudicial to Austria; as some people sourly remarked, Metternich could not so much as have a headache without having some ulterior motive. (A revealing little incident is recorded by Stratford Canning when he first met Metternich while en route to Russia in 1824 at an evening party: 'The same sofa held us both, and I had not been long seated when he said rather curtly "You have a bug on your sleeve". Whether he meant to try me, or provide for his own security, I know not, but the remark was not pleasing and I could only defend myself at the expense of the hotel.')

Was it naive of Castlereagh to believe that in a Europe ruled by autocrats, good personal relations were the way to guarantee peace and prosperity? Was he duped by Metternich into accepting legitimacy as the only basis for recog-nizing a government – a policy which Metternich would later claim to have been why revolutions in Naples, Piedmont, Greece and Spain had been put down without flaring up into a general conflagration? Perhaps. But by then (1820) Castlereagh was having doubts about the system he had himself created. The turning-point for him probably came at the end of 1819 when a Russian royalist named Kotzebue was assassinated by a university student at Jena, thus giving Metternich an excuse to get the various German principalities to agree to set up a bureaucratic system, including spies and secret police, which contin-ued to serve as the glue that held the Austrian Empire together until 1918. These 'Carlsbad Decrees' caused alarm in Britain, where the Peterloo Massa-cre, when an ill-led squadron of Yeomanry had charged a peaceful demonstra-tion in Manchester with considerable loss of life, had provoked a strong public reaction against using force to maintain order.

A few months later Spanish troops in Cadiz, under orders for South America to put down a colonial revolt, mutinied, sparking off a general rising against the absolutist King Ferdinand. Metternich and the European sover-eigns condemned these rebel 'Constitutionalists', but Castlereagh refused to join their protest, and on 5 May 1820 wrote an important state paper. While admitting that the 'Representative Principle menaces the stability of all exist- ing government' it also stated that to repress a popular uprising 'by foreign force' would be 'as dangerous to avow as it would be impossible to execute'. In other words, a country has no business to interfere in the internal affairs of another, however deplorable those affairs might seem. Castlereagh realized, as Canning already had, that you cannot put a genie back in its bottle; the Paris- ian mob by storming the Bastille had shown that the common people were more powerful than the King, so Europe could never be the same again – a fact that Metternich never recognized. His Carlsbad Decrees kept the lid on reform, and it is no coincidence that when the lid finally blew off in 1914 with a force that convulsed Europe, the explosion was triggered by the assassination of an Austrian Grand Duke by a dissident Serb who did not wish to be a subject of the Austrian Empire.

ↈ

Castlereagh served as Foreign Secretary for just over ten years, until he died suddenly and unexpectedly in August 1822 (of which more anon). When Metternich heard the news he wrote that it was, 'A great misfortune. The man is irreplaceable, above all for me. ... Castlereagh was the only man in his country who had experience in foreign affairs. He had learned to understand me. ... Now several years will elapse until somebody else acquires a similar degree of confidence.'[3] Castlereagh's successor was Canning, who in reply to a query from Granville, the British ambassador in Paris, would write (11 March 1825), 'What I think of Metternich? That he is the greatest rogue and liar on the Continent, perhaps in the civilised world.' Canning was ahead of his times in that age of aristocracy in seeing that the aspirations of ordinary people, once aroused, could not be suppressed indefinitely. Towards the end of his life (when Wellington was trying to amend a Corn Bill that landlords disliked) Canning told his private secretary, 'It is a great misfortune that the Lords take so narrow a view of their present situation, that they cannot see we are on the brink of a great struggle between property and population and that such a struggle is only to be averted by the mildest and most liberal legislation.' Canning knew instinctively that if England was to avoid the fate of France, then high Tory policies must be rejected – the first six years of his life had given him something that almost all his contemporaries lacked: an experience of what life was like for those who were not of the privileged classes.

When Canning became Foreign Secretary, he had been out of office for 18 months. Since 1812 he had been MP for Liverpool, where he had been asked to stand despite his opposition to the slave trade on which the city's prosperity was founded. His election seems to have boosted his morale, judging by a letter to Mrs Leigh:

> Liverpool, 17 Oct. My election here took place yesterday, after a severe contest, by a majority of 500 over my opponent Mr Brougham. I have just been chaired round the Town – and I send you a ribbon, such as the ladies here wear in honour of my victory.
> Numbers at the close of the Poll on Wed. Oct. 16
>
> | | |
> |---|---|
> | Canning | 1631 |
> | Gascoigne | 1532 [Canning's running-mate] |
> | Brougham | 1131 |
> | Creevey | 1068 [the diarist][4] |

But his electoral success had done nothing to advance his career, and when the war ended he decided to take his family to Portugal, as the doctors had advised that the only hope for his beloved son George would be a spell in a warmer climate. This was meant to be a private visit, but when Lord Liverpool heard of it he asked Canning to go to Lisbon as ambassador in order to have a high-profile minister to welcome the Portuguese Regent back from Brazil. This appointment did Canning no good either politically or financially: his opponents condemned it as 'a job', especially when the Regent decided not to return after all, yet far from saving money by going to Lisbon at the taxpayers' expense Canning lost heavily financially, as he resigned the embassy before he had time to recoup the initial outlay (which for an ambassador was enormous; Stratford Canning in 1821 was still £5,000 in debt after a year as minister in Washington, and reckoned it would take two years of strict economy 'to set all to rights'[5]).

At the end of 1815 Lord Buckingham died, and Liverpool asked Canning to come back to England and succeed him at the Board of Control – a considerable come-down for a former Foreign Secretary, but Liverpool badly wanted him in the cabinet to counterbalance its more conservative members. Because the workload was light Canning was able during the long parliamentary recesses to travel extensively on the Continent – Germany, Austria, Italy and above all Paris, where his morale was again boosted by being fêted almost as if he were still Foreign Secretary:

> 9th [October 1816] Arrived at Paris. Dined with Mr & Mrs Hammond [Under-Secretary]. ... Fri 11th Dined with the Russian Minister. Present: the Sardinian, Neapolitan, Spanish & Portugese ambassadors, Russian, Saxon, Hanoverian Ministers, the Duc d'Evian, the Duc de la Chastres, the Count de

Cazes [sic], Minister of Police (NB the Minister of most influence & talents) who sat next to me. ... Tuesday 22 Went to Court. The King's levee first, then I had the Dss. of Angoulême, then the Duc d'Ath, then Monsieur [the heir presumptive] then the D. & Dss. of Berry – in all about 3 hours worth. ... Wednes. 23. Went to the Thuileries [sic] by appointment to see Monsr – a long tête a tête. Thursd. 24. Pozzo di Borgo the Russian Minister called on me by appointment to have a long talk re Politicks. ... Monday 28th I dined at De Cazes', a huge dinner of Ministers and men in Office. After dinner abundance of politicks with some of the leading People questioning me about the English Parliament and Government.[6]

It seems to have taken Canning longer to get over the duel than it did his opponent, and this is not surprising. Not only did he receive a physical wound, which though he made light of it had put him out of action just when it was most important politically for him to be up and doing, but the psychological trauma of looking down the barrel of a pistol held by someone who intends to kill you is bound to leave its mark, whereas Castlereagh had been in no more danger from Canning than if he had been pheasant shooting next in line to a notoriously wild shot. Perhaps his memory of the duel may have been partly why Canning had refused to become Foreign Secretary again in 1812 if Castlereagh remained leader of the Commons – a decision he bitterly regretted, for, as the Prince Regent remarked at the time, his skill in debate would soon have made him leader in all but name. But after Canning rejoined the cabinet in 1816 any psychological scars from the duel seem to have healed; Castlereagh went out of his way to be friendly to Canning, who in turn defended his colleague ably and vigorously when he was attacked in the House of Commons. Another sign of a better relationship was their concerted efforts on behalf of Canning's cousin George (son of Paul Canning) who was also Castlereagh's brother-in-law. After the duel George had been in a quandary: should he support his cousin to whom he owed his parliamentary seat, or Castlereagh who had influence in Ireland and in 1807 had done his best to persuade the Viceroy to 'do something' for him: 'Mr Canning has a very good property in the counties of Cavan and Londonderry, but ... it would certainly be an object to him to be brought forward in some official situation' (i.e. a juicy sinecure). By 1816 George had set his heart on an Irish peerage (an English one was too much to hope for), but the Viceroy objected that 'Mr Canning has neither character, nor fortune, nor connection, nor service to Government to his credit'. However, a concerted shove from both Castlereagh and Canning eventually prevailed, Castlereagh telling the Viceroy, 'it is much too late to urge these objections now. I have been authorised by Lord Liverpool to tell Mr Canning that ... he is to have it', and on 28 October 1818 George duly became Baron Garvagh in the peerage of Ireland.

Before long it seems that Castlereagh was quite happy for Canning to offer advice on foreign affairs: when during the Conference of Aix-la-Chapelle in 1818 Canning persuaded his colleagues to send instructions for Castlereagh to reject the Tsar's proposal for a 'Holy Alliance' ('we are of opinion that any new treaty of [that] nature ... would be attended by more inconveniences than it could produce advantages'), it seems that Castlereagh, far from being affronted by Canning's interference, actually welcomed it.[7]

But in 1820, Canning nearly left British politics for good. Early in that year the poor, insane George III died after ten years' inhuman incarceration at Kew, so there had to be a general election. Canning sent his aunt, Mrs Leigh, a brief note on 18 March from his Liverpool constituency: '1st I am getting quit of my cold. 2nd I am getting out of my troubles. A publick dinnier & a speech today. Tomorrow Church with the Mayor. Monday off to Welbeck. 3rd George is better.' But no sooner had he written that than he learned that George had suddenly taken a turn for the worse. Canning hurried back to London, and was at his son's side when he died a few days later (Joan was in Florence at the time with their other three children). The death of his beloved eldest son diminished Canning's zest for politics, especially as he soon had a further reason for disenchantment. With George III's death, Princess Caroline had become Queen, but her husband was determined that she should not be crowned, and made the government start proceedings against her in the House of Lords for adultery. The result was a ribald farce; clearly Caroline had committed adultery during her foreign travels (not least with her Italian courier – one of the witticisms going round London was 'Did the Queen read the Morning Chronicle?' 'No, she took in the Courier'), but her husband had notoriously been equally promiscuous. As a government minister Canning would be obliged to vote against Caroline when 'the Queen's Business' came to the Commons, and he could not bring himself to do that to the godmother of his son who had just died. Canning knew he must resign, telling his aunts on 19 December:

> Come, shall I tell you? – No, I won't – And yet I think I will
> But then, young women, mind you keep those tongues of yours quite still.
> For if, like giddy gossips, you go jabbering about,
> The secret that I tell will be, like he who tells it, out.
> 'Out! Why?' – Yes, faith, the time was come; I could stay in no longer;
> I, who had favour'd neither side, the weaker nor the stronger,
> I, who for six long months and more a neutral power had been

Must now take part, if I staid on, against our gracious Queen.
Rather than this, I must resign – don't breathe it on the Steyne.[8]
Carlo [his youngest son], his holidays expired, must hasten back to school,
But I, while Parliament is hot, at Paris shall keep cool.
The heats in Parliament, I fear, will last for many a day
The heats about the Queen, I mean. But I shall be away.

Caroline's marriage had been a tragedy from the outset: the Prince Regent was still in love with Mrs Fitzherbert whom he had married, albeit in contravention of the recent Royal Marriages Act, and he took against Caroline at first sight. To make matters worse, her wretched mother, the Duchess of Brunswick, a sister of George III, had never taught her to wash or change her underclothes so she stank (hence perhaps the Prince's alleged request when he first met her, 'My God, Malmesbury, fetch me some brandy'). When George IV's coronation took place in July 1821 Caroline was forcibly prevented from entering the Abbey, and soon afterwards she died. Not long before, George IV had been told of Napoleon's death – 'Sire, your enemy is dead' – and assumed they meant his wife.

The 'Queen's Business' affected both Castlereagh and Canning but in different ways. Her former friendship towards Canning caused him, as we have seen, to resign, and turned the new King into his implacable enemy. As for Castlereagh, since the public were on the Queen's side against the government, he became very unpopular. Soon after her arrival in London, the radical Alderman Combe lent Caroline his house which, by bad luck, was close to Castlereagh's in St James's Square, so that when the mob came to cheer the Princess, as they frequently did, they broke Castlereagh's windows while they were about it. However, unpopularity did not worry Castlereagh unduly, any more than it did the Duke of Wellington – their Anglo-Irish upbringing had taught both of them to despise the mob; and as it happened poor Caroline was the indirect means of enabling Castlereagh to get on better terms with the King. News of her death reached her husband just before he embarked at Holyhead for his visit to Ireland, accompanied by Castlereagh, and because the royal suite was in mourning they spent some days at Viceregal Lodge with little else to do than talk to one another.

Although Liverpool would have liked to have Canning back in his cabinet once the 'Queen's Business' was out of the way, he realized that the King would not accept him, so instead proposed that he should succeed Lord Hastings, who wanted to come home, as Governor-General of Bengal. The offer was tempting. Being in office had impoverished Canning, not enriched him as it did some politicians (by bad luck he had just missed a valuable sinecure that came up only a month after his resignation in 1809), and India would restore his finances and Joan's depleted fortune. But Joan hated the idea: their daughter Harriet was just 'coming out' and if she went to India it would ruin her matrimonial prospects and probably her health too, while if she stayed behind then Joan would have to stay with her and be separated from her husband for several years. After much agonizing, Canning accepted India, since he had no prospect of office in England. He wrote resignedly to his cousin Bess on 28 March 1822, 'You will be sorry for the appointment, <u>perhaps</u> – but I am sure you will be glad to know that it passed in the most satisfactory manner God bless you. G.C.'

But Canning never went to India. Lord Hastings delayed his return and Canning had not yet sailed for India when news came that Castlereagh had committed suicide. What led him to do this may have been the same mental instability that had led him 13 years earlier to challenge a colleague to a duel; certainly it is ironic that the two most extraordinary actions in Castlereagh's life were responsible both for displacing Canning as Foreign Secretary and for restoring him to that office 13 years later. In a sense the second event cancelled out the first: if Castlereagh had not died when he did, just before Canning boarded his ship for India, their duel would have had far greater consequences for England and the world.

Liverpool was determined to have Canning as Castlereagh's successor despite the King's threats to dismiss the whole government rather than accept him. Canning was genuinely reluctant; he had made up his mind to go to India, and as he told Granville (25 August), 'Ten years have taken away all that was desirable, and ... almost the desire itself.' The peace settlement had been made, the important decisions taken. However, when Liverpool offered him 'the whole heritage' – being Leader of the House as well as Foreign Secretary – he felt he must accept. The King's violent objections were only overcome by Wellington persuading him that the 'private honour' of a gentleman (George affected to believe that Canning had had an affair with his wife) mattered less than the royal prerogative of exercising 'mercy and grace' – a well-judged appeal to the 'First Gentleman of Europe' that allowed Canning to kiss hands and become His Majesty's Secretary of State.

The Opposition, afraid that Canning might steal their Whig clothes, deplored Castlereagh's loss. Brougham remarked, 'Put all their men in one scale together, and poor Castlereagh in the other – single, he plainly weighed them down. ... Also, he was a gentleman, and the only one amongst them.' The equally radical Byron, on the other hand, not being a politician, pronounced that 'Canning is a genius; and no man of talent can pursue the path of his predecessor'. The immediate matter for his attention was the Congress that had been planned for Vienna but was instead to meet at Verona. Castlereagh had intended to attend in person, so Wellington went instead (it may be that Bathurst asked him before the new Foreign Secretary was in place), and Canning confirmed the instructions that Castlereagh had prepared for himself.

The Congress was expected to concentrate on Greece, where a nationalist uprising the previous year had massacred 6,000 Turks and the Sultan had retaliated by nailing a quantity of Greek ears to the door of his seraglio, hanging the Patriarch of Constantinople and sending a Turkish force to massacre thousands of Greeks at Chios (Byron had been a little unkind to Castlereagh, who had after all made a strong formal protest to the Sultan). But it was not Greece but Spain that unexpectedly took up most of the Congress's time. Wellington was in full agreement with Canning that there should be no foreign intervention to help the absolutist King Ferdinand against the Constitutionalists, but nonetheless he found Verona a very frustrating experience. He was not feeling well. Just before he set off he had been at a review of artillery and stood too close to a howitzer when it fired. That deafened him, and he went to Dr Stevenson, an ear specialist, whose 'cure' was a caustic solution that caused agonizing pain and loss of balance. But the undaunted Duke set off for Vienna (making his first voyage in a steam packet), only to find that the conference was now being held at Verona, where he had nothing to do except reiterate that Britain was against intervention in Spain. At least, that is not strictly true. Metternich, ever eager to find diversions for any delegate who might prove awkward, introduced the Duke to Napoleon's wife, the Empress Marie Louise, and the two of them got on very well.

On his way home Wellington stopped in Paris and flattered himself that he had managed to dissuade the French from invading Spain. Canning was sceptical, and, annoyingly for Wellington, was proved right when the French did in fact invade. To rub salt into the wound, against all the Duke's confident military predictions the French had no difficulty in marching straight into Madrid. The Spanish people had resisted to the death Napoleon's armies bringing liberty and enlightenment, but welcomed with open arms the Duc d'Angoulême's army coming to restore the authority of Church and King.

The French success put Canning in a difficult position. Either he would have to go to war to uphold the Constitutionalists against the absolutist Bourbon King Ferdinand, or accept that Spain would become a satellite of Bourbon France. His opponents, both in the Opposition and within the cabinet, were not displeased to see Canning discomforted, but his response took the wind out of their sails. Rather than try by threats or diplomacy to get the French to withdraw, Canning sent a naval squadron to the West Indies to protect British commerce, on the grounds that Spain was no longer capable of doing so because it no longer had control of its colonies which were in revolt. Canning had realized that Spain without the wealth of the Indies was no asset to France, but would become a burden instead. As he told Wellington on 25 September 1823, 'I am morally convinced that if France is allowed to get a way in Spanish America, not only will our ministry be overturned, and I think deservedly, but the reputation of this country will be irretrievably lowered.' Wellington disagreed: he did not want to offend France or the other powers of the Holy Alliance, and from then on he mistrusted Canning and unfortunately tried to influence the King against him.

This was made easier because George IV was also Elector of Hanover and could therefore correspond with Metternich via the Hanoverian minister Hardenberg behind the cabinet's back. Princess Lieven, wife of the Austrian ambassador in London, who loved a plot, entered eagerly into the conspiracy (though before long Canning managed to charm her into being one of his supporters). When Canning found proof of what he suspected was happening, he confronted the King, who had to back down. Canning handled George IV very astutely, using a judicious mixture of cajolery and flattery tempered with firmness, and before long turned the King from an enemy into an ally. He also persuaded the cabinet to agree to recognize the independence of the old Spanish colonies of Mexico, Colombia and Buenos Aires – Chile and Peru were still fighting Spanish armies – a remarkable achievement, since Canning's only real ally in the cabinet (until Huskisson joined it) was the Prime Minister himself. Liverpool good naturedly complained that Canning 'never came to an interview or a cabinet without bringing his resignation in his pocket'. To a greater or lesser extent, all the rest of the cabinet suspected Canning (with some reason) of being dangerously 'liberale'.

Wellington felt particularly aggrieved because it was only thanks to him that the King had agreed to Canning rejoining the government, and now here he was pursuing these dreadful liberal policies and presuming to think he knew more about Europe than the Duke did. The Duke's hostility to Canning is understandable, if mistaken. During the war they had both been on the same side politically, as they had both supported the war while the Opposition thought Britain should sue for peace. But in the 1820s the political divide was between 'liberals' wanting reform of the corn laws, Catholic emancipation and total abolition of the slave trade on the one hand, and conservatives anxious to uphold the existing order and the rule of law at a time of dangerous discontent among the labouring classes. Moreover, Wellington's reputation and his position as virtual governor of occupied France had made him a very great man indeed on the European stage, making it difficult for him now to accept that Canning might be able to deal with foreign affairs better than he could.

Canning's announcement of his South American policy to the House of Commons would have done nothing towards conciliating opponents. 'I called the New World into existence to redress the balance of the old,' he famously declared. It is a measure of his success with the King that he was allowed to present the new South American envoys at the court of St James (although 'liberale though I am,' he told Joan, he felt some qualms as he presented the 'cocoa-coloured' envoys to His Majesty). But recognizing those ex-colonies was undoubtedly a master-stroke. It give Britain a commercial advantage in South America that lasted until the world wars of the twentieth century wiped out her overseas investments. It also held the French in check, and for over a hundred years restrained the United States from dominating the countries of South America (a domination that since 1945 has not always been to the advantage of their inhabitants).

But the Spanish colonies were not the only ones that Canning had to deal with. Portugal, too, was in crisis. King John, who had sailed to Brazil in 1808 to escape Soult's invading army, had still not returned. The Regency at Lisbon was so corrupt that in 1820 Beresford – who had stayed on as commander-in-chief of the Portuguese army after the war – sailed to Rio and tried to persuade the King to return. He failed, and when he got back to Portugal found the country in turmoil, all his British officers arrested and he himself not allowed to land. It had fallen to Castlereagh to handle the crisis, which he did calmly and firmly, saying that unless the royal family returned he would have to 'reconsider' Britain's treaty obligations (which were vague, dating back to medieval times, but important to Portugal). King John duly returned, and accepted a Constitution, but the Assembly then tried, to Castlereagh's irritation, to bring Brazil (where the King's eldest son Don Pedro was in charge) back under their own control. When Canning took office the Assembly was demanding a British force to deter the French army in Spain from invading Portugal. Canning replied (as Castlereagh would probably have done) that Britain was ready to *defend* Portugal, but would not send troops unless any attack had taken place. In the diplomatic wrangling that ensued Canning was handicapped by Thornton, British Minister in Lisbon (whom Canning called 'that henpecked diplomat'), being no match for the Frenchman Hyde de Neuville. Thornton fell in with the suggestion of asking the Holy Alliance to mediate and Canning had to repudiate and recall him. Canning then sent a naval squadron to the Tagus, and that did the trick; he was fully alive to the persuasive force of the Royal

Navy, and realized that a frigate or a squadron was both more powerful and less provocative than a battalion or two of troops (which were not available anyway). First with Spain and Portugal and later with Greece, quiet use of sea power proved far more effective than diplomacy backed by sabre-rattling. Palmerston is often thought of as the great exponent of gunboat diplomacy, but Palmerston was a political disciple of Canning; and although 'gunboat diplomacy' has got a bad name, it could be used for good purposes. Canning wanted Britain to have strong influence in Brazil, and backed Don Pedro's bid for independence partly for commercial reasons (as with the Spanish colonies), but also in order to stop the slave trade. In 1822, 20,483 slaves were shipped to Rio from Africa, of which 1,288 died en route; by 1823 the numbers had gone up to 29,211 and 2,499 respectively; gunboat diplomacy was not always a bad thing. (Incidentally, Canning was unofficially assisted by Lord Cochrane, the model for Captain Aubrey in Patrick O'Brian's series of nautical novels, who was in command of Don Pedro's navy.) And since Don Pedro was the son and heir of the King of Portugal, recognizing the independence of Brazil did not upset Metternich; he had been furious over the recognition of the Spanish colonies, but recognizing Don Pedro as ruler of Brazil did not contravene the principle of 'legitimacy'.

The third, and most tortuous, problem facing Canning was the Greek struggle for independence.[9] There was a general feeling that the Ottoman Empire was crumbling, and for some time Russia had been encroaching on the Danubian Principalities – the eastern Balkans including today's Romania. The Greek revolt of 1821 had led to the massacre of thousands of Turks, and the new Sultan, Mahmoud II, had retaliated by massacring even more Greeks than they had massacred Turks. Mahmoud's ferocity had provoked a strong protest from Castlereagh, and when Canning became Foreign Secretary he praised the British Minister in Constantinople, Lord Strangford, for persuading the Sultan to show more restraint and open up the Bosphorus to Russian shipping. But at the same time, Canning recognized the Greeks as belligerents, as that gave the Royal Navy a legal justification for policing the Aegean and protecting British shipping – something the Turks lacked the power or will to do.

All the Western powers, including Britain, felt ambivalent about 'the Eastern Question'. Turkish brutality and oppression of Christians was repugnant to them, yet the last thing they wanted was for Russia rather than the Ottoman Empire to control the Balkans. But in the case of the Greeks, familiarity with the classics combined with Christian sentiment to make educated people in the West instinctively sympathetic to their struggle for independence from Muslim rule. Byron's espousal of the cause, and his death at Missalonghi, put

British public opinion firmly on the side of Greece – even Lord Eldon of all people contributed £100 to the Greek Committee that had been formed. Canning supported the Greeks, not because he wanted them to gain complete independence from the Sultan, but as a lever to persuade the Sultan to grant virtual independence while retaining his nominal suzerainty; he was acutely aware that if the Ottoman Empire started to fall apart Russia might fill the resulting vacuum, and whoever controlled Greece would control the eastern Mediterranean and threaten communications with India.

At the end of 1825 the Emperor Alexander died and (after a rival claimant had been removed) was succeeded by Nicholas. Canning asked Wellington to go to St Petersburg to offer congratulations to the new Tsar, but not to get involved in any diplomacy. But sending the Duke off to Russia without any instructions put him in a difficult position: he was prevailed upon to sign a protocol that went further than he realized or Canning intended, as it implied that Britain was prepared to join France and Russia in using force against the Sultan unless he granted their demands. Back in London, meanwhile, the intriguing (in both senses of the word) Princess Lieven told Canning that the Sultan had encouraged his Egyptian satrap Ibraham Pasha to invade Greece, evict the Greek population and re-people the country with Muslims. Canning still hoped to save Greece without a war, 'through the agency of the Russian name upon the fears of Turks' (i.e. the threat that Russia would declare war if the Sultan did not restrain Ibraham), but the time it took to communicate between London and St Petersburg was making for confusion all round – Lord Strangford in St Petersburg received a strong rebuke for exceeding his instructions, which he greatly resented.

In the end, the protocol that Wellington had signed led 18 months later to a treaty between France, Russia and Britain to protect the Greeks from Turkish and Egyptian oppression. Wellington said, 'I did everything I could to prevail upon Mr Canning not to enter into the Treaty, but blame myself and the rest of the Cabinet for not stopping it.' He had signed the protocol without realizing its implication as he had not been properly briefed, and thought that Canning had tricked him. This was not the case, but once the protocol had been signed the resultant treaty was inevitable. On the same day (6 July 1827) that it was signed, Canning (by then Prime Minister) received a despatch from Stratford Canning, who had succeeded Strangford as ambassador in Constantinople, reporting that his best efforts to get Turkey to accept British mediation had failed. The final denouement came in October: an Anglo-French naval force under Admiral Codrington had been sent to stop Ibraham from supplying his forces on the Greek mainland, and after weeks of naval manoeuvring and political parleying Codrington led the combined fleet into Navarin Harbour where the Turkish fleet was at anchor. He ordered that 'no shot may be fired before a given signal, so that it may be the Turks who open fire'; but the provocation was too great. The Turks fired on an English sloop, and the massive retaliation from the Anglo-French fleet destroyed Ibraham's navy. This action was not what Canning had planned, but the result – Greek independence from both Turkey and Russia – was exactly what he had wanted, although by the time the battle was fought Canning was dead.

Six months earlier, Lord Liverpool had suffered a stroke, and it soon became clear that he must resign. His successor had to be Wellington or Canning, and to the Duke's fury (exacerbated it must be said by tactlessness on Canning's part) the King chose Canning. Wellington refused to serve under him, partly from pique (he also resigned quite unnecessarily from his post of commander-in-chief, provoking a caricature depicting him as Achilles sulking in his tent), but also because Canning's policy over Spain and Portugal had been far too radical for his liking. The other ultra-conservatives in the cabinet also refused to serve under Canning, with the result that his short-lived ministry – the King asked him to form a government in April and he died in August – broke the mould of British politics. The only members of the old cabinet to stay on under Canning were Huskisson, Wynn, Harrowby and Bexley, while junior ministers included the ex-Foxite Tierney and the future Whig Foreign Secretary Palmerston. History books may say that Canning's was a Tory government, but in fact it was much more like Lord Grey's Whig ministry than those of Wellington or Peel. Certainly the nations of Europe were in no doubt that the new British Prime Minister was a champion of liberty – or, as Metternich would put it, a dangerous radical; the Greek Archbishop told the Russian diplomat Capo d'Istria (25 May 1827), who was Greek by birth, that 'the new English government is for nations in general and not for Aristocracy alone'.

☙

But how much difference would it have made if Canning and not Castlereagh had been at the helm during the post-war years? A politician's outlook is determined by external events as well as by inward conviction; both Canning and Castlereagh had been all for Fox and liberty until the Jacobin terror in Paris made them change their views. Similarly, events in Spain in 1820 led Castlereagh to change his mind about the value of the Congress system – and by the same token, if Canning had been Foreign Secretary in 1814 he might have decided (as Castlereagh in fact did) that the peace of Europe would be best served by its rulers meeting together regularly. There is no doubt that the duel did affect the course of history, but it is impossible to guess exactly how things might have turned out if that encounter on Putney Heath had never taken place. The best verdict on the respective merits of the two Foreign Secretaries is perhaps that given by Professor Temperley, who deplores

> the tedious and unworthy dispute about the respective merits of Castlereagh and Canning. During the most crucial years of the nineteenth century these two men guided the destinies of England. If the one possessed constructive qualities, serene steadfastness, and cosmopolitan detachment, the other had infinite resource, intellectual imagination and a hitherto unexampled power of national and popular appeal. Both men, though in different ways, rendered immortal services to their country. It should be enough to remember that [their] two bodies lie at the foot of the grave of Pitt, whom both men acknowledged as their model and their master.[10]

CHAPTER 12

Death Comes To Us All

C anning's premiership might have lasted much longer than it did had
his health held up. As he himself had recognized when he wrote what
he thought would be a valedictory letter to Joan the night before the
duel, Canning was apt to 'feel, and fret, and lament, and hate, and despise'.
Intelligence and sensitivity are valuable gifts, but they can come at a price
– Canning was a worrier. In addition, his health had never been very robust:
he caught colds easily, and when he had one it usually hit him hard. As his
near-fatal illness during his first year as an MP proved, he was not someone
who could just ignore a cold and carry on normally until it went away. Nor was
his digestion all that good: he had learned that he could not afford to drink as
freely as many of his contemporaries without ill effects, while turtle dinners
had long since ceased to be a pleasure and had become an ordeal.

Early in 1827 the Duke of York died, and his funeral took place at Windsor
in bitter January weather. The coffin arrived at St George's Chapel nearly two
hours late, during which time the assembled dignitaries had to stand in icy
cold on wet flagstones. As a result many of them caught colds; the only actual
fatality was the Bishop of Lincoln, but as Canning wrote after the funeral
to Wellington (who like himself was quite seriously ill after the ordeal), 'I
presume that ... whoever filched the cloth or the matting from under our feet
in the aisle, had bets or insurances against the lives of the Cabinet.' [1] Canning's
cold seems to have developed into pneumonia. His aunt Hitty Canning, who
now lived at Clewer, offered to put him up for the night after the funeral, but
one of the Canons of Windsor, Mr Long, had already 'promised him a bed near
him at Mr Stopford's'. Unfortunately Canon Stopford's house 'had not lately
been occupied. I feared it must be cold and damp and that GC would probably
suffer from it. Next day his indisposition was announced in the papers. I then
had no doubt of the cause, actually the house was so forlorn that there was not
a pen and ink in it, he was obliged to send out for one.' [2]

175

Not long afterwards, whether or not as a result of the Duke of York's disastrous funeral, Lord Liverpool had a stroke, and although he made a partial recovery it was soon clear that he had to resign. George IV was both a weak man and a vain one; he seems to have made the most of this opportunity to exercise real authority, since it was the royal prerogative to decide who to ask to form a new government. The choice had to lie between Wellington, with his immense reputation and strong support from ultra-conservatives, and Canning, who was able to manage the Commons. The King invited both men to stay at Windsor, and apparently gave the impression that he would choose Wellington; but when the house party set out for an afternoon carriage drive, the King changed the seating plan at the last minute and asked Canning to go in his carriage, and then asked him to try and form a government. However, George does not seem to have made his decision generally known. When Canning wrote to ask if Wellington would be willing to serve in the new government, the Duke wrote back asking who would be Prime Minister. Canning (exasperatedly? maliciously? deliberately? carelessly?) replied tersely that he understood that when the King asked someone to form a government, he meant that person to be at its head. As we have seen, Wellington, angry and insulted, then had a fit of the sulks (just as he had 18 years earlier when the fruits of his victory at Vimeiro were thrown away by Generals Dalrymple and Burrard). Not only did he refuse to serve under Canning, but he even resigned from the non-political post of commander-in-chief.

Perhaps Canning might have handled the Duke more tactfully and patiently had he not been suffering from the after-effects of pneumonia. As it was, he had to form a government against considerable opposition when he was still not fit. The strain of being Prime Minister and being sniped at viciously both by the 'ultras' (right-wing conservatives) and by the Opposition hurt him a great deal – even at the best of times he was prone, as we have seen, to 'feel, and fret, and lament, and hate, and despise'. Lord Grey made some particularly vicious personal attacks that got under his skin and which, combined with the work and worry of forming a government, managing the House of Commons and continuing to direct foreign policy through Lord Dudley, the new Foreign Secretary, took a heavy toll on his health. He left Downing Street at the end of July to stay at the Duke of Devonshire's house at Chiswick, where he was almost immediately taken severely ill. The symptoms suggest that it may have been cancer. On 5 August he told Stapleton that if all the pain he had undergone during his whole life were collected together it would not amount to one hundredth part of what he had suffered during the previous three days. Fortunately for him, his mind then started to wander, the pain abated, and shortly before 4 am on Wednesday 8 August 1827 George Canning died, in the same room in which Charles Fox had died 21 years earlier. Lord Dudley wrote that 'what really killed him was fatigue. He died of overwork just as much as any poor horse that drops down dead in the road.'

Canning's aunt Hitty, who with her husband had been entirely responsible for his upbringing from the age of six until he went to university, was a staunch Whig and had seen her nephew's desertion of Fox for 'that monster Pitt' as apostasy. But in her letter to her daughter after Canning's death – by then she was an old lady of 78 – she wrote, 'I truly believe that the ambition of him whom we now lament, was of the purest and most virtuous kind, and that his first wish was to promote the prosperity and happiness of the Country, and the next to improve the moral and religious character of the people.' The public reaction to Canning's death was much the same: after his funeral, *The Times* reported that 'regret was exhibited in the conduct of the assembled multitude yesterday more strongly and intensely than, we believe, was witnessed at the death of any subject within the memory of the oldest person now living.' Canning's death also caused a fall on the Paris bourse and dismay to liberals all over Europe. Metternich rejoiced, but paid the reluctant tribute that it was 'an immense event, for the man was a whole revolution in himself alone'.

℘

Castlereagh's death had taken place almost exactly five years earlier, in August 1822. He was only 53 years old, whereas Canning lived to the age of 57. Both events took people by surprise, but in retrospect Canning's death was not very surprising. For the last five years he had been driving himself very hard – he himself complained that the double burden of being Foreign Secretary and Leader of an often recalcitrant Commons was too much for any man, and since becoming Prime Minister in April the burden of work and worry had become even heavier. Castlereagh's death, or rather why he was driven to commit suicide, seemed inexplicable even after the event. Montgomery Hyde's account of it is entitled *The Strange Death of Lord Castlereagh*;[3] and strange it certainly was. What could have driven so calm and self-possessed a man to commit suicide when less than a month earlier he had been displaying confident mastery of the House of Commons?

There is good evidence that for some months before his death Castlereagh's health had been causing concern. For example, in May, Lady Conyngham, the King's mistress, had tried to prevent Lady Castlereagh from being invited to a banquet for the King of Denmark. Princess Lieven persuaded her to drop her objection so as to avoid a public row, but she then rather tactlessly told

Castlereagh what she had done and he exploded in 'a paroxysm of rage'. It was not surprising that he should have hotly resented the attempted slight to Emily, but Lieven was astonished at the violence of his reaction; his rage was very much out of character. (After Castlereagh's death Princess Lieven said she thought that Emily had long realized that her husband had been behaving strangely, but had loyally covered up for him – adding, perhaps rather spitefully, that Emily did not want anything to get in the way of their projected trip to Vienna to which she had been much looking forward.)

Much more worrying than that uncharacteristic burst of anger described by Lieven in May was an incident early in July. Castlereagh was asked a parliamentary question about an English ship that had been captured by a Spaniard, and replied that this was the first he had heard of it, and he 'would be obliged to any hon. Member who could acquaint him of it'. His reply would have seemed perfectly normal, but for the fact that the incident was such a cause célèbre that it was inconceivable that the Foreign Secretary had been unaware of it. Something was certainly very much amiss.

In August it became clear beyond doubt that Castlereagh's mind was seriously deranged. At an audience with the King to take his leave before going to the Congress in Vienna, his manner and conversation was alarming: according to one account he said that the King was 'his enemy'. When the King mentioned the forthcoming Congress, Castlereagh said, 'The time has come to say goodbye to Europe. You and I have known Europe, and together we have saved her, there is no one after me left with any understanding of continental affairs,' and he ended the interview by saying 'between sobs ... I know I am mad. I have known it for some time, but no one has any idea of it.' The source for some of this is again Princess Lieven who is not totally reliable, but we do also know that on his way out from his audience someone politely said, 'So you propose leaving us for the Congress?', and Castlereagh replied, 'Propose? So you are in the conspiracy against me, to prevent me going.' He was also convinced that the Duke of Wellington, his greatest friend and supporter in the government, was plotting against him.

The King was so concerned that he wrote to Castlereagh, saying that he was 'so uneasy at the state of feverishness under which you were labouring this morning' that he wished him to see his own doctor, Bankhead, or the court physician Sir William Knighton 'before you return to the country'. Wellington, equally troubled, called at St James's Square and found Castlereagh terrified by some real or imaginary visitor and displaying all the signs of paranoia: cellars searched, windows barred against intruders. He said he was being blackmailed. Apparently he had sometimes visited a brothel on his way home from parliament and on one occasion, so he told Wellington, a prostitute had revealed 'herself' as a man and then other people arrived and threatened him with exposure. Whether this was true, or simply the figment of an inflamed imagination, is uncertain. Montgomery Hyde thinks Castlereagh really was being blackmailed, but Wellington told Lord Liverpool some years after the event that in his considered opinion Castlereagh had imagined the whole thing. This is quite likely, since everyone had been talking about the recent conviction of the Bishop of Clogher for buggery, a shocking case that could well have preyed on the mind of a man who was suffering from a persecution complex at the time.

After his visit to St James's Square Wellington told Arbuthnot, the Chief Whip, that Castlereagh was 'in a state of mental delusion'. Emily had already gone down to their country house at Cray, and her husband joined her there on Friday 10 August. Dr Bankhead went down the next day and took the precaution of removing any knives or sharp implements that Castlereagh could use to do himself harm, but unfortunately a small razor escaped his notice. Early in the morning of Monday 12 August, while Emily was out of their bedroom for just for a few seconds before the housemaid who had been summoned arrived, her husband used the razor he had hidden to cut his own throat.

The shock and grief of those who knew him was intense. The public reaction was, predictably, mixed. Byron, the radical idealist, was brutal:

So, *He* has cut his throat at last – He? Who?
The man who cut his country's long ago.

The funeral, at Emily's request, took place at Westminster Abbey. Unlike Canning's funeral, when *The Times* would report that 'regret was exhibited' by the crowd 'more strongly and intensely than, we believe, was witnessed at the death of any subject within [living memory]', Castlereagh's coffin was booed and hissed when being carried into the Abbey before the funeral. This has been taken simply as an indication of Castlereagh's unpopularity, which, as we have seen, he had incurred as a result of having had to commend the repressive measures of Lords Sidmouth and Eldon to the House of Commons. It seems, however, that the main reason for hissing the coffin was that people disapproved of a suicide being afforded a Christian burial. The coroner at the inquest (which took place in the house where Castlereagh had died – the jury being taken upstairs to view the body as it lay) had been at pains to secure a verdict of suicide 'while of unsound mind'. This was partly to enable the burial to take place in consecrated ground, especially in view of Emily's desire for a Westminster Abbey funeral, but the same verdict would surely have been given in any case. Suicide 'while of unsound mind' was an accurate description of what had happened; the only doubt about Castlereagh's suicide is not 'was he really of unsound mind?', but what exactly was the 'unsoundness'?

Various suggestions have been put forward. An article in *The Practitioner* of February 1970 entitled 'The Psychiatric Illness of Lord Castlereagh'[4] suggests that he 'suffered from involutional depression', and points to the death of his father Lord Londonderry in the spring of 1821 as the 'precipitating factor'. (Optimistically, the author claims that 'today Castlereagh's illness would be diagnosed readily and easily, the treatment would probably take three to six weeks and the prognosis ... should have been good'.) But the death of his septuagenarian father is unlikely to have precipitated any mental breakdown on Castlereagh's part. Had it been Emily, or even his brother Charles, who had died, then it might have affected him badly, but his father had reached a very ripe old age for those days and his death certainly did not come as a shock. The only reason for suggesting Lord Londonderry's death as a 'precipitating factor' is that it happened to occur at about the time when symptoms of Castlereagh's mental decay were starting to become obvious.

Long before the last couple of years of Castlereagh's life, though, there had been puzzling episodes that with hindsight can be seen as foreshadowing the eventual decline. In 1801 he was laid low for several weeks, and Cornwallis felt concerned because there were no obvious and treatable symptoms. 'I have been, and indeed am still,' he wrote, 'very uneasy about Lord C. who has had a return of his fever. They tell me there is no danger, but I have never heard of a fever of so long continuance without danger.' In 1807, when Castlereagh was Secretary of State for War at the height of the Napoleonic Wars, an unexplained but serious illness again laid him low, leaving the War Department leaderless. There was also a prolonged bout of acute depression in 1814 while he was in Paris; that could have been due to weariness and a sense of anti-climax when peace came at last after two anxious and strenuous years of hard work, but his friends had been concerned because he seemed so morbid. Once at a dinner party he enquired diligently of a doctor who was present where the carotid artery was (the one that he cut, fatally, seven years later). And for the last three or four years of Castlereagh's life, people began to notice warning signals that he was less physically robust and less mentally alert than usual. This too could be put down simply to overwork, since being both Foreign Secretary and Leader of the House of Commons was, as Canning later complained, enough to undermine any man's health. But – again with hindsight – it can be seen as a warning sign of what was to come.

But the real clue to Castlereagh's bouts of illness, and to his eventual suicide, is something that happened much earlier in his life. In the autumn of 1787, at the start of his second year at Cambridge, he was confined to his rooms by 'indisposition' for almost the whole Michaelmas term, and became unwell again in the New Year. This illness at first seemed inexplicable, like those later ones in 1801 and 1807, but a letter to young Robert Stewart from his step-grandfather, Lord Camden, reveals the cause. On 8 January 1788 Camden had written:

> I am very much concerned to know you have been so long indisposed … by your unlucky illness … [you must] quit College and change the scene, as I am sure no Medicine … can be so effectual for the establishment of your health. … Order a Post Chaise and come directly and don't let the term business detain you for a moment.

In other words, like Cornwallis 13 years later, Camden was worried because it seemed a mystery illness. But then Camden heard from his eldest son Lord Bayham who was at Cambridge, and his report put an entirely new light on Robert's illness. Accordingly, Camden wrote a second letter to his grandson on 16 January:

> My dear Rob, It is very unlucky that your present distress, which cannot be directly acknowledged before the women, and so has driven you into a solitary lodging; a circumstance that I lament more than the disorder itself, which by Bayham's account is in the fairest way of soon being cured. I am glad however to find your illness of your own [?deserving? devising?] and not constitutional.

An illness that 'cannot be directly acknowledged before the women' can only mean some form of venereal disease. This could explain not only his two subsequent 'mystery' illnesses and his eventual suicide, but also various mood swings that seem out of character for such a normally self-possessed person. For example, in 1798 he arrested Teeling with absolutely no warning at the end of a friendly morning ride, then, that same evening, entertained him to a convivial dinner, immediately after which he had Teeling imprisoned without trial for so long that it nearly killed him. That was behaviour more suited to a capricious and sadistic oriental potentate than to a man who prided himself, with some reason, on behaving like a gentleman.

Then, as we have seen, the duel of 1809 undoubtedly shows an irrational pattern of behaviour. If Castlereagh had felt his honour affronted, why delay so long before issuing his challenge? And why frame it in the form of that long, rambling and increasingly indignant letter justifying his own conduct and condemning Canning's? Why, since he was a crack shot, did his first shot miss entirely? If he had deliberately fired wide, why did he insist on a second shot (that very nearly proved fatal) against the advice of Lord Yarmouth, his second? Had Yarmouth been fighting a duel he might well have missed the first time, since he was sufficiently debauched for his aim to be erratic, and have insisted on a second shot, since he was sufficiently unprincipled to use a duel as a way of getting away with murder. But that explanation will not do for Castlereagh: calculated, cold-blooded murder was quite out of character for him.

The reader may well ask why, if some form of venereal disease was really affecting Castlereagh all his adult life, has this not been recognized long ago? The answer is simple. Hyde's *The Rise of Castlereagh* reproduces the letters from Camden about his grandson's illness, but omits the crucial sentence saying that the illness 'cannot be directly acknowledged before the women' (i.e. it was venereal disease). This is very understandable. Hyde was reading Castlereagh's private correspondence sitting in the library of Mount Stewart,[5] and he wrote his book *The Rise of Castlereagh* in the 1930s. At that time any writer would have drawn a veil over the nature of Castlereagh's 'indisposition', because to have accused him of having contracted venereal disease would have seemed a mean slur on the reputation of a great statesman. Today, 70 years later, we not only know more about the way that syphilis can affect behaviour, but also how common it was in the eighteenth and nineteenth centuries. For example, Deborah Hayden points out that in the nineteenth and early twentieth century syphilis 'was life's dark secret'.[6] It is hardly ever explicitly mentioned in memoirs, biographies or even medical records of famous nineteenth- and twentieth-century figures, yet (as Hayden shows) anyone who is alert to pick out the clues can diagnose syphilis in a great many famous men.

It would in fact have been by no means uncommon for any undergraduate to contract syphilis in the 1780s, and the fact that Castlereagh did so does not mark him out as unusually naughty or depraved. It is reckoned that in most European cities some 15 per cent of the population probably suffered from syphilis, and a university town such as Cambridge, with its large proportion of young men, would if anything have had a higher than average rate of incidence. (Incidentally, Castlereagh's mother may well have inherited syphilis; her family were certainly eccentric, and she had a stillbirth as her second child, something that was frequently caused by that disease.)

Castlereagh's own medical history, so far as it is known, would entirely bear out the hypothesis that he had acquired syphilis during his late teens (a detailed medical account of the probable effects of this undergraduate illness is given in Appendix 1). As a boy he seems to have been robust and healthy, except for concern during his time at Armagh Royal School that he seemed delicate and was 'wasted in the left arm by an issue long previously applied'.[7] Minor injuries – or, come to that, failure to treat some minor wound – would not have been surprising at Armagh School, and any damage that might have been noticed in his arm does not seem to have been permanent. For example, General Napier 'had often been engaged with him in athletic sports, pitching the stone or bar, and looked upon him as what indeed he was, a model of quiet grace and strength combined'.[8] Evidently Castlereagh was far from being a delicate boy once he had left Armagh School; the first sign that his health gave any cause for anxiety was that illness during the Michaelmas term of 1787 at Cambridge, which flared up again more briefly in the New Year.

These two bouts of illness correspond exactly with what would be expected to occur during the primary and secondary stages of syphilis. The third (tertiary) stage of this disease can produce a variety of symptoms, mental or physical, which may take anything from two to 40 years to become noticeable, perhaps with quite long periods of remission in between. Only when the disease is reaching its climax do the symptoms become obvious; it usually takes between ten and 20 years for this stage to be reached, but it could take as long as 40 years. In Castlereagh's case 35 years elapsed between his illness at Cambridge and his eventual suicide.

The two 'unexplained' illnesses of 1801 and 1807 certainly match what would be expected during the semi-dormant tertiary stage of syphilitic meningitis.[9] The 1801 illness was described as 'brain fever', and during the 1807 illness Emily noted 'increasing debility' (whether she meant physical – perhaps a loss of libido – or mental is not clear; perhaps both).

Uncharacteristic or irrational behaviour, such as Castlereagh exhibited over the duel (including the wording of that 'extraordinary document', his challenge), together with a lack of judgement and self-control, suggests a degree of paranoia that would be consistent with the tertiary stage of neurosyphilis. Similarly, for a reputed crack shot to miss the first time and only wing his man with the second shot suggests incipient physical incoordination, which again would be consistent with neurosyphilis. Any such mental derangement or physical incoordination is not easy to spot, because those whose brains are thus affected can often disguise the fact, rather as a hardened toper can usually make sensible conversation and perform routine actions satisfactorily, but be unable to cope with the unexpected. He or she could, for instance, drive home along a familiar route quite steadily, but be completely floored by an unexpected road diversion sign.

In Castlereagh's case, such ability to disguise symptoms could explain several aspects of his career that on the face of it seem puzzling. As Secretary of State he did brilliantly in establishing a successful system of army recruitment, as this was something he had been thinking about for a long time. However, when it came to war strategy, which by its nature is at the mercy of unexpected events – victories, defeats and the weather – Castlereagh made surprising blunders. Admittedly Canning was hyper-critical, but the fact that virtually all the cabinet took it for granted in 1809 that Castlereagh was not up to his work at the War Office cannot simply be ignored. One can argue the rights and wrongs of his handling of the Convention of Cintra or his failure to control or supersede Moore, but the Walcheren Expedition was a most extraordinary military bungle for even a British government to make. Castlereagh's original plan, for a diversionary attack in northern Europe to take the pressure off Austria, was sensible enough, and what might be expected from a disciple of Pitt. But once having got that plan into his head, Castlereagh was incapable of modifying it in the light of new developments – Wellington's unexpected success in the Peninsula, and the overwhelming naval and military opinion that the Walcheren plan was impracticable. Castlereagh was behaving very like the drunk driving home, who, when faced with a diversion sign, simply ignores it and drives into the roadworks. Of course his mishandling of Walcheren is not evidence of his having neurosyphilis, but it is uncannily consistent with the tertiary symptoms of that disease.

Castlereagh's illness came to its climax very much as one would expect in a case of tertiary neurosyphilis. There were bouts of rage, as with Princess Lieven in May 1822, and curious instances of forgetfulness. Particularly telling was that incident in the House of Commons when Castlereagh said he had no idea that a British ship had been seized by Spaniards; for that is a classic example of an ability to cover up failure of memory or mental grasp unless anything unexpected crops up. His calm and unruffled confession of ignorance, and request that any member who knew of the affair would inform him, displayed all his usual mastery when dealing with questions in the House; no one present that day could have guessed that the Foreign Secretary had in any way lost his grip, were it not that the incident happened to be such a *cause célèbre* that he simply *must* have heard about it.

The fact that symptoms of this disease are so hard to spot explains why, right to the end of his life, even such a close friend as Mrs Arbuthnot noticed nothing amiss about Castlereagh's behaviour. She continued to speak of his 'remarkably fine commanding figure, very fine dark eyes ... smile sweeter than it is possible to describe ... benevolent and amiable expression of his countenance ... and air of dignity and nobleness such as I have never seen in any other person ... manners perfect as those of a high-born polished gentle-man.' There must be several leading politicians of the eighteenth and nine-teenth centuries whose behaviour only seems bizarre when one is alert to possible symptoms of neurosyphilis – after all, a cynic might say that all politi-cians at times behave so crassly that it is impossible to say when they are clearly 'of unsound mind'. One politician whose mental degeneration is generally acknowledged to be a result of syphilis is Lord Randolph Churchill (and to his eternal credit Mr Gladstone always made a point of being in the House to hear his speeches even when they became embarrassingly incoherent). It is unlikely that Lord Randolph and Castlereagh were the only public men to suffer from this disease in the nineteenth century, and when we consider the sexual *mores* of many cabinet ministers today it would be invidious to single out Castlereagh for blame because he had, in the words of Lord Camden, succumbed to 'the indiscretions of a young man'. After all, Castlereagh's marriage was a loving relationship that endured to the end, and there is no evidence that he was considered a libertine. Even those who deplored his politics and thought little of his ability saw much to admire in him; the worst that Creevey could bring himself to say was that 'by experience, good manners, and great courage, he managed a corrupt House of Commons pretty well, and with some address. This is the whole of his intellectual merit. He had limited understanding and no knowledge.' And Charles Greville wrote after Castlereagh's death, 'He is a great loss to his party ... to his country I think he is none. ... I believed he was considered one of the best Managers of the House of Commons who ever sat in it ... [having] good taste, good humour, and agreeable manners.' Brougham, very much a political opponent, wrote, 'he was a gentleman, and the only one' in the cabinet.

‿

The duel was a significant historical event. Had it not happened, Castlereagh would almost certainly not have been Foreign Secretary when the peace settle-ment was being negotiated. As it was, his courtesy, calm temperament and patrician demeanour made him acceptable to the crowned heads of Europe; and as a result of the lucky accident of having to go out to the Allied headquar-ters in person, he had seen for himself, briefly but unforgettably, the horrors of war. Had Canning been Foreign Secretary at that time, as but for the duel he probably would have been, he would have been cleverer, but probably less persuasive. Tsar Alexander was more likely to listen to a tall, handsome son of a marquess than to a brilliantly intelligent man who could be dismissed as being the son of an actress and not a gentleman.

The undergraduate indiscretion that led to Castlereagh's contracting the disease thus had important consequences, not least that irrational challenge to a duel in 1809, which in turn led to his being Foreign Secretary at a moment when his aristocratic charm was just what was needed to command the respect of European statesmen and control the Tsar's wilder enthusiasms. Then, 13 years later, Castlereagh's suicide while of unsound mind led to Canning becoming Foreign Secretary just when a sharp intelligence was needed to curb the revived Bourbon alliance that threatened British trade and European peace – a threat that Canning averted by being determined to put *England* at least occasionally in place of *Europe*: as he put it, 'for Europe I shall be desirous now and then to read England'.[10] The Europe that emerged in the years following Waterloo was not perfect, and contained the seeds of the catastrophe of 1914. But it would be unreasonable to expect any statesmen to look that far ahead, and Europe did enjoy a more peaceful hundred years than ever before or since. British foreign policy got the best of both worlds: Castlereagh and Canning were, each of them, what was needed at the time. Perhaps that youthful undergraduate indiscretion was providential.

Appendix 1

Mr John Gleave FRCS (lately senior consultant neurosurgeon at Addenbrooke's Hospital, Cambridge) kindly read Montgomery Hyde's *The Strange Death of Lord Castlereagh* which contains most of the report of the coroner's inquest. (A printed contemporary copy of the account of the inquest in Cambridge University Library was presented, rather touchingly, by a graduate who had joined the Foreign Office and was clearly a great admirer of Castlereagh). Mr Gleave's considered opinion is that Lord Castlereagh suffered for all his adult life from a form of syphilis. He writes:

ROBERT STEWART, VISCOUNT CASTLEREAGH, 2ND MARQUESS OF LONDONDERRY

Medical history (so far as can been gathered from the sparse notes available)

Although he might have suffered from the congenital form of the disease in view of his family background, I think the evidence is against this hypothesis. His father came of good Scots Presbyterian stock, with no hint of hereditary disease. His mother's family, however, was known to be eccentric; her nephew was a notorious rake (the model for the Marquess of Steyne in *Vanity Fair*), and she herself almost certainly died of syphilis, but whether acquired (very likely) or congenital cannot be ascertained. Although she died of puerperal sepsis she had a stillbirth as a second child and the cause of this was frequently syphilis. Robert Stewart [i.e. Castlereagh] had none of the usual stigmata of the congenital disease, i.e. eye problems, joint problems, saddle nose, Hutchinson's teeth, etc.

The disease of syphilis is conventionally divided into three stages. Primary, this is the chancre or sore which develops about 7–10 days after infection; secondary, which is essentially a painless non-irritating generalised rash which develops after about 6 weeks and may last a similar period (in some patients it may be far more severe than this, affecting several systems of the body, and may lead to death – this was the form which affected Europe after the Siege of Naples); and tertiary.

In the case of Castlereagh, the first two stages would seem to correspond to his being indisposed during the Michaelmas term of 1787, and in January 1788.

The tertiary stage of the disease occurs at a very variable time after the onset and its clinical manifestations are protean. In the main they affect the cardiovascular and the nervous systems, though the skin, the joints, and the skeleton are all attacked in various ways. The latent period before the effects of such involvement in the disease process are manifest is extremely variable.

In the case of Castlereagh we are chiefly interested in neurosyphilis and even more specifically in the effects of the disease on the brain as affecting intellect, personality and mood. We are not concerned primarily with its effect on the control of movement, though in one form of the disease – tabes dorsalis – it was profound. The latent period before the symptoms of neurosyphilis began to be noted was very variable. This is in part because the changes in mood, temperament, memory and personality would be obvious to business colleagues and social acquaintances before they were to the patient and those close to him, and also because the changes in cognitive functions and personality were so insidious. The length of time before such changes were noticed could be as little as 2 years or as long as 40 years. The majority declare themselves between 10 and 20 years from the initial infection, but 40 or 50 years old is the usual age of presentation, and a latent period of 30 years would be entirely acceptable, especially if there had been some unexplained illness in the interim which might have been due to another manifestation of the disease process.

The physical symptoms are usually minor until the later (terminal) stages, but earlier there may be some loss of fine coordination (could this be enough for a crack pistol shot to miss a standing target at twelve paces?).

The cognitive symptoms are affected insidiously, with a slight defect of memory and of the reasoning and critical faculties, minor peculiarities of conduct, and irritability. This is succeeded by more pronounced mental impairment of both a negative and a positive kind. The former consists of deterioration in the functions already specified, loss of interest in personal appearance, and crumbling of morale; the latter comprise emotional outbursts, fits of temper or of pique, and the development of delusional ideas among which a godlike euphoria is frequently present.

The psychological symptoms are based on a relentless deterioration of the personality, both in intelligence and in character, of which depression and excitement are both accessory symptoms. Headache, fatiguability, memory failure and change of behaviour such as irritability and loss of consideration are common complaints. On the other hand they are capable of normally doing their routine work perfectly well, but they may fail when faced with a particularly difficult problem. Their attitude to failure may well be that they are ruined and blameworthy (particularly if they believe that they have been guilty of a mortal sin, e.g. that of the Bishop of Clogher) so that the one mode of escape that is left is suicide.

Personal history (so far as can be ascertained)

- Aet. 10. 'delicate, wasted in left arm by an issue long previously applied'.
- Aet. 18. Very off-colour during whole of Michaelmas term; kept to his room in St John's: 'no more than the usual consequences of a young man's indiscretion'.
- Aet. 24 (1793). While in camp with militia, had a nightmare vision of a 'radiant boy' that made a lasting impression.
- Aet. 31 (1801). 'brain fever' – lasted about two months and seems to have been a physical illness with a fever.
- Aet 38 (1807). Virtually off work for two months – 'increasing debility' according to Lady Castlereagh. Whether this was physical, loss of libido (though it must be noted that they were childless) or mental, is not clear.
- Aet. 40 (1809). The duel. This seems to have been an irrational act, provoked by what was largely an imaginary slight. Paranoia seems evident. The fact that a reputed crack-shot missed the first time and only winged his man the second time (and a second shot was insisted on against the advice of both seconds) perhaps is an indication of incipient incoordination, let alone lack of judgement and self-control.
- Aet. 45 (1814). Detailed enquiry about precise position of jugular vein (carotid artery). 'In strange mood'.
- Aet. 59 (1819). Seems to have been trapped into a very foolish act of dissolute behaviour with young man dressed as girl in brothel. May have been blackmailed (certainly believed that he was and that the police were after him following the Bishop of Clogher's buggery on 19 July 1822).
- Aet. 52–53 (1822) January. 'Began to run down'; May, obviously something amiss; August (9th) bought small knife from Jewish pedlar in Piccadilly – ? because Lady C. had hidden his pistols; told the King that police were after him; (12th) died.

Discussion and opinion

1. Although he might have suffered from the congenital form of the disease in view of his family (maternal) background, I think the evidence is against this hypothesis. The only possible point in favour is the wasted left arm which might have been due to syphilitic amotrophy. However, this condition is irreversible and so far as we know he grew up with a normal left arm. A mild attack of polio, an injury, or a chronic infection of soft tissue, joint or bone therefore seems more likely, because from all three recovery to normal function is possible.

2. Almost certainly, i.e. beyond reasonable doubt in legal phraseology, he had an attack of gonorrhoea and syphilitic infection (the two very frequently are acquired together) at the beginning of the Michaelmas Term 1787. The secondary stage of the syphilis would have occupied the rest of the term, and the whole disease process would then have become quiescent so far as symptoms went, though the spirochaete would have been steadily working its mischief.

3. Whether the 'radiant boy' nightmare (1794) was a manifestation of early cerebral syphilis or merely the result of a Celtic imagination inflamed by wine I do not know.

4. The attack of 'brain fever' (1801) was on the balance of probabilities an attack of syphilitic meningitis, occurring as a preliminary manifestation of the tertiary stage of the disease, which he is now entering.

5. Lady C. noted subtle deterioration, physical and mental ('debility') in 1807.

6. The duel (1809) manifested paranoia, lack of rational judgement, deterioration of moral standards, and, in that he missed, some loss of fine-control movement.

7. The delusions associated with his paranoia led to perverted reasoning which almost seemed sensible, as he requested (1814) precise knowledge of the course of the vascular bundle of the neck. His mood was noted to be very strange.

8. Progressive deterioration of moral judgement, swings of mood, irritability alternating with an almost godlike serenity which impresses some of his political colleagues, unwarranted self-confidence, and attacks of unreasoning panic all become apparent towards the end of his life.

9. Finally he develops headaches, his self-control and memory are seriously impaired, and all recognize that he is seriously demented and deteriorating physically. In this state he kills himself in a precise and unusual fashion,

presumably because Lady C. had hidden his pistols.

10. There was no autopsy and so a tumour of the brain (meningioma or low-grade astrocytoma spring to mind) or other pathology cannot be entirely ruled out, but on the balance of probabilities he suffered from tertiary neurosyphis (General Paralysis of the Insane).

Note: The (Cambridge) Emeritus Professor of Morbid Anatomy, Austin Gresham, when asked for his opinion, said that he had 'no doubt that Stewart had syphilis'. (Gresham is an Irishman, and is conversant with the history of that period.)

Appendix 2

About ten years ago, while sorting the Canning family papers in my possession but before becoming interested in the duel of 1809, I obtained photocopies of a few of the letters in the Harewood MSS at Leeds. One was from Castlereagh, written in July 1807 to Canning (concerning some problem in the Mediterranean). I showed this to a friend, Mrs Nicol Gross, who had once spent a month in Paris learning from an expert graphologist how to judge character from handwriting, and who had more than once given me an uncannily accurate character-description of people I had met, without knowing anything about them except a sample of their handwriting. In showing her this letter from Castlereagh I did not tell her who wrote it (having blanked out the signature), but simply the decade in which is was written. She knew a little but not much about the period of the Napoleonic Wars. Mrs Gross's verdict on the writer's character surprised me: she said the handwriting showed an intelligent and sensitive man, but one who was very tired – the handwriting and grammar deteriorated as the letter went on. Also, she felt quite concerned for the writer, who (she opined) knew that he was seriously ill, and was worried because no one else knew it, and also because he did not think he could carry on much longer without the illness showing itself. (I myself did not know when I showed her this letter that a month or so after it was written, Castlereagh was off work, ill, for two months.)

Since Mrs Gross is no longer alive, and gave me this character-assessment based on Castlereagh's handwriting verbally, it can hardly be adduced as evidence for Castlereagh's mental state. But it kindled my interest in the relationship between Canning and Castlereagh that led to their duel.

Appendix 3

Complete transcription of a contemporary MS copy of Canning's statement that he made (unadvisedly, because none of those who could
have corroborated it were willing or – in Portland's case, able – to
do so).

**Statement of the cause of that Transaction upon a misapprehension
of the leading facts of which Lord Castlereagh's Letter appears to
have been founded.**

It is perfectly true that so long ago as Easter Mr. Canning had represented to
the Duke of Portland the insufficiency (in his opinion) of the Government as
then constituted, to carry on the Affairs of the Country under all the difficulties of the times, and had requested that, unless some changes should be
effected in it, he might be permitted to resign his Office. It is equally true
that, in the course of the discussion which arose out of this representation, it
was proposed to Mr. Canning, and accepted by him, as the condition of his
consenting to retain the Seals of the Foreign Office, that a change should be
made in the War Department.

With respect to the concealment, Mr. Canning some short time previous
to the date of Lord Castlereagh's letter, without the smallest suspicion of the
existence of any intention on the part of Lord Castlereagh to make such an
appeal to Mr. Canning as that Letter contains, but upon information that some
misapprehension did exist as to Mr. Canning's supposed concurrence in the
reserve which had been practised towards Lord Castlereagh, transmitted to
one of Lord Castlereagh's most intimate Friends to be communicated whenever he might think proper, the copy of a Letter addressed by Mr. Canning to
the Duke of Portland in the month of July, in which Mr. Canning requests,
'in justice to himself, that it may be remembered, whenever hereafter this
concealment shall be alleged (as he doubts not it will) <u>against him</u>, as an act of

injustice towards Lord Castlereagh, that it did not originate in his suggestion; that so far from desiring it, he conceived, however erroneously, Lord Camden to be the sure channel of communication to have been actually made'.

But it is not true that the time at which that change was ultimately proposed to be made, was of Mr. Canning's choice; and it is not true that he was party in consenting to the concealment of that intended change from Lord Castlereagh.

The copy of this Letter, and of the Duke of Portland's answer to it, acknowledging Mr. Canning's 'repeated remonstrances against the concealment' are still in the possession of Lord Castlereagh's friend.

The communication to Lord Camden to which this letter refers, was made on the 28th April, with Mr. Canning's knowledge and at his particular desire. Lord Camden being the near connection, and most confidential Friend of Lord Castlereagh, it never occurred to Mr. Canning, nor was it credible to him till he received the most positive asseveration of the fact, that Lord Camden had kept back such a communication from Lord Castlereagh.

With respect to the period at which the change in the War Department was to take place, Mr. Canning was induced, in the first instance, to consent to its postponement till the rising of parliament, partly by the representations made to him of the inconveniences of any change in the middle of a Session, but principally upon a consideration of the particular circumstances under which Lord Castlereagh stood in the House of Commons after Easter; circumstances which would have given to his removal at that period of the Sessions, a character which it was certainly no part of Mr. Canning's wish that it should bear.

Mr Canning however received the most positive promise, that a change in the War Department should take place immediately upon the close of the Session.

When that time arrived, the earnest and repeated intreaties of most of Lord Castlereagh's friends in the cabinet, were employed to prevail on Mr Canning to consent to the postponement of the arrangement.

At length, and most reluctantly, he did give his consent to its being postponed to the period proposed by Lord Castlereagh's friends; viz the termination of the Expedition then in preparation. But he did so upon the most distinct and solemn assurances that, whatever might be the issue of the Expedition, the change should take place at that period; that the Seals of the War Department should then be offered to Lord Wellesley (the Person for whose accession to the Cabinet Mr Canning was known to be most anxious); and that the interval should be diligently employed by Lord Castlereagh's Friends in preparing Lord

Castlereagh's mind to acquiesce in that arrangement.

It was therefore a matter of astonishment to Mr Canning when, at the issue of the Expedition, he reminded the Duke of Portland that the time was now come for His Grace's writing to Lord Wellesley, to find that, so far from the interval having been employed by Lord Castlereagh's Friends in preparing Lord Castlereagh for the change, the same reserve had been continued towards him against which Mr. Canning had before so earnestly remonstrated.

Being informed of this circumstance by the Duke of Portland, and learning at the same time from His Grace, that there were other difficulties attending the promised arrangement, of which Mr Canning had not before been apprized, and that the Duke of Portland had himself come to a determination to retire from Office, Mr Canning instantly & before any step whatever had been taken towards carrying the promised arrangement into effect, withdrew his claim for its execution, and requested the Duke of Portland to tender his (Mr Canning's) resignation, at the same time with His Grace's, to the King. [Marginal note inserted at this point]: This was on Wednesday the 6th of September previously to the Levy of that day.

All question of the performance of the promise made to Mr. Canning being thus at an end the Reserve which Lord Castlereagh's friends had hitherto so perseveringly practised towards Ld Castlereagh, appears to have been laid aside. – Ld. Castlereagh was now made acquainted with the nature of the arrangement which had been intended to have been proposed to him.

What may have been the reasons which prevented Ld. C's friends from fulfilling the assurances given to Mr Canning, that Ld Castlereagh's mind should be prepared by their communications, for the arrangement intended to be carried into effect; and what the motives of the disclosure to Lord Castlereagh, after that arrangement had ceased to be in contemplation, it is [later pencilled insertion *not*] for Mr Canning to explain.

Notes

Chapter 1. Origins

1. Elizabeth Longford, *Wellington: Pillar of State* (London: Weidenfeld and Nicolson, 1972), p 97.
2. George Canning to John Beresford, 13 May 1766, Harewood MSS.

Chapter 2. Boyhood and Youth: Castlereagh

1. Sheridan wrote a charming little (unpublished) poem to console Canning's nine-year-old cousin Bess on the death of an avadavat (a small bird) given to her by Fox, containing a verse:

    The prisoner insolvent, who dies in the Fleet
    From death gets his Habeas, as Wilkes did from Pratt;
    When cag'd up for life, no joys could be sweet
    And this was the case with the Avadavat.
2. 6 October 1777, Londonderry MSS.
3. Letter to Mrs Leigh, 18 March 1788, Harewood MSS.

Chapter 3. Boyhood and Youth: Canning

1. 11 September 1782, Harewood MSS.
2. 11 October 1787, *Anglo-Saxon Review*, 1901.
3. Letter to Bess Canning, 29 August 1790, Harewood MSS.

Chapter 4. The Young Politician: Castlereagh

1. Letter to his Under-Secretary, Cooke, 21 June 1800, quoted in H. Montgomery Hyde, *The Rise of Castlereagh* (Macmillan, 1933).
2. Rosebery's *Pitt* (John Murray, 1891) has the advantage of being written by a prime minister who had himself had to grapple with the 'Irish Question' just as Pitt had done; his chapter on Ireland shows a deeper understanding of the issues and personalities involved than a study of history on its own could ever give.
3. Charles Teeling, *History of the Irish Rebellion of 1798 etc.* (Shannon: Irish University

199

Press, 1972).

4. *Correspondence of Charles, first Marquis Cornwallis*, ed. Charles Ross (London: John Murray, 1859), vol. 2, p. 371.

5. *Ibid.*, 9 July 1798.

6. Some years later Lord Liverpool complained that few earls wished to become marquesses – a favour that cost nothing – because it would mean their younger sons would be called 'Lord' and be precluded from a career in the law. Irish peers had no such inhibitions.

Chapter 5. The Young Politician: Canning

1. Letter to Bess Canning, 29 May 1799, Harewood MSS.

2. It is not clear when the definite offer was made. Gabrielle Festing's *John Hookham Frere and His Friends* (London: Nisbet, 1898), p 28, suggests it must have been *before* he had 'joined Pitt' in August 1792, but a letter to Wallace of 13 March 1793 suggests that it had only just been made.

3. Letter to Mrs Stratford Canning, 5 July 1793, Harewood MSS.

4. *Lady Bessborough and Her Family Circle*, ed. Earl of Bessborough and A. Aspinall (1940), 4 July 1793.

5. Pitt to Pretyman, quoted in John Ehrman, *The Younger Pitt* (London: Constable, 1996).

6. Canning's Letter Journal, 1793–95, Harewood MSS, printed in 1991 by the Camden Society and edited by Peter Jupp, is a constant source for this chapter, together with his correspondence with his cousin Bess Canning.

7. Letter to Bess Canning, June 1794 (from Christ Church, Oxford), Harewood MSS.

8. Letter to Bess Canning, 27 February 1796, Harewood MSS.

9. *Private Correspondence of Lord Granville Leveson-Gower*, ed. Castalia, Countess Granville, 2 vols. (London: John Murray, 1917).

10. Festing, *John Hookham Frere and His Friends*, p 31.

11. *A Series of Letters of the First Earl of Malmesbury*, 2 vols. (London, 1870), 8 February 1801.

Chapter 6. Contrasting Fortunes

1. Festing, *John Hookham Frere and His Friends*, p 53.

2. *Diaries of Sylvester Douglas, Lord Glenbervie*, ed. F. Bickley, 2 vols. (London, 1928), 15 April 1801.

3. *Letters of the First Earl of Malmesbury*, 18 August 1812.

4. J. Bagot (ed.), *George Canning and His Friends* (London: John Murray, 1909), 14 March 1801.

5. *Correspondence of Charles, first Marquis Cornwallis*, 26 February 1801.

6. Rosebery, *Pitt*, p 199.

7. *Correspondence of Charles, first Marquis Cornwallis*, 22 April and 7 May.

8. Pretyman MSS 108/44, 45, quoted in William Hague, *William Pitt the Younger* (London: HarperCollins, 2004), p 497.

9. Elizabeth Longford, *Wellington: The Years of the Sword* (Weidenfeld and Nicolson, 1972), p 86.

10. *The Creevey Papers: A Selection from the Correspondence and Diaries*, ed. Sir Herbert Maxwell (John Murray, 1904), vol. 1, p 43.

11. Sidmouth MSS, quoted in Hague, *William Pitt the Younger*, p 550.

12. William Napier Bruce, *Life of General Sir Charles Napier* (London: John Murray, 1885), p 28, quoted in Hague, *William Pitt the Younger*.

13. John Ehrman, *The Younger Pitt*, vol. 3, pp 92–7, felt obliged by current literary fashion to consider whether there might have been a homosexual element in Pitt's friendship with Canning, but rightly ruled it out (as Lord Holland did in his *Memoirs*), although he did not point out that as well as never having known his father, Canning had also at the age of 17 lost the uncle who had largely filled the gap left by his father's death and had become his guardian.

14. Duke of Buckingham, *Memoirs of the Court and Cabinet of George III*, 4 vols. (1853–55), 16 March 1801.

15. *Ibid.*, 20 March 1801.

Chapter 7. Cabinet Colleagues

1. Satire on the Duke of Portland in the *Morning Chronicle*, 31 March 1807.

2. Letter to Lord Temple, 18 March 1807, *Memoirs of the Court and Cabinet of George III*.

3. David Wilkinson, *The Duke of Portland: Politics and Party in the Age of George III* (New York: Palgrave Macmillan, 2003), to which I am indebted for the quotation at the head of this chapter.

4. *Ibid.*

5. *DNB*.

6. *DNB*.

7. A. Aspinall and E.A. Smith (eds), *English Historical Documents*, vol. 8 (1783–1832) (London: Methuen), p 92 (letter of 27 December 1807).

8. Carola Oman, *Nelson* (Hodder and Stoughton, 1947), pp 587, 597.

9. 'Private', 25 May 1807, Harewood MSS.

10. Napier's *History of the Peninsular War* states incorrectly that Canning failed to issue that instruction.

11. Duke of Buckingham, *Memoirs of the Court and Cabinet of George III*, 11 October 1808.

12. 22 August, Camden Miscellany, XVIII, 1948.

13. *Ibid.*, Berkeley to Temple, 14 October.

14. Giles Hunt, *Mehitabel Canning: A Redoubtable Woman* (Royston: Rooster Books, 2001), p 222.

15. Quoted in Rory Muir, *Britain and the Defeat of Napoleon* (New Haven and London:

Yale University Press, 1996).

16. Charles Esdaile, *The Peninsular War: A New History* (London: Allen Lane, 2002), p 146.

Chapter 8. The Year of the Duel

1. 28 February 1809, Harewood MSS, bundle 48.
2. Rory Muir, *Britain and the Defeat of Napoleon*, p 84.
3. A. Aspinall (ed), *The Later Correspondence of George III* (London: Cambridge University Press, 1970), 13 September 1809.
4. A brother of Canning's aunt Hitty, Major Robert Patrick, had died in the West Indies, and it was evidently thanks to Chatham that his son was given a commission in the 4th Foot of which Chatham was colonel. See Giles Hunt, *Mehitabel Canning*, pp 166, 168, 232.
5. Stanley Lane Poole, *The Life of the Right Hon. Stratford Canning* (London: Longmans & Co., 1888), vol. 1, p 213.
6. There is a detailed account of the campaign in Gordon Bond, *The Grand Expedition: The British Invasion of Holland in 1809* (Athens: University of Georgia Press, 1979), to which I am much indebted.
7. Iris Butler, *The Eldest Brother: The Marquess Wellesley, the Duke of Wellington's Eldest Brother* (London: Hodder & Stoughton, 1973).
8. *Wellesley Papers*, vol. 1, pp 268ff (28 October, 1809).

Chapter 9. The Duel

1. John Ehrman, *The Younger Pitt*, vol. 3, p 128.
2. J.A. Atkinson, *The British Duelling Pistol* (London: Arms & Armour Press, 1978).
3. Letter to Charles Stewart, 21 September 1809 (PRO Northern Ireland).
4 *The Diaries and Correspondence of the Rt. Hon. George Rose*, ed. L.V. Harcourt (London, 1860), p 422.
5. See, for example, *The Times*, 26 September 1809.
6. But in Fox's duel it had been 14 paces.
7. See, for example, Longford, *Wellington: The Years of the Sword*.

Chapter 10. The Aftermath

1. Henry Richard Fox, *Further Memoirs of the Whig Party, 1807–1821*, ed. Lord Stavordale (London: John Murray, 1905).
2. Raglan MSS No. 25, 22 October 1809, quoted in Longford, *Wellington: The Years of the Sword*, p 206.
3. I have not found this among Castlereagh's letters to his father in the Northern Ireland Record Office.
4. *Morning Post*, 2 June 1798.
5. *The Times*, Monday, 25 September 1809.

6. Public Record Office of Northern Ireland, April 1827.
7. *Memoirs of the Court and Cabinet of George III*, 16 January 1821.

Chapter 11. Long-Term Consequences: The Two Foreign Secretaries

1. *Eton College Chronicle*, 5 July 1794.
2 BL Add. Mss 38.566, 23 March 1814.
3. *Nesselrode Papers*, vol. 3, p 522, quoted in Henry Kissinger, *A World Restored* (New York: Grosset and Dunlap, 1964), p 312.
4. Harewood MSS.
5. Giles Hunt, *Mehitabel Canning*, p 312 (letter to William Canning, 12 April 1821).
6. Letter to Frances Canning, Harewood MSS.
7. *Supplementary Dispatches, Correspondence and Memoranda of 1st Duke of Wellington* (London, 1858–72), 13 November 1818.
8. George IV's Pavilion at Brighton was by the river Steyne, pronounced 'Steen'.
9. In what follows I have leaned heavily on Charles Crawley's *The Question of Greek Independence: A Study of British Policy in the Near East, 1821–33* (Cambridge University Press, 1930), not only because it was considered worthy of re-publishing in New York in 1970, but because I was fortunate enough to have the author as my supervisor – which does not of course make him responsible for any errors I may make.
10. Harold Temperley, *The Foreign Policy of Canning, 1822–1827* (London: G. Bell and Sons Ltd, 1925).

Chapter 12. Death Comes To Us All

1. *Supplementary Dispatches of 1st Duke of Wellington*.
2. Giles Hunt, *Mehitabel Canning*, p 331.
3. H. Montgomery Hyde, *The Strange Death of Lord Castlereagh* (London: Heinemann, 1959).
4. By W.D. Henry M.B., B.Ch, D.F.M. Wendy Hinde kindly drew this to my attention.
5. I am very grateful to Lady Mairi Bury for telling me where it is now lodged, in the Public Record Office in Belfast.
6. Deborah Hayden, *Pox: Genius, Madness, and the Mysteries of Syphilis* (New York: Basic Books, 2003).
7. Montgomery Hyde, *The Rise of Castlereagh*.
8. Bruce, *Life of General Sir Charles Napier*, as quoted in Chapter 6 above.
9. Montgomery Hyde thinks that a nightmare Castlereagh had in 1793, when embers of a dying camp fire seemed to take the shape of a 'radiant boy', was a significant pointer to future mental instability, but this seems rather far fetched: men can have vivid nightmares without becoming unbalanced or suicidal.
10. Letter to Charles Bagot, 5 November 1822.

Select Bibliography

Original sources

The Canning papers are in the Public Record Office in Leeds, where they form the bulk of the Harewood MSS. Castlereagh's private papers in the Public Record Office of Northern Ireland in Belfast are obtainable on microfilm. Many of the Portland papers at Nottingham University are now online. There is of course much more manuscript material of the period, which I have not attempted to delve into – I have not, for instance, seen any of Castlereagh's official papers in MS form apart from one or two letters that happen to be with those of Canning in the Harewood MSS (now sometimes called the 'Canning MSS'). Most contemporary newspapers – *Courier*, *Morning Chronicle*, *Morning Post*, *Observer*, *Times* – are on microfilm in Cambridge University Library (perusal takes time as one gets side-tracked by reading some fascinating advertisements). Most of the important diaries and correspondence have been printed and published, and are in the following list.

Abbot, Charles, *Diary and Correspondence of Charles Abbot, Lord Colchester* (John Murray, 1861)

Aspinall, Arthur (ed.), *The Hobhouse Diary* (London, 1947)

——, *Politics and the Press* (London: Home and Thal, 1949)

——, *Correspondence of George III / of George Frederick Prince of Wales / of George IV* (all published by Cambridge University Press)

Bagot, John, *George Canning and His Friends* (John Murray, 1909)

Bell, *Early Days of the Rt. Hon. George Canning* (London, 1828)

Bessborough, Earl of, and Arthur Aspinall, *Lady Bessborough and Her Circle* (John Murray, 1940)

Bond, Gordon C., *The Grand Expedition* (University of Georgia Press, 1979)

Bor, Margot, and Clelland, Lamond, *Still the Lark: Life of Elizabeth Linley* (Merlin Press, 1962)

Bryant, Sir Arthur, *The Years of Endurance* (Collins, 1942)

——, *The Years of Victory* (Collins, 1944)

——, *Jackets of Green* (Collins, 1972)

Buckingham, Duke of (ed.), *Memoirs of the Court and Cabinet of George III* (Hurst & Blackett, 1853–55)

Butler, Iris, *The Eldest Brother: The Marquess Wellesley* (Hodder & Stoughton, 1973)

Chambers, James, *Palmerston* (John Murray, 2004)

Cornwallis, 1st Marquess of, *Correspondence of Charles, first Marquis Cornwallis*, ed. Charles Ross (London, 1852)

Crawley, C.W., *The Question of Greek Independence* (Cambridge University Press, 1930)

Derry, John W., *Castlereagh* (London: Allen Lane, 1976)

Dixon, P, *Canning: Politician and Statesman* (Weidenfeld & Nicolson, 1976)

Ehrman, John, *The Younger Pitt*, vols. 2 and 3 (Constable, 1983 & 1996)

Esdaile, Charles, *The Peninsular War* (Allen Lane, 2002)

Festing, Field Marshal Sir Francis *see* Wilkes, Lyell

Festing, Gabrielle, *John Hookham Frere and His Friends* (James Nisbet, 1899)

Fortescue, the Hon. J.W., *A History of the British Army*, 13 vols. (London: Macmillan, 1899–1930)

Frere, W.E., and Sir Bartle, *Works of John Hookham Frere*, 2 vols. (Basil Montagu Pichering, 1872)

Fulford, Roger, *Royal Dukes* (Duckworth, 1933)

Gash, Norman, *Mr Secretary Peel* (Longmans, 1961)

——, *Lord Liverpool* (Weidenfeld & Nicolson, 1984)

Glenbervie, Lord (Sylvester Douglas), *Diaries*, ed. F. Bickley, 2 vols. (London, 1928)

Glover, Michael, *Britannia Sickens* (Leo Cooper, 1970)

Gray, Denis, *Spencer Perceval: The Evangelical Prime Minister* (Manchester University Press, 1963)

Guedalla, Philip, *The Duke* (London, 1931)

Hague, William, *William Pitt the Younger* (HarperCollins, 2004)

Hanwell, Major, *Short History of the Ninth Queen's Royal Lancers* (Gale & Polden, 1949)

Harcourt, L.V. (ed.), *George Rose, Diaries* (London: Richard Bentley, 1860)

Harris, Rifleman, *Recollections of Rifleman Harris* (London, 1829)

Hibbert, Christopher, *George IV*, 2 vols. (Longmans, 1972; Allen Lane, 1973)

——, *Wellington: A Personal History* (London, 1997)

——, *George III* (Viking, 1998; Penguin, 1999)

Hinde, Wendy, *George Canning* (Collins, 1973)

——, *Castlereagh* (Collins, 1981)

Hobhouse, Christopher, *Fox* (London, 1952)

Holland, Lord, *Memoirs of the Whig Party* (London, 1852–54)

Hunt, Giles, *Mehitabel Canning: A Redoubtable Woman* (Rooster Books, 2001)

Hyde, H. Montgomery, *The Rise of Castlereagh* (London, 1933)

——, *The Strange Death of Lord Castlereagh* (London, 1959)

Iremonger, Lucille, *Lord Aberdeen* (Collins, 1978)

Jupp, Peter (ed.), *The Letter Journal of George Canning* (Camden Soc., 4th Series, vol. 41)

——, *Lord Grenville 1759–1834* (Oxford: Clarendon Press, 1985)

Kissinger, Henry, *A World Restored: Metternich, Castlereagh and the Problems of Peace* (Weidenfeld & Nicolson, 1957)

Lane Poole, Stanley, *Life of the Rt. Hon. Stratford Canning*, 2 vols. (Longmans, 1888)

Liddell Hart, Basil (ed.), *The Letters of Private Wheeler* (Michael Joseph, 1952)

Londonderry, 3rd Marquess of (ed.), *Correspondence, Despatches and Other Papers of Viscount Castlereagh, Second Marquess of Londonderry* (London, 1848–53)

Longford, Elizabeth, *Wellington: The Years of the Sword* (Weidenfeld & Nicolson, 1969)

——, *Wellington: Pillar of State* (Weidenfeld & Nicolson, 1972)

Maxwell, Sir Herbert, *The Life of Wellington*, 2 vols. (London, 1899)

——, *The Creevey Papers*, 2 vols. (John Murray, 1903–4)

Napier, Sir William, *History of the War in the Peninsula*, 6 vols. (London: Thos. & Wm. Boone, 1853)

——, *Life and Memories of Sir Charles Napier*, 4 vols. (John Murray, 1857)

Nicolson, Harold, *The Congress of Vienna 1818–22* (Constable, 1946)

Oman, Carola, *Life of Nelson* (Hodder & Stoughton, 1947)

——, *Sir John Moore* (Hodder & Stoughton, 1953)

Pakenham, Thomas, *The Year of Liberty* (Hodder & Stoughton, 1969)

Pearce, Robert, *Memoirs & Correspondence of Richard, Marquess Wellesley*, 3 vols. (London: Richard Bentley, 1843)

Perkins, Bradford, *Prologue to War: England and the U.S. 1805–12* (University of California Press, 1968)

Plumb, J.H. *The First Four Georges* (Batsford, 1956)

Price, Cecil, *The Letters of Sheridan* (Clarendon Press, 1966)

Rose, J.H., 'Canning and the Spanish Patriots in 1808', *American Historical Review*, vol. 16 (1906–7)

Rosebery, Lord, *Pitt* (Macmillan, 1908)

Ross, General C., *Correspondence of Charles, First Marquess Cornwallis* (John Murray, 1859)

Stapleton, Augustus, *George Canning and His Times* (London: John W. Parker & Son, 1859)

Teeling, Charles, *History of the Irish Rebellion* (Irish University Press, 1972)

Temperley, Harold, *The Foreign Policy of Canning 1822–27* (London, 1925)

——, and Webster, Sir Charles, 'The Duel Between Castlereagh and Canning in 1809', *Cambridge Historical Journal*, vol. 3 (1929), pp 83–95, 314

Thompson, Neville, *Earl Bathurst and the British Empire* (Leo Cooper, 1999)

Trench, W.S., *Realities of Irish Life* (London, 1868)

Walpole, Spencer, *The Life of the Rt. Hon. Spencer Perceval*, 2 vols. (London: Hurst and Blackett, 1874)

Webster, Sir Charles, *The Foreign Policy of Castlereagh 1812–15* (London: G. Bell, 1931)

Wellington, 2nd Duke of (ed.), *Supplementary Despatches, Correspondence and Memoranda of Field Marshal Arthur, Duke of Wellington* (London, 1858–72)

Wheeler, Charles, *The Letters of Private Wheeler*, ed. B.H. Liddell Hart (Michael Joseph, 1951)

Wilberforce, R.I. and S.W., *The Life of William Wilberforce* (John Murray, 1838)

Wilkes, Lyell, *A Study of Front-Line Frankie (Field Marshal Festing)* (Lewes: Book Guild)

Windham, William, *The Windham Papers* (Herbert Jenkins, 1913)

Ziegler, Philip, *King William IV* (Collins, 1961)

——, *Addington* (Collins, 1965)

——, *Melbourne* (Collins, 1987)

Index

Abbot, Charles *see* Colchester, Lord
Abercromby, Lieutenant-General Sir Ralph, 40, 41–2
Aberdeen, George Hamilton Gordon, 4th Earl of, 155–7
Adam, William, 127, 139
Adderley, 52
Addington, Henry (later 1st Viscount Sidmouth), xii, 45, 65, 67, 70, 71, 72–4, 77–81, 84, 87, 159, 179, 160, 201
Addiscombe, 55
Aix-la-Chapelle, Congress of, 164
Alexander, Tsar, 156–7, 164, 171, 185
Amiens, peace of, 73, 75, 77, 155
Ancaster, Duchess of, 15
Anti-Jacobin, 60
Antwerp, 119, 120, 121, 155, 157
Arbuthnot, Charles, 84, 179
Arbuthnot, Harriet, 129, 184
Arden, Lord, 24, 122–3
Armagh Royal School, 9, 10, 29, 183
Armistead, Mrs, 25
Ashbourne Hall, 48, 50
Aspinall, Arthur (historian), 115, 200
Assaye, battle of, 75
Asturias, 94
Atkinson, J.A., 134, 202
Austerlitz, 93
Austria, 59, 60, 110, 119, 156–8, 161–2, 184

Bagot, Charles, 63, 134, 200, 203
Bagot, Lady, 46
Baird, Lieutenant-General Sir David, 103–4, 106, 110
Ballylawn, 1, 2
Baltinglass, 3
Bandon, 10, 39

Bankhead, Dr, 178–9
Bantry Bay, 39
Bath, 13, 82, 92–3
Bathurst, 2nd Earl, 90, 92–3, 114
Bayham, Viscount *see* Camden, 1st Marquess of
Belfast, 11, 30, 32, 28, 38
Bellingham, John, 152
Bentinck, Henry *see* Portland, 3rd Duke of
Bentinck, Lord William, 103
Beresford, Lord, 36, 39
Beresford, Major-General William Carr, 111, 169
Berkeley, Admiral, 201
Berlin Decrees, 93
Bessborough, Countess of, 30, 49, 83, 200
Bootle Wilbraham, 66
Boringdon, Lord, 50
Borrowes, 18
Bowles, Captain, 102
Bragge Bathurst, 80, 81
Brazil, 169, 170
Bristol, Earl/Countess of, 12, 56
Brooks's Club, 47, 51, 59
Brougham, Henry (later Lord), 162, 166, 185
Brownrigg, Lieutenant-General, 119
Buchanan, Sir Andrew, ix, 61
Buckingham, Earl (later 1st Marquess and Duke of), 133, 162, 200–1
Buckinghamshire, 2nd Earl of, 33
Bulstrode (home of Duke of Portland), 112, 113, 118
Buonaparte, Joseph, 94
Burke, Edmund, 25, 31
Burrard, Lieutenant-General Sir Harry, 95–9, 102, 176
Bury, Lady Mairi, ix, 203

Butler, Lady Eleanor, 12
Butler, Iris (historian), 202
Byron, Lord, 166–7, 170

Cadiz, 91, 101–4 *passim*, 110, 113, 160
Cambridge University, 11–13, 21, 29,
  181–3
Camden, 1st Earl of, 7–12 *passim*, 27, 30–3,
  40–2, 144, 181, 185, 199
Camden, 2nd Earl of (1st Marquess of),
  13, 32, 36–9, 42, 89, 114–18, 126–8,
  130–3, 135, 145–8, 150, 181
Canning, Bess (Canning's cousin), 18, 25,
  58, 62, 63, 144, 147, 149, 196, 199, 200
Canning, Charles (Canning's cousin), 18,
  25, 49, 52, 58, 63, 66, 80
Canning, Charles ('Carlo' – Canning's third
  son), 70, 134, 165
CANNING, George, *passim* (*see* chapter
  headings)
Canning, George (1st Lord Garvagh) *see*
  Garvagh, 1st Baron
Canning, George (Canning's father), 3–6
Canning, George (Canning's eldest son),
  69–70, 83, 134, 162, 164
Canning, Harriet (Canning's daughter, *m*
  Lord Clanricarde), 70, 134, 166
Canning, Harry (Canning's cousin), 18, 19,
  80, 134
Canning, Joan (née Scott – Canning's wife),
  62–7, 83, 118, 122–3, 125, 133–4, 146,
  164, 166
Canning, Laetitia (née Newburgh
  – Canning's grandmother), 3, 19
Canning, Mary Ann (née Costello
  – Canning's mother), 5, 6, 15, 16, 22–3,
  56–7, 134
Canning, Mehitabel (Mrs Stratford
  Canning), 5, 15, 16, 18, 20, 22, 24, 26,
  50, 54, 57, 80, 97, 144, 175, 177
Canning, Paul (Canning's cousin), 5, 163
Canning, Stratford (Canning's grandfather),
  3, 5, 18
Canning, Stratford (Canning's uncle), 5, 6,
  15, 21, 27, 83, 115
Canning, Stratford (Canning's cousin,
  Viscount Stratford de Redcliffe), 18, 57,
  80, 113, 144, 153, 160, 162
Canning, William (Canning's cousin), 18,
  23, 57, 80, 113, 144, 143, 153, 171, 202
Canning, Revd Canon William (Canning's
  cousin), 18, 54, 74, 153

Canning, William (Canning's second son),
  70, 134
Carew (MP for Waterford), 44, 135
Carhampton, Major General Lord, 39, 40
Carlisle, Earl of, 53
Carlsbad Decrees, 160–1
Caroline, Princess of Wales (later Queen),
  53, 69, 79, 164–5
Castaños (Spanish general), 95, 104
Castlereagh, Lady (née Emily Hobart), 33–
  5, 39, 45–6, 152, 159, 177–80, 189–91
CASTLEREAGH, Viscount, *passim* (*see* chapter
  headings)
Cathcart, General Lord, 156–7
Charlemont, Lord, 40
Charlotte, Princess, 89
Charmilly, Colonel, 107
Chatham, 2nd Earl of, 90, 101–2, 113–14,
  118–21, 123
Chiswick, 176
Christ Church, Oxford, 20–7 *passim*, 50,
  52, 57
Cintra, Convention of, 97–101 *passim*, 109,
  114, 184
Clancarty, Lord, 114, 128
Clanricarde, Marquess of *see* Canning,
  Harriet
Clare (previously Fitzgibbon), Lord, 35–7
Clarke, Mary Anne, 112
Cleland, Revd James, 10, 39
Clogher, Bishop of, 179, 189
Cloncurry, Lord, 30, 38
Cochrane, Lord, 170
Colchester, Lord, 112
Combe, Alderman, 165
Constantinople, 98, 156, 167, 170–1
Conyngham, Marchioness of, 177
Cooke, Edward, 38, 44, 72, 128, 130, 145,
  150, 199
Coote, Sir Eyre, 121
Copenhagen, 73, 92–3, 97
Cornwallis, General Lord, 41–5, 65–6, 75,
  180, 199, 200
Corunna, 94, 104, 106–7, 110, 114
Costello, Mary Ann *see* Canning, Mary Ann
Costello, Mrs (Canning's grandmother), 57
Courier, 138–9, 144, 164
Cowan, Mary (Castlereagh's grandmother),
  1
Cradock, General, 110–11
Crawley, Charles, 203
Creevey, Thomas (diarist), 77, 151, 162,

185, 201
Crewe Hall, 23–4, 27, 49
Crewe, Mrs, 22–4, 49, 51, 63–4
Cruikshank, George (cartoonist), 142
Cuesta, General, 101

Dalrymple, General Sir Hew, 39, 95–8, 100–3, 176
d'Angoulême, Duc, 167
Devonshire, Georgiana, Duchess of, 26
Dogharty (Canning's Irish agent), 19
Downshire, Marchioness of, 76
Downshire, Marquess of, 29, 20
Doyle, Lieutenant-General Sir John, 101, 111
Dropmore (Grenville's country house), 59
Drummond, Sir William, 95
Dublin, 30ff, 76, 81, 137, 148
Dudley, Lord, 67, 176–7
Dundas, General Sir David, 119
Dundas, Henry, 1st Viscount Melville, 35, 47, 51–2, 63, 65–6, 69, 82–3
Dundas, Lady Jane, 63

Egmont, 2nd Earl of, 87
Ehrman, John (historian), 200–2
Eldon, Lord Chancellor, 89–90, 114, 117, 160, 171, 179
Eliot, Sir Gilbert *see* Minto, Lord
Ellis, Charles, 50, 52–3, 55, 60, 64, 132–5, 139–40
Ellis, George, 50, 55, 60, 140
Errol, Lady, 159
Erskine, William, 100, 140
Esdaile, Charles (historian), 202
Eton College, 18–22, 27, 57, 90, 203

Falmouth, Lord, 127
Ferdinand, King, 94, 160, 167
Festing, Field-Marshal Sir Francis, 11
Festing, Gabrielle (historian), 200
Fingall, Lord, 44
Fitzgerald, Lord Edward, 26, 43
Fitzgerald, Lady Lucy, 23
Fitzgibbon *see* Clare, Lord
Fitzharris, Lord, 62, 82
Fitzwilliam, Earl, 35–6
Fleming (Canning's manservant), 56
Flushing, 119–21
Fortescue, J.W. (historian), 90, 111–13
Fouché (Préfet de Paris), 158
Fox, Charles James, 18, 22, 25–6, 33, 35,

47, 49, 53, 79, 82, 84–5, 127, 139, 172, 177, 199, 202
Frere, John Hookham, 49–52, 64, 66, 69, 78, 101, 104–7, 109, 110, 117, 200

Gale, Daphne, 17
Garrick, David (actor), 15
Garfit, Guy, ix
Garvagh, 2, 3
Garvagh, 1st Baron, 163–4
George Frederick, Prince of Wales (George IV), 24, 87, 151, 153, 163–72 *passim*, 176, 178, 203
George III, King, 57–8, 65–6, 73, 82, 84–7, 93–6, 100, 111, 113–18, 123–4, 126–8, 132, 136, 143, 148–51, 164–5, 197
George IV *see* George Frederick
Gibraltar, 91, 95, 101, 111, 113, 15
Gleave, John, ix, 187
Glenbervie, Lord, 15, 66–7, 71, 200
Gloucester Lodge, 70, 132, 134, 139
Gordon, Colonel J.W., 119
Gordon, Duchess of, 53
Gower, Lord, 51, 56
Granville, Lord (Leveson-Gower), 27, 50–1, 63, 71–2, 116, 118, 161, 166, 200
Grattan, Henry, 31–2, 36
Greece, 160, 167, 170–1
Grenville, Lord, 35–6, 50–1, 58–60, 62, 66, 77–9, 82, 84–7, 90, 143, 151
Grenville, Thomas, 84
Gresham, Austin, 191
Greville, Charles, 185
Grey, Charles (later Lord Grey), 26, 52–3, 143, 151, 172, 176
Gross, Eileen, 193
Gustavus, King of Sweden, 96

Hague, William, 201
Haliday, Dr, 33, 40
Hammond (u/Secretary, Foreign Office), 59, 162
Hanover, 60, 168
Hardenberg, Baron, 168
Harris, Rifleman, 105
Harrowby, Lord, 53, 115, 172
Hastings, 1st Marquess of *see* Moira, Lord
Hastings, Warren, 74
Hawkesbury *see* Liverpool, 2nd Earl of
Hayden, Deborah (author), 182, 203
Hazlitt, William (essayist), 129

Helder Expedition, 94, 96, 119
Hely Hutchinson, 23
Herbert, A.P., 53
Hertford, Earl of, 2, 12
Hervey *see* Bristol, Earl of
Hervey, Lord Frederick, 12
Hervey, Lady Louisa (later Lady Liverpool), 56
Hillsborough, Lord *see* Downshire, Marquess of
Hinchcliffe, John *see* Peterborough, Bishop of
Hinckley, 70, 90, 98, 122, 125
Hinde, Wendy (historian), 152, 203
Hobart, Emily *see* Castlereagh, Lady
Hobhouse Diaries, 74
Holland, 110, 112, 115
Holland, Lady, 89
Holland, Lord, 25, 89, 144
Home Popham, Admiral, 120
Hope, Major-General Alexander, 119
Hoppner (portrait painter), 48, 61
Hunn, or Hunne (Canning's stepfather), 16, 21, 23
Hunter, John, 80, 94, 101
Huskisson, William, 168, 172
Hyde Abbey, 18
Hyde, H. Montgomery, 2, 42, 177, 179, 182, 187, 199, 203

India, 74ff, 166

Jackson, Dr (Dean of Christ Church), 20–1, 50, 112
Jenkinson *see* Liverpool, 2nd Earl of
Junot, Marshal, 97–8

Kellerman, General, 97–8
Kilkenny, 19
King, John, 44
Kissinger, Henry, 203
Knight, Gally, 19
Knighton, Sir William, 178

Lake, General, 39, 42, 76
Lane Poole, Stanley, 202
Lawrence (portrait painter), 21, 34, 124, 125, 129
Legge, Edward, 50, 52–3, 55
Leigh, Revd William (and Mrs), 20, 21, 56, 58, 63–4, 69, 162–4, 199
Leinster, Duchess of, 23

Lennox, Colonel, 139
Leveson-Gower *see* Granville, Lord
Lieven, Princess, 168, 171, 177–8, 184
Lincoln, Bishop of *see* Pretyman
Lisbon, 106–7, 110, 113, 162, 169
Littlehales, Colonel, 45
Liverpool (city), 161–2, 164
Liverpool, 2nd Earl of, 10, 22, 27, 50–6, 67, 71–5, 78–9, 81, 83, 89, 90, 118, 144, 151–3, 158–9, 161–3, 165–6, 168, 172, 176, 179, 200
Llangollen, 12
Londonderry, 1, 2
Londonderry, 1st Marquess of *see* Stewart, Robert (Castlereagh's father)
Londonderry, 2nd Marquess of = Castlereagh, *passim* (*see* chapter headings)
Londonderry, 3rd Marquess of *see* Stewart, Charles
Longford, Elizabeth, Countess of (historian), 4, 75, 199, 200–2
Loughborough, Lord Chancellor, 41, 45, 65, 89

Macartney, Lord, 20, 21
Madrid, 104, 106, 123, 167
Malmesbury, Lady, 51, 54, 55
Malmesbury, Lord, 51, 58, 60, 62, 65, 71, 73, 82, 144, 165, 200
Malta, 73, 100
Marie Louise, Empress, 167
Markham, William *see* York, Archbishop of
Maurice, Colonel J.F., 109
Melville, Viscount *see* Dundas, Henry or Robert
Metternich, Prince, 155, 157–8, 160–1, 167–8, 172, 177
Microcosm, 19, 57
Minto, 1st Lord, 86, 87, 95, 97
Miranda, 94
Moira, Lord, 86–7, 97, 102, 109, 165–6
Moore, Lieutenant-General Sir John, 94–6, 102–10, 156, 184
Morier, David, 153
Morning Chronicle, 139, 143–4, 164, 201
Morning Post, 127, 202
Mornington *see* Wellesley, Marquess of
Morpeth, Lord, 27, 50
Mount Stewart, 2–9 *passim*, 30, 34, 182
Muir, Rory (historian), ix, 111, 201–2
Mulgrave, Lord, 51, 83, 90, 92–3, 122

Napier, Charles, 78–9, 201, 203
Napier, William (historian), 94, 113, 183
Napoleon (Buonoparte), xii, xiii, 73, 77–8, 81–2, 92–3, 94, 97, 104–5, 107, 119, 154, 156, 158–9, 165, 167
Navarino Bay, 172
Nelson, Horatio, Admiral Viscount, 73, 80–1, 91, 93, 95, 120–1, 127
Newburgh, Laetitia (Canning's grandmother) *see* Canning, Laetitia
Newtown or Newton, Isle of Wight, 51, 62
Newtownards, 1, 9, 10, 40, 44, 76
Ninth Light Dragoons, 121
North, Frederick, 50

Observer, 140
Oman, Carola (historian), 73, 80, 201
Orange Order, 36
Orders in Council, 92–3
Owen, Captain, 120
Ouseley, Sir Gore, 158
Oxford University, 12, 20–1, 49, 115

Palmerston, Viscount, 50, 170, 172
Paris, 153, 159, 161, 162, 167, 177
Patrick, Elizabeth (Bess) (Canning's aunt), 80
Patrick, Mehitabel *see* Canning, Mehitabel
Patrick, Paul, 56
Patrick, Major Robert, 80, 101, 202
Payne, Sir Ralph, 24
Pedro, Don, 169, 170
Pelham, Thomas, 38, 41, 43
Peninsular War, 94–114 *passim*, 184
Perceval, Spencer, 10, 71, 84, 87, *88*, 90–3, 98–100, 112, 116–18, 122–5, 126, 130, 145, 148, 151–3
Perkins, Bradford (historian), 93
Peterborough, Bishop of, 23
Peterloo, 160
Pitt, William, xii, 22, 27, 31–3, 35, 40–4, 47–9, 51–4, 57–84 *passim*, 87, 90–1, 109, 110, 113, 127, 139, 146, 156, 173, 177, 184
Planta, Joseph, 153
Ponsonby, Sarah, 12
Portaferry (school), 9
Portland, 3rd Duke of, 35–6, 44, 49, 58, 63, 74, 85, *86*, 87–9, 91, 110–152 *passim*, 162, 169, 170
Portugal, 96–102 *passim*
Practitioner, The, 180

Pratt *see* Camden, 1st Earl or 1st Marquess of
Pratt, Frances (Castlereagh's stepmother), 7, 9
Pretyman (Bishop of Lincoln), 16, 73, 83, 175, 200, 201
Putney, xi–xiii, 18, 78, 83, 127, 135–8, 153, 173

Reddish, Charles and Samuel, 16, 23, 27, 56–7
Reddish, Samuel (father of the above), 16
Reynolds, Sir Joshua (portrait painter), 17, 21
Richman, Dr, 18, 20
Robinson, Crabbe, 106
Rockingham, 1st Marquess of, 7
Romaña, Marques de la, 104–5
Romney (portrait painter), 17
Rose, George, 73, 114, 123, 130, 145, 202
Rosebery, Earl of, 35, 66, 70, 72, 190, 199, 200
Ross, General, 43, 45, 72
Ryder *see* Harrowby, Lord

Sahagun, 104
St George's Chapel, 175
St James's Square (Castlereagh's London house), xi, 130, 135, 165, 178, 179
St John's College, Cambridge, 12
St Mary Cray (Castlereagh's home in Kent), 76, 179
St Vincent, Lord, 80–1
Salamanca, 103–4, 106
Sardinian Treaty, 52
Scheldt, 116, 120–3
Scott, Joan *see* Canning, Joan
Scott, Sir John (father of the above), 63
Seymour-Conway, Lady Sarah (Castlereagh's mother), 2, 182
Shelley, Percy Bysshe, xi, 159
Sheridan, Eliza (née Linley), 22, 24, 26
Sheridan, Richard Brinsley, 18, 21, 24, 26, 49, 52, 71, 82, 84, 199
Sheridan, Tom, 52
Seville, 104
Sidmouth, 1st Viscount *see* Addington, Henry
Smith, Bobus, 50
Smith, Easely, 50
Smith, Sir George, 39, 110
Smith, Sydney, 50

Sneyd, Revd John, 69, 71
Soult, Marshal, 80, 104–5, 169
South Hill (Canning's farm), 69
Souza (Portuguese minister), 97
Spain, 94–112 *passim*, 149, 160, 167, 170, 184
Spencer, Countess, 30
Spencer, Earl, 26, 35, 66
Spencer, Jane (wife of Paul Canning q.v.)
Spencer, Lord Henry, 22, 27
Spencer, Lieutenant-General Sir Brent, 5, 94, 113
Stafford, Lady, 71
Stafford, Marquess of, 51, 53
Stanhope, Lady Hester (Pitt's neice), 78, 102, 106
Stapleton, Augustus, 102, 176
Stewart, Alexander (Castlereagh's grandfather), 1, 2, 9
Stewart, Charles (later 3rd Marquess of Londonderry), 10, 97, 99, 100, 145, 149, 152, 156–9, 180
Stewart, Robert (Castlereagh's father, 1st Marquess of Londonderry), 1, 2, 7, 29, 76, 145–6, 148, 180
Stewart, Robert = Lord Castlereagh (later 2nd Marquess), *passim* (*see* chapter headings)
Strachan, Admiral Sir Richard, 120–1
Strangford, Lord, 62, 93, 170–1
Stratford de Redcliffe, Viscount *see* Canning, Stratford
Stratford, Robert (of Baltinglass – Canning's great-grandfather), 3
Sturges Bourne, 50, 52
Sutherland, Countess of, 51, 56
Sweden, 86, 113
Sydenham, Benjamin, 123–5

Talavera, 101, 143
Talbot, Lord, 139, 158, 160
Tallyrand-Perigord, duc de, 158
Teeling, Charles, 38, 39, 181, 199
Temperley, Professor, 150, 173, 203
Temple, Lord, 84, 87, 98, 201
Thurlow, Lord, 24–5, 65
Tierney, George, 127, 130, 139, 146, 172
Times newspaper, xi, 81, 105, 138, 139, 148, 177, 179
Titchfield, Lord, 53–5, 63–4, 69
Tregony, 33
Trench, W.S., 9

Trentham, 51, 56
Trotter, Alexander, 81–2
Troy, Bishop, 44

United Irishmen, 36, 38

Verona, Congress of, 167
Vienna, 155, 167, 178
Vienna, Congress of, 10, 155–60 *passim*
Villeneuve, Admiral, 91
Villiers, Sir John (ambassador at Lisbon), 111
Vimeiro, 96, 98–9, 109, 176

Walcheren Expedition, 112, 117–23, 128, 133, 144, 146 143, 150, 184
Waldegrave, Lord, 156
Walmer Castle, 63, 78
Walpole, General, 130, 146
Wanstead, 50, 52, 54, 59, 62–3
Wardle, Colonel, 112
Webster, Professor, 150
Welbeck, 65, 164
Wellesley (Sir) Arthur *see* Wellington Duke of
Wellesley, Henry, 132–3
Wellesley, Richard, Marquess Wellesley, 51, 75–6, 113, 117–18, 123–6, 132, 151, 196, 202
Wellesley Pole, William, 123–4, 132, 144
Wellington, Duke of, xi, 4, 18, 70, 75, 93–8, 101–2, 109, 111–14, 121, 127, 135, 143–4, 149, 156, 165–8, 171–2, 175–6, 179, 201, 203
Wendover, 62, 70
Westmoreland, Earl of, 89
Windsor, Canons of, 175
White's Club, 51
Wilberforce, William, 12, 49, 65, 89, 112, 127, 132, 144–5
Wilkes, John, 4, 7, 10, 139, 199
Wilkinson, David (historian), 85, 201
Winchelsea, Lord, 127
Wyndham (or Windham), William, 26, 35, 66, 80, 82, 95, 144

Yarmouth, Lord, 130–8 *passim*, 182
Yawkins, 120
York, Archbishop of (William Markham), 51, 54
York, Duke of, 95–7, 112, 114, 139, 175–6
Yorke, Charles, 50